«ART IS REALLY THE SURPLUS OF
LONGING THAT CANNOT FIND EXPRESSION
IN LIFE OR IN OTHER WAYS»

ERLING DAHL JR.

My Grieg

A personal introduction
to his life and music

EDVARD GRIEG MUSEUM

Copyright © 2014 by Erling Dahl jr.
and Edvard Grieg Museum, Troldhaugen

Norwegian version published in 2007
by Vigmostad & Bjoerke, Bergen

The book is published thanks to financial support from:
Norwegian Hull Club, Bergen
Steinway & Sons, New York
Grieg 07 / Municipality of Bergen
NORLA (support to Norwegian literature abroad)

Photos and material have been lent out from Edvard Grieg Museum, Troldhaugen
and Bergen Public Library, The Grieg Collection

Layout: Tønnes H. Gundersen, Bergen
Cover photo: Anders Beer Wilse (EGM)
Print and binding: John Grieg AS, Bergen

Translation: Felicity Burbridge Rinde, Bergen
and Sarah Lustig, London

ISBN: 978-82-9173-851-2

Paper: 100 gr Silk
Typesetting: Goudy 11/14

Questions about this book can be addressed to:
MusInvest / Erling Dahl jr. Teatergaten 7, NO-5010 Bergen, Norway
Email: dahljr2@me.com – Tel. +47 9180 9753
or
Edvard Grieg Museum, Troldhaugen
att. Dir. Sigurd Sandmo
Troldhaugveien 65, NO-5232 Paradis, Bergen, Norway
Email: info@troldhaugen.no – Tel +47 559222992

Preface

IN SPRING 2001 I was given the opportunity to travel to Italy to kick off a project I had long been planning to get around to – namely, sifting through all my thoughts and ideas about Edvard Grieg's life and music. I spent thirteen years as manager and director of the Edvard Grieg Museum at Troldhaugen working with this material on a daily basis, and I have derived great pleasure from presenting it to all kinds of people from all over the world.

The process which started in Rome resulted in this book – a travel guide to the musical world of Edvard Grieg. The starting point for my book is Edvard Grieg's music. The book deals with a fairly large selection of Grieg's works, but far from all of them. As is the case with all composers, Grieg's output varies in character and quality. The works I have concentrated on in this book are not necessarily simply his most popular pieces, but pieces that have something to tell us today about Grieg and the times he lived in.

When approaching Grieg's music, I feel it is important to listen and to seek. Listening and seeking – rather than simply listening and seeing – is absolutely vital if we are to get to the core of any material. I have found 'my' Grieg by listening and seeking with as open a mind as possible, given my background. What I have discovered so far is an artist with such a complex, multifaceted corpus of work that I could happily continue studying and reflecting on this theme for the rest of my life.

I owe a debt of gratitude to many individuals and institutions in connection with this project. First and foremost, the Edvard Grieg Museum, Troldhaugen, whose activities, staff and property have enabled me to pursue and develop my interest in Edvard

Grieg's life and music. In the spring of 2001 I was able to follow in Grieg's footsteps to Italy, via Copenhagen, in order to collect my thoughts and write the first draft of this book.

The book is richly illustrated, and this would not have been possible without the generous help and cooperation of various institutions and archives. Special thanks go to the Bergen Public Library and its director Trine Kolderup Flaten, to the Edvard Grieg Archives and their head Siren Steen, and to the Edvard Grieg Museum, Troldhaugen and its chief curator Monica Jangaard. Their help in lending materials, their suggestions and corrections, and their encouragement throughout my work on this book have been invaluable.

Thanks also to all my former colleagues at Troldhaugen, and particularly Eilif B Løtveit for his help in uncovering facts, proof-reading, work on the indexes and registers, and much more. A huge vote of thanks must go to the person most closely involved in the writing of this book, Tønnes H Gundersen – historian, photo-grapher, text author and designer par excellence. He designed the book, proofread the text, and contributed to the conceptual lay-out. For over ten years he has helped create a consistent, stylish profile for all Edvard Grieg Museum's products, as well as being the driving force behind the touring exhibition *Edvard Grieg – Art and Identity*. I am pleased and proud that he carried on this work in this book.

But above all, thanks to Edvard Grieg – for who he was, for what he created and for all the joy, wonderment and reflection he has inspired.

Bergen, February 2007
ERLING DAHL JR.

CREDITS & ABBREVATIONS
BOB: The Grieg Collectiom, Bergen Public Library
ED: Erling Dahl jr.
EGM: Edvard Grieg Museum – Troldhaugen
FIB: Festspillene i Bergen
THG: Tønnes H. Gundersen
TUB: The Theatre Archive, Bergen University
UBB: The Photo Collection, Bergen University

Contents

The Edvard Grieg statue in Bergen by the sculptor
Ingebrigt Vik. The monument was unveiled
on 4 September 1917, exactly ten years
after the composer's death. (THG)

This silhouette of Edvard Grieg was created by Dr Otto Böhler some time before 1900, and published in 1914. Otto Böhler (1847–1913) was an Austrian silhouette artist who specialized in portraits of many great conductors, composers, and pianists of his time. (EGM)

Introduction

I F WE ARE ever tempted to start comparing Grieg with the great composers, we should remember his own words:

'I make no pretentions of being in the same league as Bach, Mozart and Beethoven. Their works are eternal, whereas I have written for my day and generation.' (Interview with Arthur M Abell in 1907)

Nor was Grieg a master of large-scale musical works, a fact that was used to criticise him and his importance as a composer by some of his contemporaries (in the turgid age of romanticism) and later on when the symphonic form dominated music life. Grieg himself believed that his music would be forgotten a hundred years later, or perhaps sooner. But for once he was wrong: his music has proved to have an incredible power of survival, and continues to gain in popularity with musicians and audiences. Grieg's music is played and listened to all over the world, and the massive performance of, and research into, his music bear witness to widespread interest in his life and works.

A glance at Grieg's list of compositions shows that large works in terms of instrumentation and duration are few and far between; for the most part his creativity was expressed through the small-scale forms of songs and piano pieces. Some people have therefore called him a miniaturist, but that is a misleading label, for Grieg's many musical poems, short pieces and songs have a clear, unique (and at times innovative) style, in terms of form, rhythm and harmony. What's more, the way in which he combined songs or piano pieces within each opus shows a clearly cyclical approach, and in his larger chamber and orchestral pieces he shows that he was every bit on a par with his contemporaries, and fully able to explore new directions. Grieg's starting point was in many ways the same as that

EDVARD GRIEG'S SYMPHONY IN C MINOR

The story behind the fact that Edvard Grieg's *Symphony in C minor* is played today, against Grieg's will, is as follows. The manuscript of the 'Forbidden Symphony' is kept at the Grieg Archives at the Bergen Public Library. The library respected Grieg's comment 'Must never be performed' for many years. However, music scholars have been allowed access to the material and in the early 1970s parts were produced from a copy of the material in the library. An 'illegal' first performance took place in Moscow in 1980. Since Grieg's veto had been broken, the directors of Bergen Public Library decided to release the material to allow a Norwegian first performance at the Bergen International Festival in 1981. Naturally there was much debate as to whether this decision was right or wrong, and critics were divided in their judgment of the symphony.

I recommend Kjell Skyllstad's article on the symphony in *Studia Musicologica Norvegica* no. 19, Oslo 1993 (*Nordic Symphony, Grieg at the Crossroads*). One thing is certain: Grieg was highly self-critical in his own assessment of this work, which has many good qualities.

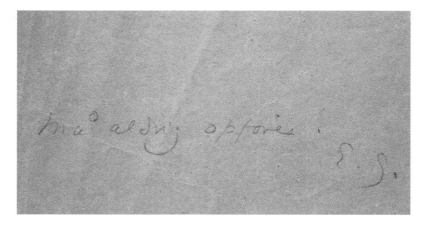

After hearing Johan Svendsen's first symphony, Grieg went home and wrote on the title page of his own Symphony in C minor: 'Must never be performed. E.G.' (BOB)

of Robert Schumann; that is, the romantic idea of expressing that which is universal through distinctly individual works with a national or local flavour. However, he was not Schumann, neither in his mastery of the large musical form nor in expression. Grieg forged his own personal path, concentrating on small, intimate forms and a national tonal language.

Grieg's output was not very extensive, just 74 opus numbers, plus a few works not included on his opus list. There are several reasons why his production was not larger.

Firstly, he was an extremely sensitive artist, who needed ideal conditions and surroundings in order to be able to compose. Such conditions proved more difficult to achieve than he would have liked, and as a result he was not always able to compose even when he felt inspired to do so. It was quite a challenge combining a hectic existence touring as a pianist and a conductor with finding the necessary peace and quiet for composing.

Another reason was that he suffered poor health throughout adulthood, constantly coming down with colds and other ailments (which he was susceptible to due to suffering from tuberculosis in his youth), which hampered his creative work on many occasions.

The third, perhaps most important, reason was his self-censorship. Grieg made extremely high demands upon himself as a composer. *'The music that I come up with one day I tear out of my heart the next – because it isn't genuine!'* he once wrote in desperation to his friend Frants Beyer.

We know, for instance, that after hearing Johan Svendsen's *First Symphony* performed in Oslo in 1867, he went home and wrote on the front page of the score of his own symphony: *'Must never be performed.'* He was fully aware of the shortcomings of his own work, poor instrumentation and insufficient thematic development, and he may also have felt that it was not 'Norwegian' enough. The symphony had already been performed on several occasions while Grieg lived in Copenhagen, and he had also arranged two of its movements for piano duet, but from that moment on he ceased all work on it.

Although Edvard Grieg was highly critical of his own work, we can discover a lot of his own thoughts on music and life in general in the huge body of written material he left behind him. He was an avid correspondent, writing on average ten to twelve letters a week throughout his adult life, as well as a fair number of speeches and articles. He also kept a diary for two distinct periods, one right at the start of his career and one towards the end of his life.

WANDERING THROUGH ROME WITH GRIEG'S DIARY AS A TRAVEL GUIDE

This journey through Edvard Grieg's music starts in Rome. Grieg always felt the pull of Southern Europe, feeling that the local beauty in art and nature and the Latin temperament provided a welcome and necessary counterbalance to the rational, cooler temperament of the Germanic tradition. He visited Italy several times, and during his first trip there in 1865–1866 he kept a diary. Visiting Rome does something to most people, and I was certainly no exception when I arrived in Rome 135 years after Grieg, and was able to follow in his footsteps, with his diary as my guide.

From Via Sistina where Grieg stayed on the second floor of no. 100 during his first visit to Rome in 1865–66. (ED)

I start my wandering at the top of the Spanish Steps. To the right of the church of Trinita dei Monti, the Via Sistina leads down to Piazza Barberini. It was here, on the second floor of Via Sistina 100, that Grieg stayed on his first trip to Rome in 1865–1866. Today this is a busy road with cars and scooters roaring past at high speed. Some of the houses must have been demolished, for I cannot find the one in which Grieg lived – there are no buildings between numbers 94 and 101.

Back again to the Spanish Steps. This area is always crowded, but despite the mass of people on all sides, everyone seems to feel

The Spanish Steps in Rome. (ED)

a special sense of peace here. They sit quietly, soaking in the beauty around them, smiling. There are beautiful old buildings on all sides of the piazza, including a pink building on the left which houses a museum to the great English poets Keats, Shelley and Byron. Keats himself lived in this building, and died here at just 25 years old.

Straight ahead we see down Via Condotti, which these days is a busy, fashionable shopping street – best to leave your credit card in the hotel safe! At number 86 we find the famous Caffè Greco, established in 1760, oozing tradition from its walls and furnishings.

The Trevi Fountain. (ED)

Caffè Greco has always been a meeting place for artists and the intelligentsia, ever since it first opened its doors, and it was here that Grieg and all the other Nordic celebrities used to come. From the mid-1800s there were particularly many Danish artists and scientists in Rome, but there were also quite a few Norwegians, including Bjørnstjerne Bjørnson, Henrik Ibsen, Andreas Munch and Edvard Grieg. Later generations of artists followed in their footsteps, including Nobel Prize winner Sigrid Undset, who also frequented Caffè Greco. She had very close ties to Rome, and even has a street named after her here. She lived in Via Frattina, which runs parallel to Via Condotti.

Old photo of Caffé Greco in Via Condotti.

The walls of the café are covered with greetings from all the great names who have visited the café: Goethe, Gogol, Berlioz, Stendahl, Taine, Baudelaire, Thorvaldsen, Wagner and of course famous Norwegians such as Bjørnson, Ibsen, Grieg and Undset. (Hans Christian Andersen stayed in rooms over the café on the third floor in 1861.)

Today Caffè Greco is a major tourist attraction, both because of its history and its unusual interior. Sitting here enjoying a pot of tea and a tiramisu, it is not unusual to hear a dozen different languages being spoken around you. Everyone is keen to find their own national heroes on the walls, just as I eagerly sought out Grieg and Bjørnson in a collage of postcards, photos, a newspaper cutting and a small musical greeting from the two of them in the

Piazza del Popolo seen from Monte Pincio. (ED)

The author in front of a collage of pictures and texts by Bjørnson, Grieg and Kröyer at Caffé Greco, Rome. Grieg's salute to the cafe is the opening phrase of The First Meeting. *(text B. Bjørnson).* (ED)

form of the opening bars of *The First Meeting* in Grieg's own handwriting. The atmosphere in the café is just like that in any European city that attracts tourists; here you will find Germans, Japanese, Frenchmen and not least Americans, along with many other nationalities, united in their enjoyment of a cup of coffee and a piece of cake.

Despite the steady stream of tourists, the café has managed to retain its special atmosphere. The taste of the classic cake some-how melts away and fades into the background, and you are left with a myriad of impressions, which make you feel suddenly much closer to the days of old.

It is easy to lose your heart to this gem of a café, but you could easily overrun your holiday budget! However, if you open all your senses to the atmosphere as well as the food and drink, you will experience the many 'tastes' which hang in the air here. And that is definitely worth the money!

The historic centre of Rome is so concentrated that you can easily cover most of it on foot. From Piazza di Spagna it is only a stone's throw to the Trevi Fountain, one of Rome's top tourist attractions. The water for this fountain and many others comes via the Acqua Vergine, an aqueduct which the Roman general Agrippa built in 19 BC.

There are signs of carnival on the steps and in the streets – confetti strewn all around, and many shops have displays of carnival costumes and decorations. In my head I hear Grieg's *From the Carnival*. What better surroundings in which to experience and understand this music? The introduction is just like the sound of footsteps on the many stone steps. The clattering of shoes, the whirl of costumes, the jumbled mass of figures of all ages, it all suits the quick 3/4 opening perfectly.

Confetti from carnival on the cobbled streets of Rome. (ED)

From the Carnival.

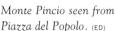

Monte Pincio seen from Piazza del Popolo. (ED)

View of St Peter's Basilica from Monte Pincio. (ED)

Following this intermezzo I wander back up the Spanish Steps, still in the company of Grieg. I am in Rome here and now, but my sense of time is muddled: the past is here, right in front of me, while the future lies hidden in the unknown and the invisible. The history right under my feet provides a basis for understanding all that has gone before, as well as a sighting point for mapping out what has gone before and what is yet to come. Goethe said that, 'He who cannot draw on 3000 years [of thinking] is living hand-to-mouth'. As I stand here, I start to understand what he meant.

With this feeling still strong, I carry on up to Monte Pincio, 46 metres above sea level, where the visitor is raised a little above the city and can see the roofline of Rome, church spire after church spire gleaming in the sunset. Far, far off I see the magnificent St Peter's Basilica. To my left is the beautiful, forested Janiculum which stretches right to Trastevere. Down on Piazza del Popolo the crowds are still bustling busily about. But up here among the busts of the nation's greatest artists and people taking an evening stroll, between the poplars and cypresses, up here, Bjørnson and Grieg sing the praises of the 'eternal city'.

Setting sun glowing, evening is nigh;
Warm, gentle rays from the heavens descending
Shower the earth with a radiance unending,
Soft gleams the mountain 'gainst blue evening sky.
Rooftops illumin'd, but off in the valley
Dark churning fogbanks beginning to rally
Cover a land whose great caesars and seers
Govern'd the world for a thousand long years.
Eventide, fill'd with life! Hear the drum! Hear the fife!
Laughing and loving sighs, flowers and teasing eyes.
Thoughts intermingling as mem'ry invites them,
Faithful to that which unites them.
Eventide, fill'd with life! Hear the drum! Hear the fife!
Laughing and loving sighs, flowers and teasing eyes

Hush to the stillness as darkness descends;
Heaven o'erarching is watching and waiting,
Biding the future that time is creating,
Stirrings of hope a new vision portend.
Surely the day will dawn; Rome will awaken,
City eternal, too long left forsaken;
Bells will be tolling, and canons will roar!
Rome will be greater than Rome was before!
Hark to the minstrel's call: Courage, young lovers all!
Hear the band, hear the lute, zither and piping flute.
Longings profound now recede from my fancy,
Lighter thoughts waken to dancing.
Courage, young lovers all! Hark to the minstrel's call:
Hear the band; hear the lute, zither and piping flute.[1]

Edvard Grieg's first trip to Rome

Edvard Grieg's father, consul Alexander Grieg (1806–1875). (EGM)

Ole Bull (1810–1880). (EGM)

IN THE LATE autumn of 1865 Edvard Grieg set out on a journey southwards. He had spent a couple of years in Copenhagen after graduating from the Leipzig Conservatory, and was now undertaking a study trip to Rome. The original plan had been to travel with his fellow artist Rikard Nordraak. The trip was being paid for by Grieg's father, Alexander Grieg, since Grieg's application of 12 June 1862 to the King of Norway for a travel grant had been turned down. His father was not altogether enthusiastic about Grieg's choice of travelling companion, since Nordraak was, in his opinion, an impetuous young man. However, he agreed to finance the trip, remarking on Grieg's departure that Edvard was an *'expensive young puppy, without a doubt!'*

This trip to Rome was not just Grieg's idea, it was very much the order of the day, and Ole Bull, himself the greatest Norwegian musician of his day, had impressed upon him that he must travel to Italy in order to understand how art music could grow out of folk music. Contemporary Italian opera was really just an elevated form of folk music that had evolved from Neapolitan folk songs, and Ole Bull felt sure that Edvard Grieg was just the man to be able to bring about a similar transformation in Norwegian music.

From Copenhagen Grieg travelled first to Berlin, where he was to meet up with Nordraak, and from there they would travel to Rome together. However, on arriving in Berlin Grieg soon realised that Nordraak was seriously ill; the charisma that had emanated so strongly from Nordraak when they had first met in Copenhagen the previous year appeared now only in brief glimpses. Nordraak was deathly pale and very weak, but he refused to admit how ill he was, and repeated over and over again that he would soon be well enough to accompany Grieg on the planned trip to Rome.

Edvard Grieg in 1868 – the year he composed his Piano Concerto in A minor. Xylography. (EGM)

'... In Rome I discovered what I needed ... the opportunity to concentrate on myself and the greatness around me, the daily influences of a world of beauty. It is of the greatest importance for a Scandinavian musician who has received his elementary training in German to later spend some time in Italy, for in so doing he can clarify his ideas and purge them of that one-sidedness that only results in further concentration on German things. The national character of a Northerner contains so much that is heavy and introspective, which in all truth cannot be counterbalanced by an exclusive study of German art. In order to serve national interests, we need mental balance, a spiritual vitality that can be acquired only by discovering what can be learned in southern Europe. ... But what for me personally has been of the greatest importance is my acquaintance and association with Franz Liszt, who was staying in Rome at that time. In him I have got to know not only the most brilliant of all piano players but, what is more, a phenomenon – intellectually and in stature – unmatched in the sphere of art. I brought him several of my compositions, which he played; and it was of supreme interest for me to observe how the national element in my work at first made him hesitant, but then enthusiastic.'

Rikard Nordraak (1842–1866). (BOB)

The Spanish Steps in Rome in Grieg's day (from the composer's private album). (EGM)

Rikard Nordraak was born in Oslo, 12 June 1842. From early childhood he showed exceptional musical talent, but he was sent to Copenhagen to study trade and business. However, the pull of music became too strong, and he went on to study music →

After a few days in Berlin, Grieg went on his own to Leipzig, where he had been booked to give a few concerts, including a performance of his first *Violin Sonata*. The concerts were well received – even the dreaded Eduard Bernsdorf gave a positive write-up in the music journal *Signale für die musikalische Welt*, although his attitude to Grieg's music would change later on. During his stay in Leipzig Grieg also met Johan Svendsen, and the two men struck up a lifelong friendship.

Piazza del Popolo in Grieg's day (from the composer's private album). (EGM)

Grieg had promised Nordraak that he would return to Berlin from Leipzig, but when it came to it, he changed his plans. He realised that his friend was dying of tuberculosis, and he was nervous of returning to Berlin. He was probably worried about contracting the disease himself, for he had been very ill with tuberculosis in his student days in Leipzig, and had had to take a year off his studies. Thanks to careful nursing he had survived the illness, but he never recovered full health, and was hampered by the effects of the illness for the rest of his life.

So instead of returning to Berlin, he travelled with a Professor Grotze from Leipzig via Vienna to Italy. They stopped off in Venice and Florence, before arriving at Rome by train from Civitavecchia on 11 December 1865.

'Grotze's friend Preller, a painter, met us at the railway station and drove us to Grotze's lodgings, where we ate our first Roman meal: ham, soup, eggs and radishes, wine and apples.' (Diary entry, 11 December 1865)

Grieg rented a room in the artists' quarters near the Spanish Steps, at Via Sistina 100, on the second floor. The very next day he hired a piano for his room.

in Copenhagen, Oslo and Berlin. From Berlin he returned home to Norway, aged 21, and his music started to be published. Nordraak is best known for setting to music his cousin Bjørnstjerne Bjørnson's national poem *Yes, we love with fond devotion* (1864), which was later adopted as Norway's national anthem. Nordraak also wrote incidental music for the theatre, piano pieces and songs. After a few years in Norway he returned to Berlin in 1865 to pursue further studies. Sadly he contracted tuberculosis and died on 20 March 1866. Since Nordraak only lived to be 24, his catalogue of works is fairly short (approximately 40 pieces), but he developed a distinctly personal, national style. His melodies are full of scale passages, and his music is of a dramatic character. Nordraak was a huge inspiration and encouragement to his fellow Norwegian artists – he has been described as a mixture of Ole Bull and Bjørnstjerne Bjørnson. Nordraak was buried in Berlin, but his remains were later taken back to Norway and interred at Vår Frelsers Gravlund cemetery in Oslo. There is still a monument commemorating Nordraak at the graveyard in Berlin, erected by, among others, Bjørnson and Grieg, and each year Norwegians gather there on 17 May, Norway's National Day.

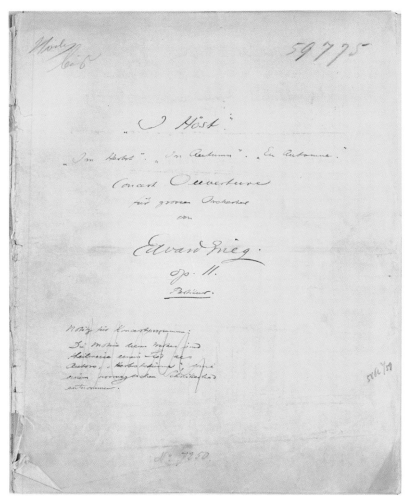

Henrik Ibsen (1828–1906) in the early 1860s. (BOB)

Title page of the overture to In Autumn; *one of the few works Grieg composed during his first stay in Rome.* (BOB)

Grieg made good use of his time in Rome, not so much for composing, but absorbing the numerous artistic and cultural impressions. It took him just a few days to see most of the sights. He wrote of his first visit to see Raphael's frescoes in the Vatican Museum: '*The first impression was almost too overpowering to even think of enjoyment.*' (*Diary entry, 11 December 1865*)

He also visited Caffè Greco, Caffè Roma, the Spanish Steps, Monte Pincio, Villa Albano, St Peter's Basilica, the Scandinavian Society, the Capitoline Hill, the Roman Forum, the Colosseum, the triumphal arches of Titus and Constantine and many other sights.

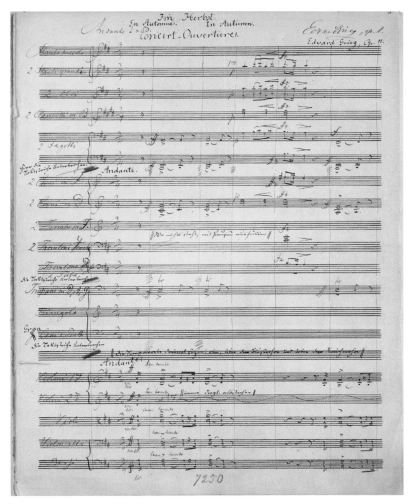

First page of manuscript of In Autumn. (BOB)

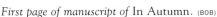

Front page of printed edition of In Autumn. (BOB)

The four months Grieg spent in Italy provided him with enough spiritual stimulation to last a lifetime. His meetings with the Nordic artists and scientists, with Classical art and with the beautiful countryside made an indelible impression on him, and in later years Grieg (who, wherever he was, frequently longed to be elsewhere) often yearned to return to Italy.

Grieg's first visit to Rome and Italy, and his encounters with the art and artists here, had precisely the effect Ole Bull had predicted: being so far away from Norway reinforced Grieg's feeling for and understanding of his native country's rich cultural heri-

Diary entry 6 April 1866. Edvard Grieg has just received news of Rikard Nordraak's death. (BOB)

tage. The great artists he met here encouraged Grieg to believe that he really did possess the necessary talent and power to achieve his innermost dreams and objectives. Grieg's meeting with Henrik Ibsen in particular would have a profound effect on his future career. Although the two men never became close friends, Ibsen was quick to see the potential of this diminutive, intellectual artist from Bergen. While in Rome, Grieg put Ibsen in touch with his German sister-in-law, Marie Grieg, who later translated *The Pretenders* into German. A few years later Ibsen and Grieg worked together on *Peer Gynt,* and they remained in contact, albeit at a distance, for the rest of their lives.

Grieg did not compose much during his first visit to Rome, but he did complete the orchestral overture *In Autumn,* op. 11. He also set to music lyrics by Andreas Munch (op. 9), whom he met in Rome. Later on he wrote two lovely pieces clearly associated with this trip, *From the Carnival* in *Pictures from Folk Life,* op. 19, and the music to Bjørnson's eloquent poem about Rome *From Monte Pincio,* op. 39 no. 1.

On 6 April 1866 Grieg received news of the death of his friend Nordraak. He wrote in his diary:

The Roman Forum. (ED)

'The saddest news that could strike me – Nordraak is dead! He, my only friend, my only great hope for our Norwegian art! And I do not have a single person here who can truly understand my sorrow. [...] Composed a Funeral March in honour of Nordraak!'

MEETING THE GREAT ARTISTS OF THE DAY

As already mentioned, one of Grieg's motivations for travelling to Italy was to discover a new perspective on his own culture. From his arrival in the 'eternal city' just before Christmas 1865, we can trace his movements through these hectic months in Italy thanks to the diary he kept. Most of the entries in this diary were very short and concise, sometimes merely lists of names and places, but they give us a clear impression of how busy Grieg kept throughout his stay. He visited the sights, studied great works of art and went to concerts. In addition he met many of the great artists of the day for the first time, some of whom were from Norway, including of course Henrik Ibsen, and others from other countries. Artists and scientists from the Nordic countries tended to gather in the Scandinavian Society in Rome.

*Johan Bravo
(1797–1876), Danish
painter and art agent.
From 1855 Swedish-
Norwegian consul in
Rome.* (EGM)

The young Edvard Grieg. (EGM)

His notes from his first day in Rome are typical of his entire trip: *'Bohlmann. Consul Bravo. Ravnkilde. Villa Albano with Dr Münster (Danish) and Bohlmann. Noon meal with Scandinavians. St Peter's Basilica. Scandinavian Society. Evening with Bohlmann. Read Bjørnson's speech to the University Student Association in Oslo, Nordraak's song mentioned. Rented a piano.'* (12 December 1865)

And so it goes on, a relentless round of activity, day after day. *'Terrible music in Chiesa Nuova. Bellini, Donizetti, Rossini. Two castratos, unnatural, repugnant.'* (17 December 1865)

He saw and heard Franz Liszt for the first time at a concert with Pinelli.

'… saw Liszt strutting about for some young ladies.' (20 December 1865)

Ibsen gets another mention in Grieg's diary on Christmas Eve. After the meal at the Scandinavian Society, a great many after-dinner toasts were made in honour of kings, nations and individuals, including Ibsen. Ibsen responded by proposing a toast for the inhabitants of Schleswig. He was irate that Norway and Sweden had not come to the aid of Denmark when the Danish duchies of Schleswig and Holstein had been annexed by the Prussians. His famous poem *A Brother in Need* and the fact that he chose to leave Norway for good are clear indications of Ibsen's deeply held political convictions.

After the meal there was a *'Festival march by Bohlmann for piano and children's instruments. Christmas tree with lottery (2 pairs of kid gloves). Dance. Ended 2 am.'*

On Christmas Day Grieg visited St Peter's Basilica with Niels Ravnkilde, and watched as Pope Pius IX was carried around St Peter's Square under a canopy to give the blessing to the scores of kneeling Catholics gathered there.

'In the evening a party on the leftovers in the Scandinavian Society. Played for Molbech. Nordic Dance by (?). Ibsen dead drunk.'

Grieg celebrated New Year's Eve 1865 very quietly. He and his friend Bohlmann went for a moonlit walk to the Roman Forum, which proved to be an eerie experience in the ghostly ruins, where assaults on visitors' wallets and persons were far from infrequent. Later they went to the Scandinavian Society, but they found the atmosphere there so formal and uncomfortable that they left without telling anybody and went on to the Caffè Greco:

'… drank our chocolate in the Caffè Greco and talked about our loved ones at home. By 11 pm I was sound asleep, so I did not experience that singular hour of transition ushering in the new year.'

On 13 January they all gathered once more in the Scandinavian Society to mark the Nordic Memorial Day, a day of recollection and promise. Ibsen made a speech on the subject of the Norwegians' weakness in the Prusso–Danish war, which caused quite a stir.

'He reminded his listeners of all the solemn promises that are given on this day by all the Scandinavian student societies – promises about solidarity and determination in the time of danger – and how without exception the entire younger generation had failed to come through when distress threatened. It was high time, he said, to end such empty talk as long as it never found expression in deeds, and he wanted most earnestly to advise that we stop celebrating a memorial day such as this under the present circumstances.'

This sparked a lively discussion, and *'… after a few exchanges of opinion and sharp outbursts the party ended at 11 pm.'*

Franz Liszt (1811–1886). In his diary Grieg noted that he had seen Liszt 'strutting about' for some young ladies. (BOB)

Gesine Judithe Hagerup Grieg (1814–1875) was daughter of Edvard Hagerup, a chief administrative officer in the county of Hordaland. She was the best piano teacher in Bergen and introduced Edvard to the mysteries of music. Her favourite composers were Mozart and Weber.(BOB)

Edvard Grieg in his student days in Leipzig. (BOB)

Prelude to life as a 'wizard in the kingdom of music'

'YOU ARE TO GO TO LEIPZIG TO BECOME AN ARTIST!'

T HESE WORDS would alter the life of Edvard Hagerup Grieg. He was nearly fifteen, and the family was spending the summer at Landås Manor, their beautiful estate at the foot of Mount Ulriken, a couple of miles out of Bergen. The family usually spent the summer months there, and the winter months at Strandgaten 152 in the city centre. Edvard was on summer holiday from Tanks School. We know from the school records that the young Edvard was not a particularly studious pupil, although he did well enough in the subjects that interested him. There can be little doubt that he felt that his schoolwork got in the way of his real interest – music.

Edvard Grieg, 11 years old. First known photo of the young Edvard (1854). (EGM)

CHILDHOOD

Edvard Grieg grew up in the middle of the busy city of Bergen, and from his home in Strandgaten he had a grandstand view of the working life and pleasures of the city's inhabitants. Around 25,000 people lived in the compact city centre around the bay, making Bergen one of Norway's largest cities at that time. The city centre was a warren of narrow alleys and passageways, all buzzing with life – fishermen and farmers with their barrows of wares, fish-wives, young girls and dockworkers, merchants and errand boys – a paradise for small boys in search of adventure. It was just a stone's throw from Edvard's home to the fish market and the Hanseatic wharf, and he knew each alleyway like the back of his hand.

It was typical of Bergen society that Gesine Hagerup studied music abroad – sons of well-to-do Bergeners were sent to Germany, the Netherlands or Britain to study trade and shipping, while daughters received training in music and the arts. Europe was thus a natural part of Bergen – both economically and culturally.

Manuscript of Larvik
Polka *(EG 101)*, *one of
Grieg's earliest extant
compositions.* (BOB)

The estate at Landås.

The Grieg family owned
Landås Manor from 1853
to 1870. Edvard's mother,
Gesine Hagerup Grieg,
inherited the manor from
her father, Edvard Hagerup.
The family lived here
during the summer months
and Edvard loved this
place. He set up his first
'composer's hut' in the
henhouse here. Landås
Manor now belongs to the
municipality of Bergen,
and is currently in use as
a vicarage.

Edvard Grieg's parents, Gesine Hagerup and Alexander Grieg. (BOB)

No doubt the young Edvard played all the usual children's
games of the day, with such enticing names as Not Full, Cock-a-
doodle and Pick the Last One (which is still played in the school
playgrounds of Bergen today). Edvard's family lived in Strandgaten, the busy main street. His father, Alexander Grieg, was in
the fish export business, specialising in lobster, and was also the
British consul in Bergen. He and his wife, Gesine Hagerup, a
trained musician, had two sons and three daughters. Edvard was
the second youngest of their children.

Edvard Grieg (in hat) grew up in a well-to-do merchant family with his brother John (born in 1840) and his sisters Maren (born in 1837), Ingeborg Benedicte (born in 1838) and Elisabeth (born in 1845). Front row, from left: Elisabeth Grieg, Benedicte Grieg, Alexander Grieg and Gesine Grieg. Back row: Fanny Riis, Edvard Grieg, Oscar Riis and Marianne Riis. Standing: John Grieg. (BOB)

Ole Bull (1810–1880) – a Norse Norwegian from Norway. (BOB)

From early childhood Edvard showed a decided interest in music, particularly improvisation and composition, and this interest soon brought him into contact with the professional musicians in Bergen. At school he was taught by the agreeable singing tutor Ferdinand G Schediwy, who moved to Bergen from Prague at the age of 21 to make his living as a violinist, composer for the city theatre, organist and singing teacher. Schediwy was one of the first people to recognise Grieg's musical talent, and he kept in touch with his pupil right up to his death in 1877.

However, Grieg's foremost teacher in his early years was his mother, Gesine Hagerup Grieg, herself a very accomplished pianist and distinguished piano teacher, who had studied music at the Hamburg Conservatory. She gave recitals, was a soloist with the Harmonien Orchestra and took private piano pupils. Gesine Hagerup Grieg was held to be the best (and most expensive) piano tutor in Bergen.

As Edvard's teacher she was strict and demanded discipline, and yet at the same time she nurtured his imagination and his need for artistic freedom. Both his parents must have had a pretty liberal attitude to schooling, since Edvard was allowed so much

The big name in Norwegian cultural circles at that time was Ole Bull. This amazing violinist had his debut with the Music Society Harmonien's orchestra at the age of eight or nine. His father subsequently allowed him to drop his academic schooling to seek his fortune as a musician in Europe. And he certainly made his fortune, through years of hard work and much self-sacrifice. Following his breakthrough in Bologna in 1834 he quickly gained international renown. One critic wrote that Ole Bull could now play wherever he wanted, whenever he wanted and name his price. He was the Paganini of the North. Despite his extensive touring all over the globe, Ole Bull often returned to Norway. He spent many summers at his farmhouse in Valestrand, on the large inland island of Osterøy, north-east of Bergen. This farm had been in the family for many years, and Ole Bull was extremely attached to the place. When he inherited the farm, which →

was known locally as 'The Bull House' he channelled his creativity into designing imaginative new buildings, and introduced modern agricultural methods. But more important was the way Bull helped raise awareness of Norway's cultural heritage. He himself had become familiar with Norwegian folk music through music making with local folk fiddlers from Osterøy and other rural communities. Ole Bull recognised that this music was genuine and of great artistic value, and it helped him to realise that Norway was capable of producing national literature, art, theatre and music that were uniquely Norwegian. And so in 1850 he founded the country's first Norwegian-language theatre, in Bergen (the precursor of Den Nationale Scene). This theatre was dedicated to promoting Norwegian drama and employed only Norwegian-speaking actors. The first 'stage poet' to be appointed there was the young, unknown Henrik Ibsen. Ibsen worked at the theatre for six years, when he was succeeded by another up-and-coming young writer, Bjørnstjerne Bjørnson. Ole Bull was particularly keen to bring to the city dwellers' notice all the musical jewels to be found among people and artists in rural Norway. It was he who discovered the greatest Hardanger fiddler player of the century, Torgeir Augundsson, also known as 'Myllarguten' (the Miller Lad), whom he invited to perform at some of his own concerts in Oslo and Bergen.

The Grieg family visit Ole Bull at his home in Valestrand, in the late summer of 1869. (Ole Bull in top hat. Alexander Grieg seated on the veranda. John Grieg (Edvard's brother) standing by the steps.) (BOB)

freedom and given ample opportunity to pursue his passion for music. They do not appear to have been worried that his focus on musical activities had an adverse effect on his studies.

At their summer residence, Landås Manor, Edvard was allowed to set up his first 'composer's hut' in the henhouse, where he tried out and noted down his first compositions. It was when Ole Bull visited the family at Landås and heard some of these that he uttered the famous words quoted at the beginning of this chapter.

Although a large city by Norwegian standards, most of the families of Bergen were related or associated with one another in some way: Edvard was related to Ole Bull by marriage on the maternal side of his family, while Edvard's father, Alexander Grieg, was chairman of the Harmonien Music Society, and Gesine Hagerup Grieg was, as already mentioned, a fine pianist. So it was hardly surprising that Ole Bull visited the Grieg family when in Bergen.

Edvard Grieg wrote in his autobiographical article *My First Success* in 1905:

'*The end of my school days – and with it my departure from home – came more quickly than I had expected. I was almost fifteen years old but was still far from achieving senior class standing. Then one*

First page of manuscript of Edvard Grieg's delightful autobiographical article My First Success. (BOB)

'I have been strongly urged to write about my first success! The task appears so complicated that I am almost tempted to say that it would be my first success if I got through this enterprise unscathed! The subject puts forth its antennae in many directions. For which success is the first one? Is there any success at all? Is it not true that when we have achieved something that for the moment seems to be of value, we are confronted by the heavy, dark glower of life's disillusion that says: 'It is nothing, nothing'? Our entry into the world is undoubtedly a success, but chiefly for that great artist whom we call Nature. Whether it is a success for ourselves, on the other hand, might certainly be disputed. And the very concept of success! Does it not vary greatly in the minds of different people? What others would call a success is not so for me, and *vice versa*. What constitutes a success – if there is such a thing? This is the interesting part of the question. Is it what is called winning the applause of a random group of people – is that the real, the decisive success for the artist himself? Or is it a matter of satisfying the few whose judgment he highly respects?'

summer day at Landås a rider on a galloping horse approached from the road below. He drew near, reined in his magnificent Arab, and leaped off. It was that fairytale idol of whom I had dreamt but had never before seen: it was Ole Bull. There was something in me that didn't like the fact that this god, without further ado, dismounted and acted as if he were a mere mortal, came into the living room, and smilingly greeted us all. I remember distinctly that when his right hand touched mine, something like an electric shock went through me. But at last the god began to tell jokes, and then I realised – with quiet sorrow, to tell the truth – that he was only a human being after all.

'Unfortunately, he didn't have his violin with him. But he could talk, and that he did in full measure. We listened speechlessly to his hair-raising accounts of his travels in America. That was something

Edvard Grieg enrolled as a pupil at Tanks School in Bergen on 1 April 1853, aged nearly 10. (THG)

The plaque at Tanks School commemorating former pupil Edvard Grieg. (THG)

Grieg's music teacher and friend in Bergen, Ferdinand G Schediwy (1804–1877). (EGM)

Edvard Grieg's self-portrait. Pencil sketch. (BOB)

for my childish imagination. When he heard that I liked to compose and improvise, there was no getting away from it: I had to go to the piano.

'I don't understand what Ole Bull could have found at that time in my naïve, childish pieces, but he grew very serious and talked quietly to my parents. What they discussed was not disadvantageous to me; for suddenly Ole Bull came over to me, shook me in his peculiar way and said: "You are to go to Leipzig to become an artist!"

'Everyone looked tenderly at me, and I understood only this one thing: that a gentle fairy was stroking my cheek and that I was happy. And my parents! Not a moment's objection or even hesitation. Everything was settled, and it seemed to me the most natural thing in the world.'

Afgaaede med „Nordstjernen" den 16de Septbr.

Til Mosterhavn: Sagfører Steen. — Haugesund:
Jfr. B. Monsen, L. Johnsen, 4 Lodser. — Stavanger:
Nelander, J. Johnsen, K. Jørgensen, J. Jørgensen, Aadne
Olsen, Hermsen, Krüger, C. Paulsen, Md. J. Juul, Anna
Olsen, Th. Barnes. — Farsund: C. P. Johannesen, B.
Asbjørnsen, A. Berentsen, Jfr. A. Brun. — Kleven: N.
Pedersen. Christiansand: J. C. Møller, Peter Blytt, Ran-
dulf Nielsen, Lorenz Kärling, Ryning, J. Irgens, Marstran-
der. — Hamburg: Frøken Jahns, Hals og Datter Edv.
Grieg.

Edvard Grieg travelled to Leipzig on the steamship Nordstjernen. 'Departing with Nordstjernen 16 Sept: … Bound for Hamburg: Miss Jahns, Hals and Daughter, Edvard Grieg. Facsimile of Bergensposten, 17 September 1858. (BOB)

FROM THE PROVINCIAL CITY OF BERGEN TO THE MUSICAL METROPOLIS OF LEIPZIG

Edvard Grieg was not a stranger to foreign travel when he boarded the steam passenger ship *Nordstjernen* on 16 September 1858, bound for Hamburg and from there by train to Leipzig. He had accompanied his father and uncle several times before on business trips in Norway and abroad, but it was quite a different matter to set out on his own to become a student in a foreign city many times the size of Bergen.

The Leipzig Conservatory where Edvard Grieg studied. (EGM)

The railway station in Leipzig in Grieg's day.
(EGM)

Felix Mendelssohn-Bartholdy (1809–1847).
(BOB)

A friend of the family accompanied him to his lodgings in Leipzig, but once there he was left to his own devices – and his loneliness.

'*I was overcome by homesickness. I went into my room, and I sat crying continuously until I was called to dinner by my hosts. The husband, a genuine Saxon post-office official, tried to console me: "Look here, my dear Herr Grieg, it is the same sun, the same moon, the same loving God you have at home."*

'*Very well intended. But neither sun nor moon nor loving God could compensate for my father's vanished friend, the last link that had bound me to my home. Children's moods change quickly, however. I soon got over the homesickness, and although I didn't have the foggiest idea of what it really meant to study music, I was nonetheless cocksure that the miracle would happen – that in three years after completing my studies there, I would return home as a wizard in the kingdom of music!*' (From My First Success)

Actually, Edvard Grieg did know quite a bit about what to expect as a student of music; he had talked at length with, and been

The famous Gewandhaus concert hall (a converted textile factory) where Grieg went to concerts in his student days, later to return as visiting soloist and conductor. (BOB)

Concert programme from Grieg's student days in Leipzig. (BOB)

given advice by, musicians in Bergen, especially his teacher and life-long friend Ferdinand G Schediwy. He had already composed a number of piano pieces by this time, several of which we find in his list of compositions without opus numbers (labelled EG).

Although this undersized lad from the far North was gently teased by his fellow students at first for his childlike appearance (they threw him back and forth between them), Grieg soon proved that his puny appearance hid a musical talent that far exceeded that of his classmates at the Conservatory.

The Leipzig Conservatory was founded in 1843 (the year of Grieg's birth) by the composer Felix Mendelssohn-Bartholdy. It quickly achieved a sound reputation thanks to the quality of the teaching staff, and it was considered one of the most progressive conservatories in Europe.

The Conservatory attracted students from all over Europe and America; in Grieg's year there were 45 students from Germany, Britain, America, Russia and Scandinavia. Grieg got on best with the other students from the Scandinavian countries, and

Grieg was a regular visitor to the Leipzig Opera. (BOB)

*Richard Wagner
(1813–1883).*

*Clara Schumann
(1819–1896), wife of
the composer Robert
Schumann, was the fore-
most pianist of her day.
She made a lasting im-
pression on Grieg when
he heard her playing her
husband's Piano Con-
certo in A minor in
Leipzig in 1858.*

*Ignaz Moscheles
(1794–1870) was one
of the finest pianists in
Europe. 'I studied dozens
of Beethoven sonatas
with him.'*

became particularly close friends with CF Emil Hornemann from Denmark.

The syllabus at the Conservatory consisted of music harmony, composition and piano playing, as well as lectures on the history of music, music aesthetics and acoustics.

Grieg's attitude towards his studies, hard work and competition had not changed much from his school days in Bergen – he later described himself as lazy and uninterested in what he was being taught. He also commented many times in later life on what he felt to be the shortcomings of the teaching and syllabus at Leipzig.

'I must say, in contrast to Svendsen, that I left the Conservatory in Leipzig as stupid as I was when I arrived there. I had learned something, of course, but my individuality was still a closed book for me.' (Letter from Grieg to his biographer Aimar Grønvold, 1881)

Grieg also complained that he did not receive training in the treatment of musical material in large-scale forms and for larger ensembles.

'YOUTHFUL IMPRESSIONS DO NOT LIE'

In Leipzig Edvard Grieg came face to face with a music environment of such intensity and high quality that it had a formative effect on his receptive young mind. As a music student he could attend all dress rehearsals of the Leipzig Gewandhaus Orchestra. In addition to orchestral concerts, there were regular solo and chamber music recitals given by top performers of the day. A successful concert with a good write-up by the Leipzig critics was the very best springboard for the career of any aspiring young musician – 'everyone' had to perform in Leipzig.

The Leipzig Opera, which already had a long and distinguished reputation for traditional works, put on contemporary opera, providing Grieg with a wealth of experience and setting the standard for his music appreciation. During his first year in Leipzig, Wagner's *Tannhäuser* was on at the Leipzig Opera, and Grieg saw all fourteen performances.

He was also lucky enough to hear Clara Schumann play her husband's *Piano Concerto in A minor*, which was a model for Grieg's own piano concerto ten years later. Clara Schumann's performance was a revelation for Grieg. When he heard Schumann's concerto performed in Oslo in 1907, he was outraged by the pianist's exaggerated, stylised manner which he called 'Wagnerian',

Edvard and John – 'Little Grieg and Big Grieg' – at the Conservatory in Leipzig.
(EGM)

Frederik Kuhlau (1786–1832) was a Danish pianist and composer with an extensive output spanning all the current genres of the day. He is best known for his opera Elverhøj, but he also wrote a number of small pieces for piano which are used in piano teaching.

Muzio Clementi (1752–1832) was an Italian virtuoso pianist and composer. His collection of instructional piano pieces Gradus ad Parnassum became a byword in piano tuition, and his numerous sonatas and sonatinas are still widely used for teaching purposes.

by which he meant that the soloist could not manage to string together four bars at the same tempo. After this dreadful performance he wrote the following account of the first time he heard the Schumann piano concerto:

'When the first, and to some extent the second, movement of Schumann's A minor Concerto is performed as it was yesterday, the noble master must turn over in his grave. It was like a rubber mask that was

Carl Czerny (1791–1857) was an Austrian pianist and composer. He was a renowned piano teacher, and his pupils included Franz Liszt. His contribution to the piano teaching repertoire is still acknowledged.

Moritz Hauptmann (1792–1868).

'Finally, I had lessons from Moritz Hauptmann; and I am still grateful to that amiable old man for all that he taught me through his sensitive and insightful comments. Despite his erudition, he represented to me the essence of non-scholastic learning. For him, rules were important only because they embodied essential laws of nature. I will mention here an episode that in a weak →

distorted beyond recognition by being pulled in all directions; it was like the music of a drunken man. [...] This is a crime. The tradition here is not in doubt. Schumann died in 1856. I came to Leipzig in 1858, and a few months after my arrival I heard the bewitching Clara Schumann play the Concerto, and each tempo remains indelibly on my soul. Youthful impressions like that do not lie. The brain is as soft as wax to receive impressions, and the imprint remains for life.' (Diary entry, 20 January 1907)

'GO HOME AND PRACTISE!'

Grieg was very taken with Schumann's music. Schumann, like Wagner, was not held much in account by the professors in general at the Leipzig Conservatory, who thought these two composers too radical. But Grieg was lucky enough, after a short period with Louis Plaidy as his piano teacher, to be taught by 'Schumann's brilliant friend' Ernst Ferdinand Wenzel.

This switch of teachers shows us something of Grieg's strong will and determination. He found his lessons with Plaidy extremely uninspiring, and when Plaidy set him to work on the studies of Kuhlau, Clementi and Czerny, it all became too much (or rather too little) for Grieg. As he wrote:

'In other words: I became lazy. Clementi's sonatas bored me. So did the rules about fifths and octaves. The things that excited me – the compositions of Chopin, Schumann and Richard Wagner – were things that an ambitious student at the Conservatory could not begin to study without committing a mortal sin ...' (Quoted in an article by J de Jong in De Tijdspiegel, 1881)

Louis Plaidy no doubt noticed his young pupil's apathy and lack of interest in these works. Grieg describes one of his lessons with Plaidy.

'One day, as I sat pounding away at what I considered an abominable Clementi sonata that he had forced me to study, he suddenly grabbed the music off the piano and pitched it in such a way that it flew through the air in a great arc and came to rest in the farthest corner of the classroom. Since he couldn't very well do the same thing with me personally, he contented himself with thundering, "Go home and practise!" I must admit that he had a right to be furious ...' (My First Success)

Grieg took it upon himself to go to the director of the Conservatory, Conrad Schleinitz, and ask to be assigned a new piano teacher, and the director agreed to his request. The amiable Ernst Ferdinand Wenzel led Grieg into the Classical world of Beethoven and Mozart, and introduced him to the modern tonal art of Schumann. Grieg greatly appreciated his new teacher, and dedicated his *Four Piano Pieces*, op. 1 to Wenzel.

Grieg also received piano lessons from Ignaz Moscheles, one of the very best pianists and teachers of his day. Moscheles was a great interpreter of Beethoven, and Grieg studied *'dozens of Beethoven sonatas'* under his instruction. Moscheles's edition of Beethoven's 32 Piano Sonatas that Grieg used as a student in Leipzig can be seen today on the piano stool in the composer's hut at Troldhaugen.

His studies with Wenzel and Moscheles sparked Grieg's ambition, as he realised that his classmates were surpassing him in technical skill. This triggered his competitive spirit and he recognised that the way to success was through hard work.

ARTISTIC AMBITIONS OVERCOME ILLNESS

It may be that Grieg's newfound industriousness was one of the reasons that he neglected his health. What he thought was merely a bad cold at the end of 1859 proved to be tuberculosis. He was so hard hit by the disease that, had he not returned home in the spring of 1860 to be nursed back to health, the outcome could have been fatal. Although he survived the illness, Grieg's health had taken quite a knock. One of his lungs was permanently damaged, and for the rest of his life he was bothered by chronic breathing problems and was very susceptible to infections in his airways.

However, his artistic spark of genius had been aroused, and against the express advice of his doctor and his parents, he returned to Leipzig that autumn. This time he was accompanied by his older brother, John, who was to study the cello. They soon became known as Little Grieg and Big Grieg.

Grieg studied theory and composition under Ernst Friedrich Richter, Robert Papperitz and Moritz Hauptmann. In his final year he had Carl Reinecke, the conductor of the Gewandhaus Orchestra, as his professor of composition. Reinecke took a very conservative approach to the teaching of composition, and Grieg did not get a lot out of these classes. *'What Reinecke failed to teach me, I tried to pick up from Mozart and Beethoven, whose quartets I diligently studied on my own initiative.'* (My First Success)

moment I might call a success. Even before I knew Hauptmann – I was not yet sixteen years old, and I still wore a boy's blouse – I had received the honour, in a *Privat-Prüfung* (a kind of annual private examination in which all the students without exception were required to take part), of being allowed to play a piece that I myself had composed. When I had finished, and was leaving the piano, to my surprise I saw an old gentleman rise from the professors' table and come towards me. He laid his hand on my shoulder and said, 'Good day, young man! We must become good friends.' That was Hauptmann, and naturally I loved him from that moment on. Sickly as he was in the last years of his life, he gave lessons in his own home – the Thomasschule, Johann Sebastian Bach's old residence. Here I had the pleasure of getting to know him better. I well remember him sitting on his sofa, wearing a bathrobe and a skullcap, his spectacles buried deep in my exercise book, which still contains more than one drop of the yellowish-brown liquid that dripped from his snuff-filled nose. He sat with a big silken handkerchief in one hand with which to catch the drips – but it didn't work. So it was used as a washcloth to clean the exercise book, which still clearly shows evidence of such wiping.'
(MY FIRST SUCCESS)

Louis Plaidy (1811–1874).

Carl Reinecke, Grieg's teacher of music theory and composition. 'What Reinecke failed to teach me I tried to pick up from Mozart and Beethoven.' (EG)

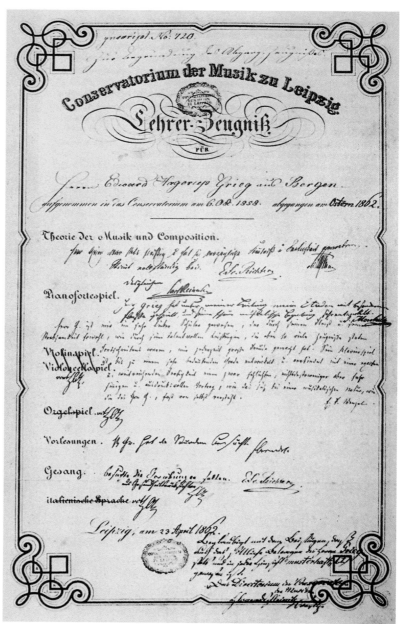

Edvard Grieg's diploma from the Conservatory in Leipzig. (BOB)

Later in life Grieg was at times highly critical of the training he had received in Leipzig, but this may not give a fair picture of what he actually learned there. These critical comments were probably his way of expressing the frustration he felt at not having been guided along the path that he was really seeking (although he may not have had a clear picture of this path himself at that stage). Nor is it likely that the Conservatory had the necessary resources to provide for such a talented student as Edvard Grieg.

When Edvard Grieg graduated from the Leipzig Conservatory, he was highly commended by all his teachers. There is no sign that they regarded him as lazy or inattentive. Moritz Hauptmann wrote Grieg the following commendation a few days before his final exam:

'Mr Grieg from Bergen, a student at this conservatory who stands out as an excellent pianist, must also be counted among the best students in composition with respect to both theoretical mastery and practical application. An exemplary diligence and love of study have always undergirded his natural talent. He has, therefore, acquired an exceptional level of training that promises great success in the future.'

This commendation was endorsed by Carl Reinecke, his professor of composition, who wrote:

'I testify with pleasure that Mr Grieg possesses a most considerable musical talent, especially for composition. It is much to be desired that he be given the opportunity to develop this talent to the fullest in every possible way.'

These teachers, and those who signed Grieg's official diploma, obviously had a high opinion of Grieg's work and talent. It is particularly interesting to note Reinecke's comment that he hoped that Grieg would get the chance to study and continue his development in other stimulating surroundings after graduating.

Concert programme from Grieg's student days in Leipzig. (BOB)

STRENGTH OF CHARACTER

In Grieg's memoirs of his student days in Leipzig we find vivid descriptions of his teachers and fellow students and some great artistic experiences. But it was not just his serious illness in 1860 that could have put an abrupt end to his stay in Leipzig, for Grieg also managed to get into a heated argument with Conrad Schleinitz, the director of the Conservatory.

Each week student concerts were held, which all students of the Conservatory were required to attend. When the appointed time came, the doors were closed. On one occasion Grieg and a few other students arrived after the start of the concert. At the

Grieg – 'a wizard in the kingdom of music'. (BOB)

Another of Edvard Grieg's diplomas from the Conservatory in Leipzig. (BOB)

Grieg used his former teacher Ignaz Moscheles' edition of Beethoven's 32 piano sonatas as a cushion on the piano stool in his composer's hut at Troldhaugen. (THG)

next concert they were given a very public reprimand in front of all the other students while the director made it clear that it was always the laziest, least talented students who arrived late. Grieg took great offence and the next day he marched into the director's office, saying that he refused to be treated like that in public. The director started to threaten Grieg with expulsion from the Conservatory, at which Grieg claimed his right to freedom of speech. Schleinitz burst out laughing at this candid, unafraid attitude; the two of them shook hands, laughed the whole thing off, and remained firm friends from that day onwards.

This was the first recorded example of Grieg's attitude to authority and his ability to speak up when he felt authority was being abused, and he continued in the same vein throughout his life.

His student days in Leipzig were now over, and Grieg had indeed become a *'wizard in the kingdom of music'*. But the most important task yet remained – to find himself, to find the music within, and to dare to stand on his own two feet. He went home to Bergen and Norway, then travelled to Denmark, then returned home again. He found his own unique music and personal style, yet he remained a restless soul all his life, forever in search of something, seeking all that is genuine and true.

Throughout this incessant physical and spiritual wandering, Leipzig remained at the centre of Edvard Grieg's life and work. It was here that he found his own publishers, Max Abraham and Henri Hinrichsen at Edition Peters in Thalstrasse 10. Grieg was given an attic apartment there, which he used a great deal.

On graduating from Leipzig, Grieg returned to Bergen, but there was too little artistic stimulation to be found there, and his father supported him financially so that he could move to Copenhagen, where he became a central figure among the musical avantgarde of the city. He also had close contact with his uncle Hermann Hagerup's family, particularly his three lively, intelligent cousins Nina, Tonny (Antonie) and Yelva (Julie). His stay in Copenhagen bore many fruits – it was here he met Bjørnson and Nordraak, and here his first trip to Rome was planned and brought to fruition. On his return from Rome his feelings for Nina grew, and in 1867 they married and moved to Oslo. The marriage was frowned upon by both families, but the young couple were not to be swayed.

KUHLAU, CLEMENTI
AND CZERNY.
These three composers'
piano pieces were – and
still are – extensively used
by piano teachers. Their
names are often associated
with rather uninspiring
studies.

Moritz Hauptmann taught
music theory and composi-
tion. 'For him, rules were
important only because
they embodied essential
laws of nature.' (EG)

Edvard Grieg as a student, 19 years old. (BOB)

Piano Concerto in A minor, opus 16

A SINGLE WORK – A SINGLE THOUGHT

Pietà *by Michelangelo in St Peter's Basilica, Rome.*

Madonna *by Edvard Munch.*

WITHIN ALL the arts there are certain works that stand out and attract particular attention and admiration for their artistic, aesthetic or human qualities. When you come face to face with a true work of art, you feel it instinctively, although you may not understand why. It is as if you say to yourself: 'That's just how it should be! That is so true! I hadn't thought about it until now, but I can see that it is so.'

Art is not necessarily true, but it is *about* truth – just think of the world's folklore. Artistic ability is about being able to concentrate a boundless amount of information in a single expression – in a confined space – on a small canvas – or within a few moments.

For the audience or observer, a work of art appears to consist of a whole, made up of a multitude of details. But it is not a definitive entity, since all works of art are interpreted by both the performer and the person watching/reading/listening. A piece of music, for instance, engages the emotions and experiences of the performer and the listener, and these emotions and experiences are continually added to the perception of the piece. For this reason, each performance can add something new. The real proof of any work of art is how well it stands the test of time. Michelangelo's Pietà in St Peter's Basilica in Rome, for instance, literally stands as hard as rock – even though a madman tried to smash it to pieces in 1972. The figure was hewn and polished from a single huge block of marble, and it expresses despair and recent death in an incredibly moving way, but above all it expresses love.

Christian Frederik Emil Horneman (1840–1906) and Edvard.(EGM)

Johan Svendsen, Edvard Grieg and Edmund Neupert photographed in Copenhagen in the 1870s. (BOB)

Edvard Grieg in 1865.
(BOB)

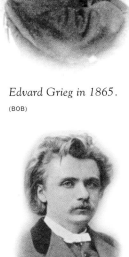

Edvard Grieg in 1868, aged 25, the year he wrote his famous Piano Concerto in A minor.
(BOB)

There is always something new to be found in this great work of art, just as there is in a string quartet by Beethoven or a painting by Munch. If we allow our own feelings and thoughts to blend with the expressions in the work of art, new feelings, thoughts and insights may arise.

If we look at Grieg's entire output, it is certainly true to say that not one of his pieces was mediocre, although not all his works were equally original or powerful.

However, one of his works has always been deemed to be in a class of its own, both in Grieg's day and today: the *Piano Concerto in A minor*, op. 16 will always stand out as a shining example of a single great thought captured and expressed in music. From start to finish the concerto contains one single idea that is constantly expanded upon and given new colour and nuance. Whichever part of the concerto you listen to, there can never be any doubt that it is the *Piano Concerto in A minor* being played. Grieg chose the most daring of openings for this work – a whole bar of expectant roll on the timpani. As the first chord sounds, in some magical way it contains the entire concerto with all its intensity of colour and shading.

Try this simple experiment: put on a CD of the concerto, but sit with your finger on the pause button. As soon as the opening chord sounds, press pause. Can you hear the whole concerto in your head?

THE GRIEG MOTIF – A NORWEGIAN GEM

The opening notes of the *Piano Concerto in A minor* (A–A–G#–E) have become the archetypal Grieg motif. We find this motif in a number of his pieces, but it is used to greatest effect in the opening of the *Piano Concerto*. He spans several octaves with this motif linked by a minor triad (E–C–A). The leitmotif is just like Grieg himself – neither major nor minor, or perhaps both at the same time.

After this majestic opening Grieg presents the first theme in the orchestra in characteristic fashion. The first two bars are in A minor, then these bars are repeated almost exactly, but transposed up to C major. In the exposition the theme is presented concisely with rhythmic suppleness, before it is set free in long billowing phrases.

In the transition between the first theme and the second theme, the piano bounces around to rhythms Grieg borrowed from the Norwegian folkdance called the *halling*, until the beautiful second theme is heralded by the cellos, first in the major, then in the minor.

Grieg displays great mastery and imagination in his development of the thematic material. The tension mounts towards the end of the first movement, culminating in the soloist's embellishment of the material in the cadenza. And then, quite unexpectedly, Grieg makes the piano leap over the edge of a harmonic abyss. The jump, the falling through thin air and the landing are all so masterfully crafted that it is easy to understand why the audience at the first performance broke out in spontaneous applause.

In the second movement, *Adagio*, this unbroken stream of inspired thought continues, albeit in a different direction. Beauty, tranquillity, cessation of time and gravity – everything just *is* in this beautiful space. Grieg explores it with melodic, rhythmic and harmonic genius, without ever leaving its confines. He was so confident of the inherent quality of this material that he had the courage to stick to a single tempo throughout the entire movement, creating a musical still life.

The Grieg motif.

Franz Liszt. (BOB)

Robert Schumann (1810–1856). His music and philosophy made a lasting impression on Edvard Grieg, who loved Schumann's music all his life. (BOB)

Memorial plaque at Mothsgaarden. (THG)

Mothsgaarden at Søllerød, not far from Copenhagen.(EGM)

Mothsgaarden is now part of Søllerød Museum. In 1868 it was owned by Copenhagen merchant Carl Gottlieb Hildebrandt.(THG)

Detail from christening photo of Alexandra, Nina and Edvard Grieg's only child. She was born on 10 April 1868 and died on 20 May 1869. 'She was a beautiful, lovable child, who instantly became calm whenever Edvard started playing the piano.' (Nina Grieg) (EGM)

The last movement, *Allegro moderato molto e marcato*, is heralded quietly but rhythmically by the wind section, before the piano enters with its playful *halling*-dancing main theme, where you can almost hear the Hardanger fiddles and see the folk dancers. The second theme is closely related to the first theme, and it is only as it is pulled this way and that that the contrast between the two becomes clear. The lyrical melody in the flute is reminiscent of *Morning Mood* from *Peer Gynt*; it leads us up into the Norwegian mountains, where it floats for a moment and then vanishes into thin air. The recapitulation brings the theme back in full force, and the movement draws to a grandiose conclusion. Grieg described Franz Liszt's reaction when he played through the concerto for the first time, during Grieg's trip to Rome in the spring of 1870.

'There is one perfectly divine episode that I should not forget. Towards the end of the Finale, as you will remember, the second theme is repeated in a great fortissimo. In the very last bars, where the first note of the first triplet of the theme – G# – is changed to G in the orchestra, while the piano in a tremendous scale passage traverses the entire keyboard, he suddenly stopped, rose to his full height, left the piano, and with mighty theatrical steps and raised arms strode through the great monastery hall, literally roaring out the theme. When he got to the above-mentioned G, he gestured imperiously with his arm and

Today Søllerød Kro is a renowned gourmet restaurant. (THG)

Søllerød Kro – the 'head-quarters' of the piano concerto. (BOB)

cried: "G, G, not G#! Famos! Das ist so echter schwedischer Banco!"
He then went back to the piano, repeated the whole phrase, and con-
cluded.'

Grieg gave permission for excerpts from two letters to his parents to be published in the journal *Samtiden* in 1892, and added this 'divine' episode in the same article.

YOUTHFUL IDEALS

As a student in Leipzig, Edvard Grieg had been very taken with Robert Schumann's music and philosophy of art, although this was not quite the done thing at the Conservatory. He had never forgotten Clara Schumann's interpretation of her husband's *A minor piano concerto* in 1858. We may therefore assume that Grieg had Schumann's concerto in his mind when he started on his largest project so far – composing a piano concerto.

Niels Ravnkilde (1823–1890). (BOB)

The newlyweds Nina and Edvard Grieg had moved from Copenhagen to Oslo in the summer of 1867, since Grieg had an idealistic desire to help establish a professional music scene in the capital city. As it turned out it was all hard graft and Grieg was left with little time for pursuing his art. But on the home front at least this was a happy time for the Griegs, with the birth of their daughter, Alexandra, in 1868; though tragically she died aged just 13 months old.

Anton Rubinstein (1829–1894), famous Russian concert pianist and founder of the St Petersburg Conservatory. His brother, Nikolai, founded the Moscow Conservatory and was one of Peter Tchaikovsky's teachers. (BOB)

From the first performance of the Piano Concerto in A minor, *Copenhagen 3 April 1869.* (BOB)

In the summer of 1868 the whole family went on summer holiday to Copenhagen. Such holidays were a welcome break for Grieg, for it was really only at such times that he had the time and the peace and quiet he needed to get on with his composing. Grieg left Nina and Alexandra with his parents-in-law in Copenhagen and travelled on to Mothsgaard in Søllerød, a few miles further north, with a group of friends. The party consisted of the Norwegian pianist and composer Edmund Neupert, the Danish composer CF Emil Horneman and the author Benjamin Feddersen. Feddersen had rented a small garden room with a piano so that Grieg could work without being disturbed. With his friends nearby, they set up a sort of headquarters at the café at Søllerød Kro for Grieg's project – his piano concerto.

Grieg worked on the concerto all summer, and there is no doubt that inspiration flowed freely. He worked from dawn to nightfall. The weather was extremely hot, but this seems to have helped the process rather than hindered it. It was also incredibly helpful having someone as gifted as Neupert on hand to try out ideas on, and to turn to for constructive criticism and sound advice. All in all, Grieg made speedy progress, and by the end of the summer the outline of the concerto was finished. The solo part, the cadenzas, the overall structure and the thematic material were all there. However, the concerto was not completed at Søllerød, as Grieg simply ran out of time.

Given Grieg's need for continuity in the creative process, this could have been disastrous. We know that many of his works were never completed because some trifling interruption caused him to lose concentration. He would have to complete the work and orchestrate it back home in Oslo, where there was a real risk of getting bogged down by everyday life, with rehearsals, teaching and money worries during the day and the demands of family life in the evening and broken nights in the attic apartment in Øvre Voldgate. Grieg wrote to his Danish friend Niels Ravnkilde:

'I received your letter in Denmark, where I spent the summer. My wife lived with her parents in Copenhagen, while I moved out with Emil Horneman and Edmund Neupert to Søllerød, a small town with which you are no doubt familiar. The heat was unbearable, but nonetheless I think about this time with pleasure. To be sure, I felt lethargic because of the temperature, but I also felt that now I had to get down to business. So I have written a concerto for piano and orchestra that I think contains some good things. I had hoped to get time now during

the autumn evenings to orchestrate the first movement, but – time. The evenings, too, are taken from me. Neupert is scheduled to play it in the Musicians' Association in Copenhagen after Christmas.' (Letter to Niels Ravnkilde, 2 November 1868)

Despite the interruption and the many demands on Grieg's time, the life force of the *Piano Concerto in A minor* was so strong that he managed to complete it, which was just as well, since the first performance was scheduled to take place in Copenhagen just after Christmas. Edmund Neupert was to be the soloist, and the concerto was, not surprisingly, dedicated to him. And Grieg got it finished! Admittedly, not straight after Christmas, but the concerto was performed for the first time on 3 April 1869 in the Casino concert hall in Copenhagen, with Neupert as soloist and Holger Simon Paulli, conductor at the Det Kongelige Teater in Copenhagen, conducting. Unfortunately Grieg himself was unable to attend due to a prior commitment in Oslo.

Johan Peter Emilius Hartmann (1805–1900). (BOB)

However, everyone else who was anyone in the music world was there. Word got around while rehearsals were underway that there was something big going on. The conductor and the orchestra were showing exceptional interest in this work; they spent whole days rehearsing with the soloist, and everyone worked extremely hard.

The day of the concert dawned, and the air was rife with expectation. As chance would have it, the celebrated Russian pianist Anton Rubinstein happened to be in Copenhagen, and he graciously lent the use of the grand piano he had with him on tour for the concert, so naturally he was in the VIP box, watching and listening, together with the entire musical elite of Copenhagen, including Gade and Hartmann.

Niels W Gade (1817–1890). (BOB)

The concert more than lived up to expectations. The audience was exceptionally enthusiastic both during and after the concert. The performance was interrupted by spontaneous applause and cheering, not just after each movement, but even after the main cadenza in the first movement. Grieg's friend Benjamin Feddersen wrote an animated description of the whole concert.

'Your composition was listened to with considerable interest. While my ears attended to your sounds I kept my eyes on the box where the notables were sitting; I observed and understood each expression, each motion, and I can assure you that Gade, Hartmann, Rubinstein and Winding were filled with joy and admiration for your work. At the very beginning Gade said something to Rubinstein, who was lis-

Edmund Neupert (1842–1888). (BOB)

Benjamin J Feddersen
(1823–1902). (BOB)

Facsimile of the 'Søllerød letter' (quoted on page 54) from Edvard Grieg to Niels
Ravnkilde, 2 November 1868. (BOB)

tening with such rapt attention that he only acknowledged Gade's
remark by nodding his head without looking at him. When Neupert
came for the first time to the rest in the first section – the place where
the bassoons come in – Rubinstein spontaneously clasped his hands
together; and throughout, wherever it was appropriate to clap, he and
Gade, Hartmann and Winding joined in the general thunderous chorus of applause.

'How I regretted that you yourself did not have the joy and pleasure of hearing this unusual work. Believe me, it will contribute greatly to your being recognised as one of the most brilliant composers of
our time. You can believe me when I tell you that the applause was
thunderous! But Neupert also did his job exceptionally well, and you
owe him sincere thanks for the interest and the love with which he

Holger Simon Paulli (1810–1891) conductor at the Det Kongelige Theater in Copenhagen. Conducted the first performance of Grieg's Piano Concerto in A minor. (BOB)

The Casino concert hall in Amaliegade in Copenhagen in its heyday in the 1860s. (BOB)

approached the playing of the piano part. Paulli also conducted the rehearsals with great care, and Rubinstein's piano contributed a bit as well with its incomparably rich and sonorous tone.' (Letter from Benjamin Feddersen to Grieg, 4 April 1869)

Edmund Neupert, the soloist, also wrote to Grieg after the concert, and would clearly have been only too pleased to be able to share the success with the man behind the concerto.

*Bjørnstjerne Bjørnson
(1832–1910).* (BOB)

'I must not forget to mention a man who, in the musically empty Oslo during the years 1868–1872, filled me with his powerful personality. That was Bjørnson. He was a true friend to me in those years and deserves much of the credit for my survival. Although he did not understand music, he believed in what I wanted to accomplish – and that gave me courage.'

(EDVARD GRIEG IN
A LETTER TO AIMAR
GRØNVOLD 25 APRIL
1881)

'*On Saturday your divine concerto resounded through the Casino's large auditorium. The triumph that I achieved was really tremendous. Already at the conclusion of the cadenza in the first part the audience broke out in a true storm of applause. The three dangerous critics, Gade, Rubinstein and Hartmann, sat up there in the VIP box and applauded with all their might.*

'*I am supposed to greet you from Rubinstein and tell you that he is really surprised to have heard such a brilliant composition; he looks forward to making your acquaintance. He spoke very warmly about my piano playing. I had at least two curtain calls and at the end I got a big fanfare from the orchestra.*

'*You should have seen Emil and Hansen after the concert; they were nearly ready to eat me up for joy because everything had gone so splendidly. Gade thought very well of the first and second movements, less about the third. Old Hartmann was ecstatic. Feddersen, who sat in the balcony, cried the whole evening.*' (*Letter from Edmund Neupert to Grieg, 6 April 1869*)

Was this a copy of Schumann's Piano Concerto? In a sense, yes. Grieg's *Piano Concerto* was constructed around the same principles of musical form as Schumann's. But that is where the similarities end. Even though Schumann and Grieg were both romanticists, their styles were quite different from each other's. The most striking thing about Grieg's concerto is its bubbly, youthful joyfulness – just listen to the positive, life-affirming mood of the opening bars. What's more, there is this characteristic Griegian (some would say Norwegian), folkloristic feel to it. And yet through this shining happiness Grieg has a special way of sneaking in his very personal characteristic, by painting this youthful delight in a minor key.

The *Piano Concerto* was a roaring success from the word go, and the critics in Copenhagen were effusive in their praise. Grieg was inundated by letters of congratulation and recognition from his colleagues. It must have been a great encouragement to Grieg, stuck as he was in physical and artistic isolation in Oslo, that all his hard work on this great project had such a successful outcome.

'*I received five different letters from dear Denmark telling about art and friendship down there. Yours was one of them. A friendly greeting such as that is like a ray of sunshine flooding into my lonely home. For I lack anything like that here in Norway, and you know very well that the ideal life requires it. For that reason I thank God for my kinship with the Danes, as a result of which my music is understood down there. Here there is coldness and harshness both in nature and in the minds of*

Facsimile of the first page of the original manuscript of the Piano Concerto in A minor, *op. 16.* (BOB)

people. Oh yes, there is in many respects an underlying warmth of heart as well, but the artist needs to see some evidence of it. He can't use his gifts constantly searching the remotest corners in hope of finding some scrap of understanding.' (*Letter from Grieg to Gottfred Matthison-Hansen, 10 April 1869*)

The *Piano Concerto* was performed in Oslo that August. Grieg missed this performance too, as he was on summer holiday with his family in Bergen. Grieg had advised Neupert against putting on a concert in the summertime in Oslo, since it was doubly difficult to get an audience in the holiday season. Nevertheless the

Edvard Grieg (1867).
(EGM)

Edvard Grieg's own printed copy of the Piano Concerto in A minor. (BOB)

concert went ahead as planned, and drew only a very small audience. There was also very little response from the music critics – the only comment in *Aftenbladet* was that the audience had been enthusiastic, particularly after *'Grieg's new, original and inspired composition'*. Period.

The excitement following the concerto's first performance in Copenhagen and the emerging interest in this promising young Norwegian composer in musical circles throughout Europe had positive repercussions for Grieg in Norway. Immediately after Grieg's success in Copenhagen, Bjørnstjerne Bjørnson submitted an article to *Norsk Folkeblad*, in which he noted the recognition Grieg had received in other countries – with the clear subtext that it was about time that his native country followed suit.

'Grieg has not received any obvious encouragement as a composer here in Norway, but he has in fact encountered many, many kinds of obstacles. Elsewhere, however, he has received wide acclaim. In Germany, and especially in Denmark, he is regarded as the man of the hour. Moreover, when he recently solicited recommendations from Europe's most famous composers in support of his application for a fellowship, he received the most excellent encomiums. Moscheles, Rubinstein, Hartmann, Gade, Liszt, etc., have given him much encouragement in his work.' (Bjørnstjerne Bjørnson in Norsk Folkeblad, *10 April 1869*)

Grieg had applied to the king for a travel grant, which he received after waiting a long time for an answer. His application was accompanied by strong letters of recommendation from well-known figures such as Gade, Hartmann and Moscheles (Grieg's piano teacher in Leipzig), but it was no doubt the eloquent letter from Franz Liszt (in French) that tipped the scales in Grieg's favour with the tight-fisted authorities. Liszt sent the following letter of recommendation to Grieg on 29 December 1868:

'*Monsieur,*

It is with the greatest pleasure that I express to you the sincere joy that I felt upon reading through your sonata, opus 8. The sonata bears witness to a great talent for composition and shows a well-conceived, inventive and excellent treatment of the material; it demonstrates a talent that needs only to follow its natural bent to attain a high level. I hope and trust that in your homeland you will receive the success and encouragement that you deserve; surely that is not asking too much. If you should come to Germany this winter, I cordially invite you to make a visit to Weimar so that we could meet.

Receive, monsieur, the assurance of my deepest regard.

Franz Liszt.'

CONCEIVED BEFORE HE BEGAN
– PERFECTED UNDERWAY

Grieg must have had the overall structure and ideas for his piano concerto in his head before ever starting to write it. And yet a number of details in the concerto in the form in which we know it today were not added until years later by the more experienced Grieg. Thanks to its popularity, Grieg was able to hear the concerto performed a great many times, and he constantly discovered small things that could be improved on, or new ways of orchestrating certain passages to come even closer to the ideal in his head.

In the original manuscript even the opening differed from later editions, with horns, trombones and timpani in the first bar, while the string section also marked the start with a short, light pizzicato. The final version with timpani alone was altered in the 1894 edition. Grieg's own printed score is on exhibit at the Edvard Grieg Museum at Troldhaugen, and we can see how he constantly added comments and made small alterations.

There were several reasons for these alterations. Some of them were a result of Grieg himself wanting to change things he had noticed at some performance of the work, while some of them may have come from other sources. It is probable that the instrumentation of the first edition was influenced by the legendary Franz Liszt.

Although he had to miss the successful first performance in Copenhagen, his next visit to Copenhagen was gratifying for Grieg. In the autumn of 1869 he finally returned to Copenhagen and stayed there for eight weeks, during which time he conducted two concerts, including the *Piano Concerto* with Neupert as soloist, and reaped general acclaim. He later (in 1893) referred to this as his first independent concert in Denmark, remarking that he '... *really made my breakthrough down here. I conducted my piano concerto, which Neupert played superbly.*'

Following this success he was keen to travel elsewhere again. On 14 November 1869 he wrote to Niels Ravnkilde, a Danish composer friend, who was staying in Rome at that time: '*I have now spent two months in frenzied activity here in Copenhagen. I had hoped to find peace and quiet for working, but that will have to wait until my trip to Rome ...*', adding that he hoped to be able to stay at Monte Pincio.

Grieg's second trip to Rome lasted for four months, like his first. Just like the first time, he arrived a few days before Christmas. Coming face to face with Italy's art and culture was a source of inspiration and clarification for him. Grieg believed that it was extremely important for artists from Scandinavia not to limit their education and knowledge to the Germanic tradition; it was only through study of more southerly art in addition that balance could be achieved. '*Our national character is so heavy and introspective that it needs this counterbalance.*'

His stay in Italy provided Grieg with a wealth of experiences, but the highlight of this trip was undoubtedly his two meetings with Franz Liszt. He described these meetings in optimistic, animated letters to his family.

'*Dear Parents!*
[Liszt] came toward me with a smile and said in the most pleasant way, "We have exchanged a few letters, haven't we?" I told him that it was thanks to his letter that I was now here, a remark which elicited a truly Ole Bullian laugh from him. All the while he eyed with a sort of voracious expression the parcel I was carrying under my arm [...] And his spidery fingers hovered so menacingly that I decided the most prudent course would be to make a move to open the parcel without

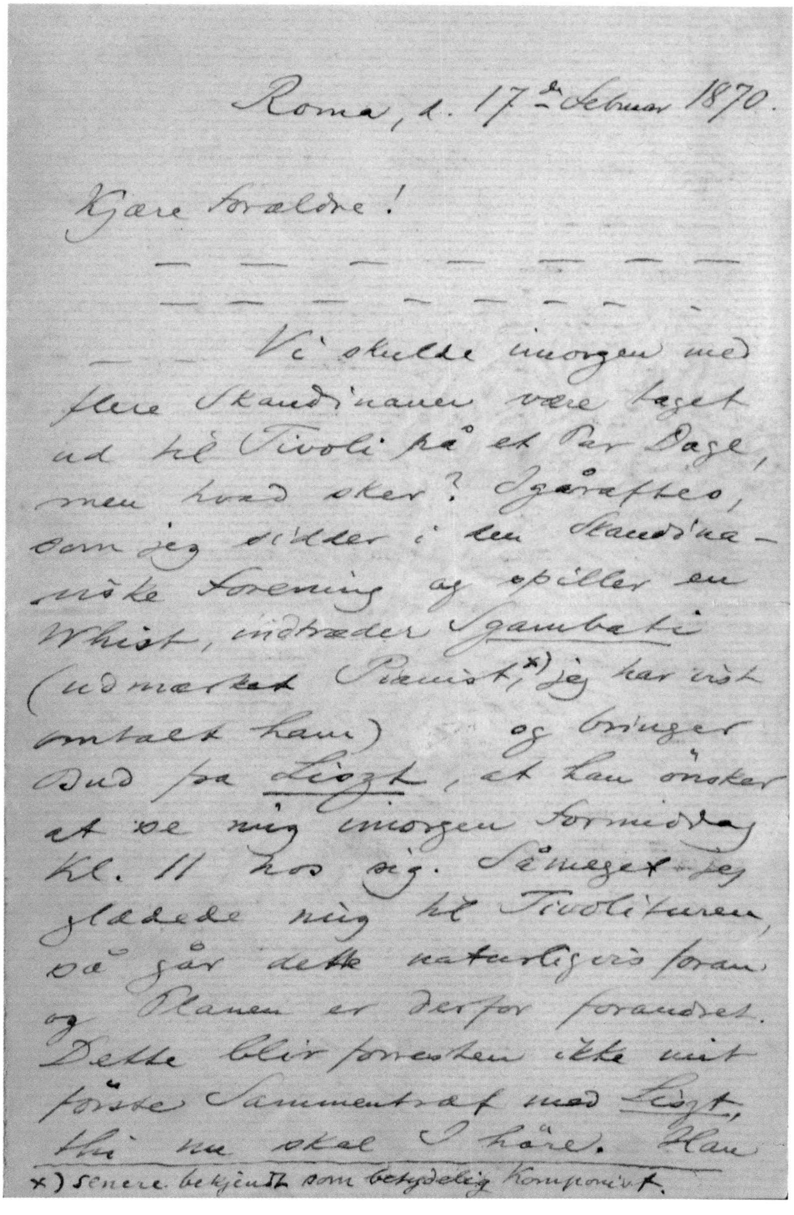

[Handwritten letter in Norwegian:]

> Roma, d. 17de Februar 1870.
>
> Kjære Forældre!
>
> — — — — — — — —
> — — — — — — —
> — — — Vi skulde imorgen med
> flere Skandinaver være taget
> ud til Tivoli på et Par Dage,
> men hvad sker? Sgambati,
> som jeg sidder i den Skandina-
> viske Forening og spiller en
> Whist, indtræder Sgambati
> (udmærket Pianist,*) jeg har vist
> omtalt ham) og bringer
> Bud fra Liszt, at han ønsker
> at se mig imorgen formiddag
> Kl. 11 hos sig. Sømeget—jeg
> glædede mig til Tivolituren,
> så går dette naturligvis foran,
> og Planen er derfor forandret.
> Dette blir forresten ikke mit
> første Sammentraf med Liszt,
> thi nu skal I høre. Han
> *) senere bekjendt som betydelig Komponist.

August Winding
(1835–1899). (EGM)

Grieg's letter to his parents about his meeting with Liszt in Rome.(BOB)

delay. He then started to leaf through it, i.e., he read quickly through
the first part of the Sonata (opus 13), and that this was no mere bluff
was immediately obvious when he indicated the best passages with a
significant nod of his head, a "bravo", or a "very beautiful". My spirits
rose, but when he then asked me to play the Sonata my mood immedi-

ately dropped to below zero. It had never occurred to me to play the Violin Sonata – both the violin and the piano part – on the piano, and on the other hand I was anxious to avoid having to sit there and mess things up. But there was no way out, so I sat down at his lovely American piano and began to play. At the very start, where the violin breaks in alone with a somewhat baroque but national passage, he exclaimed, "Ah, how daring! Listen, I like this. Let me hear it again, please." And when the violin comes in again, this time adagio, he played the violin part an octave higher on the piano, and he played with an expression so beautiful – so absolutely, amazingly authentic and cantabile – that I smiled to myself. Those were the first tones I heard from Liszt.

'And now we came straight into the Allegro, he playing the violin part, I the piano. My courage steadily increased, because I was so pleased with his approval, which in truth flowed so abundantly that I felt the most wonderful gratitude. When we had finished the first movement, I asked if I might play something for piano alone, choosing the Minuet from the Humoresques, which you of course remember. When I had played the first eight bars, and repeated them, he sang the melody with a certain heroic expression of power in his gesture, which I very readily understood. I noted, of course, that it was the national peculiarities that appealed to him. I had suspected this earlier, and for that reason had brought along a number of pieces in which I had tried to touch some national strings.' (Letter to Grieg's parents, 17 February 1870)

A few months later he wrote:

'Dear Parents!

[…] Winding and I were very eager to see if he really would sight-read my Concerto – something that I, for my part, considered an impossibility. Liszt, however, was of an entirely different opinion. He said, "Will you play?" I quickly said, "No, I can't!" Then Liszt took the manuscript, went to the piano and said with a characteristic smile to all those present, "Well, then I will show you that I can't either." And then he began. And in view of what he now achieved, I must say that it would be impossible to imagine anything of the kind that would be more sublime. Oh yes, he played the first movement somewhat rapidly, and the result was that the opening passage sounded rather slapdash; but later on, when I had an opportunity to indicate the tempo, he played as he alone and no one else can. It is typical that he played the cadenza, which is among the technically most difficult parts of the concerto, perfectly. His gestures are priceless. You see, he doesn't just play; no, he converses and criticises at the same time. He carries on a brilliant conversation, not with one person but the entire audience,

C F E Horneman and E Grieg are photographed together again. (EGM)

distributing significant nods to right and left, mainly when he is particularly pleased with something. In the Adagio, and to an even greater
extent in the Finale, he reached a peak both in execution and in the
praise he gave.

Finally, as he handed me the score, he said: "Hold to your course.
Let me tell you, you have the talent for it, and – don't get scared off!"

Virtuoso violinist and composer Johan Svendsen (1840–1911) left Paris and Leipzig to return home to Norway in the early 1870s. He later became principal conductor at Det Kongelige Theater in Copenhagen. (BOB)

This last is of infinite importance to me. There is almost what I will call a sacred mandate about it. Time and again when disappointments and bitterness come, I shall think of his words, and the memory of this hour will have a singular power to sustain me in days of adversity; that is my confident hope.' (Letter to Grieg's parents, 9 April 1870)

After returning home, Grieg also submitted a report to the Ministry of Church and Education, in which he naturally spoke warmly of his meetings with Liszt and their significance for him. *'In him I have got to know not only the most brilliant of piano players, but what's more, a phenomenon – intellectually and in stature – unmatched in the sphere of art. I brought him several of my compositions, which he played; and it was of supreme interest for me to observe how the national element in my work at first made him hesitant, but then enthusiastic. A triumph of this kind for my efforts and my views on the national element is itself worth the journey.' (Excerpt from Grieg's report to the Norwegian Ministry of Church and Education, September 1870)*

The clearest influence from Liszt in the first edition of the concerto was the use of the trumpets in the orchestration of the beautiful second theme. It was not until the 1882 edition that we find the second theme where it naturally belongs, i.e. the cello section, which is much closer to the typical Griegian sound.

Given the successful performances and Liszt's unambiguous praise, it might be expected that there was no difficulty in getting the *Piano Concerto* published. In fact it proved more difficult than expected; neither Sophus Hagen in Copenhagen nor the big Leipzig publishing houses were courageous enough to take on this major project. Despite the concerto's success in the Nordic countries, and the fact that Grieg was willing to accept a minimal fee, if any, it was not until Johan Svendsen approached his publisher EW Fritzsch in Leipzig that there was any likelihood of the work being published. Svendsen wrote to Grieg in July 1871:

'I have spoken at length with Fritzsch concerning your Piano Concerto – without being familiar with it – and made his mouth water. I am completely confident that he will publish it […] He is an honest man of the rarest kind, and he bets everything on something that he believes has a future.' (Letter from Johan Svendsen to Grieg, 14 July 1871)

The *Piano Concerto* was published for the first time in 1872 and this decision proved to be a sound financial investment on the part of the publisher.

Peer Gynt

'THE MOST UNMUSICAL OF ALL SUBJECTS'

WHEN NINA and Edvard Grieg went to live in Oslo in 1867, they were full of idealism, and they set out to establish a thriving professional music scene in the capital city. Their ambition proved somewhat optimistic – they encountered little willingness among the city's inhabitants or politicians to take any decisive steps towards raising the artistic standard or making it possible for musicians to earn a decent living. Even so, this period in Oslo meant a lot to Grieg insofar as it brought him in close contact with three of the leading lights of Norwegian culture: Bjørnstjerne Bjørnson, Johan Svendsen and Henrik Ibsen.

Henrik Ibsen. (BOB)

Grieg developed a close friendship with Bjørnstjerne Bjørnson. In 1868 he wrote to his Danish friend Niels Ravnkilde: *'But Bjørnson is here, thank God; where he is there is also life and imagination.' (Letter to Niels Ravnkilde, 2 November 1868)*

Bjørnson's wide-ranging ideas and interests stimulated Grieg far beyond the musical plane, and without a doubt Bjørnson helped awaken Grieg's political and social consciousness.

Johan Svendsen, who had returned to Norway after studying music in Leipzig and living for a time in Paris, was very different from Grieg, both in terms of temperament and music. Nevertheless the two men worked extremely well together, and were a source of mutual inspiration. Grieg and Svendsen shared many artistic successes in the Norwegian capital, which amazed people in Oslo, since they had assumed that when two great artists were forced to share the same arena, it would inevitably lead to envy and competition. In fact the very opposite happened, and the two remained almost like brothers throughout their lives.

Bjørnstjerne Bjørnson, on succeeding Henrik Ibsen as theatre director at Det Norske Theater in Bergen. (EGM)

The busy years in Oslo were not all bad, despite many difficulties. Grieg's close contact with these other great artists was a source of stimulation that rekindled his creative spark again and again. His comment that '... *that was indeed a wonderful time, in spite of everything*' is one of few positive statements on record about his years in Oslo; generally speaking Grieg did not attempt to conceal his feelings about the dreadful conditions for artists in Norway's capital city.

'*Tell Ibsen from me that things are absolutely delightful up here. It was quite a shock returning here from southern Europe this time, much more so than ever before. I was greeted with icy coldness on all fronts, and I came very close to packing my bags and leaving.' (Letter to John Paulsen, 15 November 1876)*

'I live up here frozen solid, in more than the literal sense. The music is going wrong everywhere. No music with full orchestra is to be had in our association, as two bassoons have decided to be awkward and won't join us for all the gold in the world – and they are the only ones in town. I have far too little to do, but nevertheless compose nothing.' (Letter to August Winding, 29 December 1876)

'Yes, conditions are wonderful in Oslo: the vilest cliques befoul the air there [...] Lies and slander are now being flung at me – but they can't reach me. If you come to Oslo you will first encounter a courtesy and friendliness that will surprise you so much that you will say: surely there cannot be anything lurking here! But – the sly old fox is on the prowl. Yet, what am I talking about, really? Well, it can only be intimated. If you pursue your own ideals, sooner or later you will run into this monster of prejudice, of half-this-and-half-that, of flabbiness, of egoism, of hatred, of envy – yes, of bestiality, of low slavery.' (Letter to John Paulsen, 19 August 1877)

Grieg's Oslo period culminated in his collaboration with Henrik Ibsen on *Peer Gynt*. Ibsen lived abroad from 1864 to 1891, so, with the exception of sporadic meetings in Rome and Germany, all contact between the two men was in writing. They met for the first time in Rome in 1865, but did not have much contact until several years later, and then primarily through their correspondence about *Peer Gynt*. Ibsen and Grieg never became close personal friends.

PEER GYNT – BETWEEN BJØRNSON AND IBSEN

Grieg had met Bjørnson in Copenhagen, and both he and his cousin Rikard Nordraak made a lasting impression on the young Edvard Grieg. Nordraak had set many of Bjørnson's poems to music and Grieg thought the world of these compositions. When Nina and Edvard moved to Oslo, it was only natural that they became firm friends with Bjørnson, and Grieg's artistic collaboration with Bjørnson was animated and enthusiastic from the start.

The inspired fusion of these two great artistic spirits provides us with a glimpse of Norway in the second half of the nineteenth century, and the possibilities that arose with the dawn of the new Norwegian nation. The collaboration between Bjørnson and

The young Edvard Grieg (1866). (EGM)

Grieg was extremely dynamic. According to Grieg, Bjørnson knew absolutely nothing about music, but he understood the significance of music and the power and necessity of art in human existence. Most importantly he gave Grieg, who at this stage was still rather unsure of himself and his vocation, the courage to follow his

The manuscript of Sigurd Jorsalfar. (BOB)

own instincts. Bjørnson's friendship contributed to Grieg's artistic
and political development. Bjørnson was regarded as a 'dangerous
revolutionary and anti-Christ' by much of the Oslo bourgeoisie,
and many of Grieg's relations in Oslo were uneasy about Grieg's
close friendship with such a man. However, Grieg said on many
occasions that Bjørnson was the person who meant most to him in
those musically barren years in Oslo, and he always claimed that
it was Bjørnson who had made him a democrat.

Unfortunately their great plan to write a national opera, *Olav
Trygvason*, never came to fruition, but before this project foun-
dered they had already created a number of important works of
national art. In 1871 Bjørnson started adapting his poem cycle
Arnljot Gelline as an opera libretto for which Grieg was to write

the music. Grieg immediately set to music the fourth poem in the epic, *Before a Southern Convent*, and this composition for soloists, choir and orchestra convinced Bjørnson that he and Grieg would indeed be able to create a Norwegian opera with a national theme.

Grieg regarded *Before a Southern Convent*, op. 20 as one of his best compositions to date, and frequently included it in the programme of his European concert tours. He always needed to be sure that the choirs that were to perform the work were big enough – and good enough. In most instances this turned out to be the case, after detailed correspondence with the organisers, but occasionally his worst fears were confirmed. After a certain performance of *Before a Southern Convent* in Paris in 1903 Grieg wrote to Frants Beyer: '*Then came* Before a Southern Convent. *Except for the orchestra, everything was mediocre: [Gulbranson] has none of the sensitivity that is required, the alto was abominable, the chorus tiny (twenty) and poor.*'

Grieg and Bjørnson's next collaborative project was the drama based on the old Norse saga of *Sigurd Jorsalfar*. Grieg composed incidental music to Bjørnson's text, and the first performance on 10 April 1872 was one of the greatest successes in Norwegian theatre to date. Grieg invited Bjørnson to join him at a festal performance of the drama on 17 May (Norway's national day) at the Christiania Theatre. Both men were probably a little nervous about how the audience would receive the piece and whether the performers would be up to scratch.

The audience was enthusiastic from the start, but the performance was far from in keeping with the ideals of either the author or the composer. Grieg described their ordeal during the performance in his *Festschrift* for Bjørnstjerne Bjørnson's 70th birthday in 1902. He wrote that during the first act Bjørnson sighed and grunted and mumbled under his breath about the static production. However, in the second act things began to pick up, thanks mainly to the leading actress Laura Gundersen's wonderful delivery of her opening monologue, and Bjørnson became more serene, '*… he sat there like a schoolboy in the classroom, calm and well-behaved*'.

Grieg was primarily concerned about how *The King's Song* in Act 3 would go. The man playing the court poet was a gifted actor but no great singer, as Grieg recalls:

'*He did his best, but when he sang* The King's Song *I had a strong feeling of displeasure that developed into such a torment that I wanted to slip away and hide. Instinctively I leaned forward more and more.*

Concert programme from
Ekserserhuset in Bergen,
11 August 1873. The
proceeds of the concert
went to the Håkonshallen
restoration fund. This was
the only public concert
Ole Bull and Edvard
Grieg ever gave together.
(BOB)

Ole Bull. (EGM)

By the time Edvard Grieg entered the artistic arena in the mid-1860s, Henrik Ibsen was already a household name in Norway and his reputation abroad was growing fast. Ibsen spent many fruitful years as theatre director at Det Norske Theater in Bergen (1851–1857). It was Ole Bull, with his nose for talent, who had discovered this shy young writer in Oslo. At that stage he had not made much of a mark in literary circles, but Bull's interest was aroused by Ibsen's poetry and newspaper articles. Bull was convinced that Ibsen possessed a great power, as yet unleashed. Ibsen's years in Bergen gave him experience and insight into the world of theatre. With his poetic genius he promoted drama as a highly developed art form. Norway was lucky enough to have Bjørnstjerne Bjørnson at the same time, and the theatre became the arena for these two giants and a central institution of social debate. In 1864 Ibsen decided to leave Norway, as he felt the need for greater distance from his native country, both artistically and personally. Ibsen lived in Italy (where he met Grieg in 1865–66) and Germany for many years before returning to Oslo in 1891, to the apartment in Arbiens gate where the Ibsen Museum now stands.

Henrik Ibsen's 'new' appearance, elegantly attired with his trademark sideburns. (BOB)

Finally I was so far down in the seat that, bracing myself on my elbows, I could hold my hand in front of my face. I relate this to illustrate the degree to which Bjørnson now realised what the situation required of us, for suddenly he gave me a fairly hard jab and whispered, "Sit up!" …'

However, the audience was delighted and the piece was staged several times over the next few years.

The music to *Sigurd Jorsalfar* includes *At the Matching Game. March.* Grieg had composed this piece for violin and piano a few years previously, but orchestrated it in a new version for this drama. (This piece was performed under the title *Gavotte* for violin and piano by Ole Bull and Edvard Grieg at a concert in Ekserserhuset in Bergen on 11 August 1873, in aid of the Håkonshallen restoration fund. This was the only occasion on which Grieg and Bull performed together in public.)

The drama also includes one of Grieg's very finest orchestral works, *Homage March*. This piece combines solemnity and ceremony without being pompous. The four-part cello arrangement of the beautiful melody is Grieg at his most inspired – a simple and dignified homage.

In 1892 Grieg put *Intermezzo. Borghild's Dream* with the two above-mentioned pieces to form the suite *Three Orchestral Pieces from Sigurd Jorsalfar*, op. 56. In this suite *Homage March* has a new fanfare-like introduction and Grieg expanded the trio section.

With Bjørnson, Grieg rode on a wave of national romanticism. The festal performance on the evening of 17 May 1872 was not their only success that day. Earlier in the day there had been a fundraising event at Akershus fortress in aid of the restoration fund for Nidaros Cathedral (Norway's only medieval cathedral, in Trondheim). Bjørnson had been invited to write a poem in honour of the occasion, and the result was *Land Sighting* – a poem about Olav Trygvason, who brought Christianity to Norway. The poem was completed in early May and sent straight to Grieg. Bjørnson expected 'a *big* sound', and that is exactly what he got.

Land Sighting, op. 31 for baritone, male chorus, organ and wind orchestra (arranged later in a version for orchestra or piano) received tumultuous applause. This work, which started out very much as an occasional piece, turned out to be one of Grieg's finest choral pieces. Grieg was thrilled with the fervent reception it received wherever it was performed. After a performance in the Norwegian capital in 1905 he wrote in his diary: 'Land Sighting *went so well that at the end I myself was completely enchanted.*' *(Diary entry, 7 December 1905)*

Bjørnson and Grieg were also political allies, but their greatest contribution to the building of the nation, quite apart from the other issues of the day, was to be the new Norwegian national opera *Olav Trygvason*.

As we know, the work was never completed by Bjørnson and Grieg. Following the positive start with inspired texts by Bjørnson and equally inspired music by Grieg, the process ground to a halt. Grieg did not receive any more text from Bjørnson, who had already moved on from his national romantic period. Inspired by the Danish writer and critic Georg Brandes, Bjørnson became one of the most energetic proponents of 'the modern breakthrough' in Scandinavian literature. Realistic prose drama by Bjørnson and

Henrik Ibsen. (BOB)

Danish critic and essayist Georg Brandes (1842–1927) was a highly influential cultural figure in the Nordic countries. (BOB)

75

Ibsen, followed by the younger Swedish author August Strindberg, took over at theatres throughout Scandinavia. Grieg, on the other hand, never felt at home in this new style. Although he was interested in all new ideas, he remained a national romantic at heart. He did not feel at home in the realistic, psychological and expressionistic manifestations that were becoming increasingly common in art and literature at that time. This being the case, it is hardly surprising that he grew impatient at the lack of new libretto from Bjørnson. He wrote Bjørnson a number of letters asking him for more text.

'*Is Olav Trygvason not coming?*' Grieg asked Bjørnson again and again in telegrams and letters. He also enlisted the help of others, including his good friend Frants Beyer, to whom he wrote:

'*If you should some day have an idle moment, write to Bjørnson as only you can do. He has a great heart, and he will understand you and agree with both you and me if you ask him to continue with Olav Trygvason. He really wants me to write music for* Kongen kommer *(a play that he is working on), but I told him it was not for me and I will not do it for any amount of money. I only want to do Olav Trygvason or a Norwegian fairy tale. Well, whatever will be, will be. I will write only what I want to write and am able to write.' (Letter to Frants Beyer, 26 December 1889)*

But in the end Grieg gave up waiting. Luckily he had other projects to keep him occupied, and then the invitation from Ibsen to write incidental music to *Peer Gynt* turned up out of the blue.

When Bjørnson realised that Grieg had abandoned *Olav Trygvason* in favour of Ibsen's *Peer Gynt*, he was most put out. All the warmth disappeared from their friendship and contact between the two was confined to letters.

Edvard Grieg's autograph book. (BOB)

At first he thought that Grieg was working on an opera, but he was heartily relieved when he realised it was a stage drama. '*I am very glad that it is not an opera* Peer Gynt *that you are working on. Very!*' But he could not stop himself from adding, with a dollop of irony: '*You have traded* Olav Trygvason *for* Peer Gynt; *you certainly are a modern philistine!!?? Boo!' (Letter from Bjørnstjerne Bjørnson to Grieg, 17 September 1874)*

Bjørnson suggested that they get together briefly to talk things through and get *Olav Trygvason* back on track, but Grieg replied that this was not something that could be hurried. '*It takes ten times as long to write an opera as it does to write a play, NB a modern opera.' (Letter to Bjørnstjerne Bjørnson, 1 October 1874)*

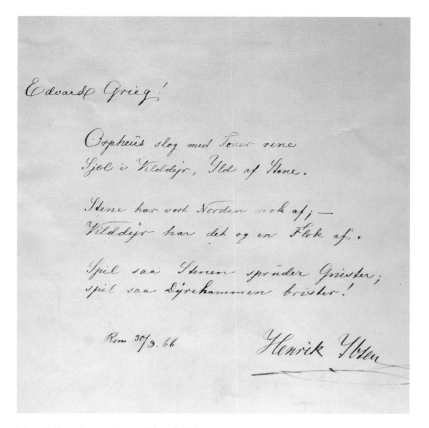

Henrik Ibsen's greeting to Edvard Grieg. (BOB)

Ludvig Josephson from Sweden was appointed director of Christiania Theater in 1873, provoking much protest (led by Bjørnson) since he was a foreigner. It was he that took the initiative to stage Peer Gynt. (BOB)

Nor could he have put his work on *Peer Gynt* to one side even if he had wanted to. He had been invited by Ibsen to undertake the task, although he baulked at the idea of '*writing music for that most unmusical of subjects*'. (Letter to Bjørnstjerne Bjørnson, 1 October 1874)

His main reason for accepting this arduous task was probably that the handsome fee would enable him to fulfil his dream of travelling to Italy again.

Bjørnson and Grieg made several more attempts to get the project off the ground, but with no luck. In letters to friends Grieg often wrote about the trouble he was having getting to grips with the material of *Peer Gynt*, but he also expressed admiration for Ibsen's wit and bile. He asked Bjørnson's opinion of this. It is clear from Bjørnson's reply that he felt a distinct antipathy for Ibsen and his manner of writing: '*… he is so damned vicious and filthy that he only provides more food for scorn, more fuel for his critics;*

it is above all the pedants who use him for their own purposes.' (Letter from Bjørnstjerne Bjørnson to Grieg, 8 December 1874)

The project grounded to a halt entirely when Grieg voiced a little cautious criticism and suggested an amendment to the text of *Olav Trygvason*:

'… the entire blood-sacrifice scene in Olav *is fine, but there are many places where I can tell that you have been thinking in terms of melodrama, not opera. Especially the beautiful monologue: it is too long, as is the chorus that follows.' (Letter to Bjørnstjerne Bjørnson, 14 May 1875)*

Bjørnson was not one to take such criticism lightly, and this was apparently the last straw for him. For the next sixteen years there was no personal or artistic contact between the two men, and what this rift may have cost Norwegian art in lost opportunities is hard to estimate. When the two men were finally reconciled, they contributed separately and jointly to the greatest project in modern Norwegian history, namely the dissolution of the union between Sweden and Norway. In 1905 Norway could finally call herself an independent nation, not only politically, but also culturally. The fact that Norway had to wait another 100 years before anyone picked up the threads of *Olav Trygvason* was a small price to pay.

THE IDEA OF WORKING TOGETHER STARTED IN ROME

Grieg's first trip to Rome was beset with problems at the start, since his travelling companion Rikard Nordraak was terminally ill and therefore unable to make the trip, but no sooner had Grieg arrived in Italy than he forgot his troubles. There were so many impressions to sink in: art and architecture of which he had only dreamed before, the captivating countryside, and a way of life very different from that in the cold north. All this, combined with his contact with artists and scientists at the Scandinavian Society in Rome, made an indelible impression on the young Edvard Grieg.

It was here that Edvard Grieg first met Henrik Ibsen, and the talented young musician soon caught Ibsen's attention. Grieg's autograph album contains a short encouraging verse written by Ibsen on 30 March 1866 which shows that Ibsen had great expectations for the diminutive composer from Bergen. This six-line verse was included in Ibsen's *Poems* published in 1871, where it was given the title *From a Composer's Album*.

Orpheus struck with purest treble
soul from beast and fire from pebble.

Stones our Norway has no lack of;
wild beasts too, we've many a pack of.

Play, that stones may spark in wonder!
Play, that hides may burst asunder! [2]

Although the two only met face to face a few times in Rome and later on, Ibsen (though he knew little about music) was convinced that Grieg was the man to tackle the greatest challenges in the field of music.

Edvard Grieg needed absolute quiet and concentration in order to compose, and had four different composer's huts at various periods: Landås (the henhouse), Elsesro (picture), Lofthus and Troldhaugen. (THG)

AN INVITATION

In January 1874 Henrik Ibsen wrote a long letter to Grieg from Dresden, inviting him to compose incidental music for Ibsen's famous dramatic poem, *Peer Gynt*. The director of the Christiania Theatre, Ludvig Josephson, had asked Ibsen to adapt *Peer Gynt* for a stage production. He had promised Ibsen the sum of 400 *spesiedaler* for this undertaking. Ibsen replied to an enthusiastic Ludvig Josephson that he would '... *arrange* Peer Gynt *as a musical drama. The music will be composed this summer.*' In his letter to Grieg, Ibsen proposed that they divide the fee equally between them.

Ibsen's casual promise that the music would be finished in the course of a few months shows how little he understood the enormity of the task he was inviting Grieg to take on. However, he already had a great deal of experience in the world of theatre, and his greatness shines through the detailed plan he drew up for Grieg in this letter. Ibsen certainly understood the role of music in drama.

'*Dear Mr Grieg,*
I am writing to you in connection with a plan that I propose to implement, and in which I wish to invite your participation.

The plan is this. I propose to adapt Peer Gynt, *which will soon go into its third printing, for the stage. Will you compose the music that*

The summer house in Sandviken, where Edvard and Nina Grieg stayed while Edvard was working on parts of Olav Trygvason *and* Peer Gynt.

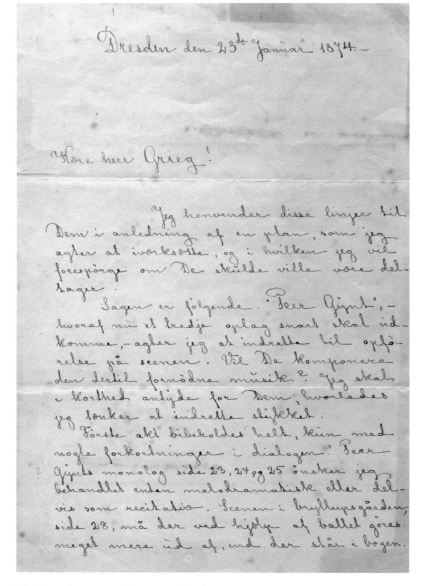

The letter from Henrik Ibsen to Edvard Grieg, 23 January 1874. (BOB)

will be required? I will indicate briefly how I am thinking of arranging the play …' (Letter from Henrik Ibsen to Grieg, 23 January 1874)

There followed a minutely detailed list of ideas and instructions which shows that the writer had a very clear picture in his mind's eye of how he wanted the stage version to be. Naturally, though, he gave Grieg free artistic rein in how to treat the material in his score.

Grieg jumped at this opportunity, not least at the promise of 200 *spesiedaler*. He was in the midst of a highly productive period and was keen to strike while the iron was hot. He accepted the invitation, although he made it clear that there was no way he could promise to have the music finished as soon as Ibsen had promised Josephson. Ibsen was not able to complete his part of the project on time either, since Josephson, who was excited at the prospect of a version by Ibsen and Grieg, had some fairly determined opinions himself about the project. Ibsen approved many of Josephson's ideas, and they decided to take however much time they needed to ensure that this project really was the masterpiece they were convinced it could be. This was a great relief to Grieg, for as he said: *'The job is proving to be much larger than I had thought, and in some places I am encountering difficulties that have me absolutely stymied.'* (Letter to Ludvig Josephson, 28 August 1874)

GRIEG'S PARENTS DIED BEFORE THE FIRST PERFORMANCE OF *PEER GYNT*

Grieg lived in his hometown of Bergen while working on the music to *Peer Gynt*. He rented a small summerhouse at Elsesro in Sandviken, just outside the city, where he found the necessary peace and quiet for composing. Even so he made slow progress. Nearly all the letters he wrote in this period contain some mention of the problems he was encountering. Sometimes it was the material itself that had him flummoxed, sometimes he was anxious about getting the music finished in time and sometimes he was most concerned about the challenge of managing to scrape together a decent orchestra for the first performance in Oslo. However, he was very glad to be in Bergen, near his dear parents, his family and friends, including his old music teacher Ferdinand Schediwy.

When he had nearly finished the music to *Peer Gynt*, Grieg travelled to Leipzig and Copenhagen. At the end of July 1875 he wrote to let Ibsen know that he had completed the task. Ibsen was very pleased and asked Grieg to send the score to Ludvig Josephson and *'… share with him any comments you wish to make.*

REFLECTIONS ON GRIEF

'I have just received the sad news of the passing of your dear mother. It is strange what can befall one in this life. That nature not only permits such agonies, but even demands them! Now you also know what is means to lose one's dearest possession. How different the world suddenly becomes, and how gloomy everything around one! But there is a consolation. It is one that heretofore you have known only in theory, but that you can joyfully depend on: that the selfsame nature that gives such deep wounds also contains a healing power, and that this wonderful healing is denied to no one. You can scarcely grasp this just now. But, praise God, it is true. I know it from my own experience. Time covers the pain of loss like beautiful, soft clouds, and you will come to acknowledge with gratitude how you →

Julius Röntgen (1855–1932). (BOB)

Edvard Grieg's parents, Gesine Hagerup and Alexander Grieg, died within a few weeks of each other in the autumn of 1875. (EGM)

[…] Play rehearsals should be hurried up as much as possible. That you yourself will be present for the music rehearsals is, naturally, a foregone conclusion; but these will probably not begin until sometime in October.' (Letter from Henrik Ibsen to Grieg, 20 August 1875) However, as it turned out Grieg was not able to be present at any of the rehearsals, since both his parents had become seriously ill at home in Bergen. He wrote to Josephson, apologising for his absence. There were so many minor details that he would have liked to have been sure of putting across, and he also had a number of small changes and adjustments in mind. Josephson was very understanding of Grieg's predicament, and as a sign of goodwill towards Grieg he put on three performances of Bjørnson's *Sigurd Jorsalfar* (with music by Grieg) that autumn. The third performance was on 12 September, and Alexander Grieg, Edvard's father, died the following day.

Grieg wrote to Josephson again on 28 September:
'As you can well imagine, I cannot leave Bergen until mother has closed her eyes. On the other hand, you can also understand that I am extremely reluctant to let the music to Peer Gynt *be performed without my being present at least for a few rehearsals in order to make sure that my intentions are realised.'* (Letter to Ludvig Josephson, 28 September 1875)

Grieg's mother died on 23 October. In the course of just a few weeks Grieg had lost two of the people most dear to him. He was absolutely devastated and was in no fit state to travel to Oslo for the final rehearsals of *Peer Gynt*. In fact he remained in Bergen for nearly a whole year before he felt able to return to the capital. Many years later, when his friend Julius Röntgen lost his mother, Grieg expressed his grief in words for the first time in a letter of condolence to Röntgen – a moving testimony from a philosophical, sensitive person.

ORCHESTRATION FOR INSTRUMENTS THAT MIGHT NOT BE FOUND

As if Grieg did not have enough on his plate worrying about the 'unmusical subject' he was working on, his rocky relationship with Bjørnson, his longing to be back in the thriving musical metropolises in Europe, and the tragic loss of both parents within a short space of time, he was also deeply concerned as to whether his music to *Peer Gynt* could actually be performed in Oslo at all.

He knew from his own experience and from what he heard from Johan Svendsen that there were huge problems involved in assembling a full orchestra in Oslo.

He poured out some of his concern in a letter to Bjørnson (just before they broke off contact):

'Yesterday I heard how things stand with respect to music in the Christiania Theatre, as a consequence of which I am today writing to both Ibsen and Josephson that I consider it my duty not to deliver anything to the Christiania Theatre so long as the orchestra is not fully staffed. It is absolutely scandalous, the worst that it has ever been, and Svendsen says that if the situation continues we will in the course of a few years have no orchestra at all in Norway's capital city – a city of nearly 100,000 people. Old Mozart operas won't be destroyed, that we know, but to deliver a score with modern orchestration to the Christiania Theatre now would be the same as wishing it to become a grand fiasco.' (Letter to Bjørnstjerne Bjørnson, 21 February 1875)

When Ibsen heard about Grieg's concerns he gave Grieg his full support and begged him to orchestrate the music in accordance with his ideal standard. Anything less than that would be unworthy of a man of his stature, and could well harm them both.

Luckily Grieg had great faith in Johan Hennum, the theatre's musical director. When circumstances forced Grieg to miss the rehearsals and the first performance, he felt it even more important that he should provide Hennum with comprehensive instructions

are matured by the law of necessity. When my mother died, my love of art died with her. But not permanently! To the contrary: when joy reawakened, it was greater than before.

'You will find, dear Röntgen, that art still carries within itself undreamed-of happiness. How certainly and beneficently is nature arranged in such a way, then, that we first reach the highest satisfaction in art through life's most traumatic shocks!'
(LETTER TO JULIUS RÖNTGEN, 4 AUGUST 1888)

Principal conductor at Christiania Theater, Johan Hennum (1836–1894) who conducted the first performance of Peer Gynt. (BOB)

Edvard Grieg's letter to Johan Hennum, dated 14 December 1875, is a godsend to all musicians, conductors and music researchers. (BOB)

and explanations of all the small, important details of the complex score of *Peer Gynt*.

Grieg's letter of 14 December 1875 to Johan Hennum is quite some epistle, with its twenty-eight pages of comments, explana-

Edvard Munch's poster for Ibsen/Grieg's Peer Gynt, Paris 1894.

Robert Henriques
(1858–1914). (BOB)

tions and suggested alternatives. Grieg wrote that the score did not always make explicit what he wanted to express. The music was not simply music; it was intended to fit closely with the dramatic performance. Ideally Grieg would have liked to discuss this at length with Hennum, but since they were at opposite sides of the country, he put pen to paper and wrote a detailed letter about his thoughts and intentions.

'There is so much that I wish we could talk about that does not lend itself to a simple summary. I will therefore set the score in front of me and go through it, and I ask you to now do the same.' (Letter to Johan Hennum, 14 December 1875)

For the first performance on 24 February 1876 the necessary reinforcements had been hired in to ensure that the orchestra could use Grieg's instrumentation. However, Grieg was not really finished with the score of Peer Gynt at this stage. He revised it a number of times, particularly each time a new production was planned. He did not always tackle the task with equal enthusiasm – when Bjørn Bjørnson (Bjørnstjerne Bjørnson's son) was to direct a new production of Peer Gynt in 1892, he asked Grieg to write some additional music for a few scenes. Grieg, however, refused to do so at first, saying quite simply: 'I am done with that period.'

'Would you, please, make sure that no trees than absolutely necessary will be cut down or destroyed during the planning and earthworks? Do you think it is better – if you find a nice tree – to move it to another place than to tear it down? If yes, please find a place where it will contribute to protecting the house against rain and wind.'
(LETTER TO SCHAK BULL, FROM LOFTHUS, 24 AUGUST 1884)

The newly built villa at Troldhaugen with Nina, Edvard and the maid at the gateway. (EGM)

Alexander Lange Kielland (1849–1906).
(EGM)

Although *Peer Gynt* met with wild enthusiasm wherever it was staged, Grieg had mixed feelings about his music. We know that while he was working on the original score he had at times been inspired by Ibsen's text and at times wished he could wash his hands of the entire project. He knew that certain passages in his score did not live up to his own expectations on a purely technical level; there were a number of instances of 'transport music' written purely to move the action on. This may explain some of his lack of enthusiasm.

Grieg undertook a major revision of the score when a new production was planned in Copenhagen in 1886; in fact he practically re-orchestrated the entire work. At the same time he added several new pieces, including *Bridal Procession*, op. 19 no. 2 before the wedding scene in the first act, and the now popular

Norwegian Dance no. 2 op. 35 was used for a dance scene in the hall of the Mountain King. This dance was orchestrated by Grieg's friend Robert Henriques.

Grieg made further changes and revisions for two subsequent productions of *Peer Gynt* in Oslo in 1892 and 1902. But perhaps the most important work he did on the music to *Peer Gynt* was to orchestrate the incidental music from eight of the scenes in what was to become the two *Peer Gynt Suites*, op. 46 and op. 55. Suite no. 1 was printed in 1888 and was an instant success wherever it was performed. After a concert in London in 1889 Grieg wrote to his friend Frants Beyer: 'At the end the noise was like the howling of animals. Well, you understand me: those primitive sounds that occur only in moments of great enthusiasm.' (Letter to Frants Beyer, 14 March 1889)

In 1891 Max Abraham of Edition Peters in Leipzig reported that the music was being played in Asia, Africa and Australia. Suite no. 2 was published in 1893, and Grieg knew now that wherever he went, he had music with him that would be a sure-fire success. The *Peer Gynt Suites* embodied the essence of the collaboration between a great poet and a fine composer, and the success of this collaboration has rarely been equalled in terms of worldwide popularity. Even so, Grieg was definitely right in saying that the music only really came into its own in its proper setting, that is in the context of a dramatic performance.

Grieg's great concern as to whether the Christiania Theatre would be able to scrape together a good enough orchestra shows once again that Edvard Grieg was not a man who was willing to compromise when it came to his art. Challenges of this sort brought out his fighting spirit. This unbending attitude in the cause of art is one of Grieg's most characteristic traits. He set a high standard for his contemporaries and his successors in this respect.

PEER GYNT IN COPENHAGEN

Within a short space of time *Peer Gynt* was in demand at theatres throughout Norway and abroad. In 1885 Grieg was summoned to Copenhagen, since a production of *Peer Gynt* was to be put on at the Dagmar Theatre in January 1886. This invitation came at the end of a very busy summer, since Nina and Edvard Grieg had moved into their new home, Troldhaugen, earlier that year.

Edvard Grieg at the top of Mount Løvstakken in Bergen with Frants Beyer.
Grieg, who is rarely seen smiling in photos, is obviously enjoying himself with a
glass of port or dark beer. (BOB)

After their yearly holiday in Lofthus and a walking trip in the Jotunheimen mountains with Frants Beyer, the Griegs travelled first to Oslo, and from there in November to Copenhagen. In Copenhagen Grieg set to work on new instrumentation of parts of the score of *Peer Gynt* for use at the Dagmar Theatre the following January. Grieg also performed at a number of concerts, and he and Nina were able to catch up with their many artist friends in Copenhagen. He wrote to Frants Beyer:

'You may well imagine what a lovely time we have after the concerts. We meet at the Viennese café in the hotel we're staying at, with musicians, painters, poets and other friends, and we pass the evenings making speeches and celebrating, usually until far too late at night. And then, of course, there's hell to pay the next morning.' (Letter to Frants Beyer, 11 December 1885)

Grieg conducted *The Mountain Thrall* in the first half of a very well-received concert at the Music Association. After the interval he joined Johan Svendsen and Alexander Kielland in the VIP box to enjoy the rest of the concert.

'We certainly represented Norway most thoroughly, and we greatly enjoyed one another's company. Kielland is a fantastic person, I feel sure that I shall care for him immensely.' (Letter to Frants Beyer, 11 December 1885)

Svendsen was very cordial towards Grieg, but he was a complex character. He had a tendency to fall out with other people with great frequency, and particularly musicians, so he was not often to be found at the receptions and parties after concerts. However, he often ate with Nina and Edvard at their hotel. Grieg wrote to Beyer:

'After dinner, Svendsen sits in our rooms pouring his heart out to Nina, while I work in my study. I am currently re-orchestrating Peer Gynt, *which is to be put on here in mid-January with Henrik Klausen (who also played Gynt at the premiere in Oslo in 1876) in the title role.'* (Letter to Frants Beyer, 11 December 1885)

Henrik Klausen as Peer Gynt. Nationaltheatret on tour at Den Nationale Scene in 1896. (Photo: H Abel).
(BOB)

Grieg threw himself into revising *Peer Gynt* with great enthusiasm. He did not only change the orchestration; he actually composed new music for parts of the drama. But, most importantly, he played an active role in rehearsals. His descriptions in letters to Frants Beyer of his escapades at the theatre are very amusing.

'This afternoon I had the first rehearsal with the singers for Peer Gynt. *As I came up the stairs of the Dagmar Theatre, I heard the herd girls yelling at the top of their lungs – naturally in the wrong tempo, exactly at half speed, so I am certainly glad that I am here. But the voices are good, and the girls appear lively, so I'm not worried about that scene, the new instrumentation for which is much improved. Then I tried Solveig's Song with Mrs Oda Petersen, but since Solveig (Mrs Petersen) is in an advanced stage of pregnancy, the illusion is not very convincing. Otherwise she handles the part well and exhibits a musical temperament. Then came the Thief and the*

Receiver, who performed their parts so stupidly that I asked them to be quiet and listen to me. Whereupon I rendered the piece, and – incomprehensibly – so masterfully that the listeners broke out in wild applause.' (Letter to Frants Beyer, 22 December 1885)

By the beginning of January, rehearsal time was running out, and it would appear from his correspondence with Beyer that Grieg had had little time for celebrating Christmas or the New Year.

'Believe me, I am floundering these days. My main failing is that I get up late, but unfortunately life here requires it. I emerge from the blankets at 8.30 am. By 9 am I have done my exercises and am sitting down in the café having breakfast. Then Nina and I take a morning walk, from which we return home at about 11 am. Only then do I get down to work. But then I keep on without a break until about 6 pm, and thank goodness I can tolerate it because otherwise I don't know what would happen.

'First I have to practise the piano (I am to perform at Svendsen's philharmonic concert at the end of January), and then I dig into Peer Gynt, many parts of which I have completely re-orchestrated. But now I am working on the last of these – fortunately, for time is very short.

'In the café I am bombarded by copyists and musical directors who grab each page from me as soon as I am finished with it. In this way we rehearse a little at a time. Two pieces gave me much satisfaction at the first rehearsal. They were the introduction to the second act and the scene with the herd girls. The latter you wouldn't even recognise. When I first conceived it I felt something, but now I know something; that is the difference. It has acquired life, colour and devilry – which really were not there before because the orchestration was so defective.

'Enormous preparations are being made for the performance, which will certainly be something totally different from the one in Oslo so far as the stage set and the music are concerned.' (Letter to Frants Beyer, 5 January 1886)

These weeks of working under intense pressure took their toll on Grieg's health. As already mentioned, in his student days Grieg had suffered a life-threatening lung disease, but thanks to his healthy lifestyle, his hiking trips in the mountains and his daily routine of walks and gymnastics, he had managed to stay in relatively good health. However, as he grew older he became increasingly prone to various ailments. After the premiere of Peer Gynt he collapsed. The doctors diagnosed anaemia and a neurological disorder, and advised Grieg to live in the countryside and bathe frequently. Not easy advice to follow in Copenhagen in January!

In a letter to Frants Beyer, Grieg complained about his poor health, and voiced concern for Nina's health, too. Naturally he also wrote about how *Peer Gynt* was going:

'*It felt very strange when I took my place in the stalls yesterday evening. Henrik Klausen was just the same as in Oslo ten years ago, a little less spry, perhaps, but it appeared to me that he handled the concluding acts better than before. Miss Aalberg from Finland was a mean Aase figure, all wrong in the first and second acts, but absolutely brilliant in her own way in the deathbed scene. The supporting roles were definitely better than those in Oslo, Cetti was absolutely perfect as the Mountain King, and a certain Mrs Krum was every bit as good in the role of Anitra. Oda Nielsen cut a comely and poetic figure as Solveig, though not the Solveig we usually think of. But she sang beautifully and naturally.*

Georg Brandes. (BOB)

'*You would have had fun watching me at the rehearsals. I was so anxious to make sure that my intentions were realised that I personally took command here and there. One moment I conducted the orchestra, another I instructed the singers, yet another I was on stage and played director.*

'*It was especially in the scene with the herd girls that I was determined not to give up. But it turned out to be quite a performance. I stood in the wings with the book open, so I could check exactly what was meant to be going on. I stopped them every moment with shouts like, for example: "It says you are supposed to kiss him – please, help yourself!" And when they finally crossed the Rubicon they became absolutely wild and crazy and everything was the way it was supposed to be.*

'*At the dress rehearsal there was great applause after this scene, but at the first performance there wasn't a single clap. The scene obviously merely astonished the audience. But as a whole the music was a great success, that I can certainly say, and the execution was quite good.*'
(*Letter to Frants Beyer, 21 January 1886*)

Ibsen and Grieg's *Peer Gynt* had taken its first important step into the international arena. The Danish critic Georg Brandes was full of admiration for the text, the music and the production. What he could not understand was how a whole generation could possibly have failed to understand the irony of the play. He wrote: '*The satire hits the audience in the face, as if it had been written about Denmark, and written quite recently.*'

At the turn of the century the play started its triumphal tour across stages all over the world. At the same time, Grieg's *Peer Gynt Suites* were a huge success in the concert halls of Europe and beyond. The extremely influential critic and musicologist Eduard Hanslick in Vienna wrote in 1891: '*Before long it may well be that Ibsen's* Peer Gynt *will continue to live only through Grieg's music, for so far as I am concerned this music contains in each of its movements more poetry and artistic insight than all five acts of Ibsen's play put together.*' This prediction did not come true, but there can be no doubt that Grieg's music contributed greatly to the play's popularity. In Germany, for instance, it was performed over a thousand times before the outbreak of the Second World War.

Right up to 1901 Grieg revised the score of *Peer Gynt* from time to time, making alterations here and there. He never seemed to get it out of his system, and he was very keen to have the entire score published. It annoyed him that Edition Peters in Leipzig was unwilling to take on this important task. It was not until the year after Grieg's death that Edition Peters gave Johan Halvorsen the task of preparing the material for printing. Halvorsen made a painstaking study of the source materials available to him (manuscripts, previously published editions of individual pieces, the orchestral suites, etc.) and Peters published the complete work in 23 numbers. Since Halvorsen was a very close friend of Grieg (he was also married to Grieg's niece) and a musician of the utmost integrity with enormous respect for Grieg, it is safe to assume that his edition came fairly close to Grieg's intentions.

Johan Halvorsen (1864–1935), violinist, composer and conductor.
(BOB)

IBSEN AND GRIEG – A LONG-DISTANCE FRIENDSHIP

Grieg met Ibsen on a number of occasions in Rome, but his diary does not give the impression that they were anything more than casual acquaintances. They stayed in touch in subsequent years, and in 1866 Grieg asked Ibsen for support for his application for the position of musical director at Christiania Theatre. This process involved a great deal of correspondence between Grieg, Ibsen and Bjørnson. In the end the position was given to Johan Hennum (who conducted the first performance of *Peer Gynt* ten years later). Grieg was extremely upset not to have got this job. Ibsen agreed with Grieg that he ought to have been offered it, but the mature, wise poet wrote a letter to Grieg that helped him recover his spirits and see things from a new perspective.

'*Write to him (Bjørnson) one more time if necessary. Tell him that he shall let you have the position. Tell him you have a right to it. Make*

(BOB)

The elderly Henrik Ibsen. (BOB)

him answerable if he refuses, and if all this is of no avail, then your musical accomplishments will demonstrate how badly people have behaved – and the whole affair will have to do only with a postponement of the time [of your triumph] …'

But Ibsen also stated that Grieg must be prepared for the possibility that the outcome might not be as he hoped, and should that happen, Grieg should be aware that '... *you have no right to say that your whole future is at stake. No, dear Grieg, your future is certainly something more and better than the position of musical director. It would be ungrateful of you to measure the talents you have received by so small a measuring stick. But of course I understand what you mean.*' (*Letter from Henrik Ibsen to Grieg, 24 August 1866*)

There is no doubt that Grieg greatly admired and respected Ibsen, but at times he was also disappointed and surprised by Ibsen's behaviour. After a successful concert in the Scandinavian Society in Rome, where Italian musicians had performed Schumann, Chopin, Tartini and Schubert quite brilliantly, Grieg tells us that:

Edvard Grieg (around 1890). (EGM)

'*Ibsen – who had drunk a few Fogliettes that had gone to his head – got the idea that we ought to dance. He then proceeded to get the table and chairs cleared out of the way and urged Ravnkilde (!) to strike up a tune. When Ravnkilde, naturally enough, declined to do as he was asked, Ibsen got so angry that he took his hat and cane and stalked off. He is accustomed, when we are alone, to having us obey his command, "Strike up a tune, you fellows!" By this "strike up a tune" he means music of any kind whatsoever, and he cannot understand how an artist can care what kind of music it is.*

'*It is remarkable that such a great man can be so tactless and, in one specific area, so limited. Just as if we were to ask Ibsen to recite some verses by Erik Bøgh, we would hear an indignant outcry. No, it is a fact: first of all an artist must maintain his own dignity, for only then does the public learn to do so. If he relinquishes that, no matter how splendidly he performs, the crowd will not recognise him for what he is.*' (*Diary entry, 9 April 1866*)

Grieg's next literary encounter with Ibsen was after the birth of Nina and Edvard's daughter. *Margaret's Cradle Song* from *The Pretenders* was a great favourite with Grieg, both in the concert hall and by his daughter's cradle. Edvard and Nina followed the Norwegian custom of naming their daughter Alexandra after her paternal grandfather, Alexander. *Margaret's Cradle Song* is the first song in opus 15, while the last song in the album is *A Mother's Grief* (text by Christian Richardt). This song is a melancholy yet beautiful pendant to the lullaby, and the very next year it took on an unexpected and tragic relevance: Alexandra contracted meningitis and died in Bergen, aged just 13 months. Nina and Edvard never had any more children.

Ibsen and Grieg rarely had the opportunity to cultivate their friendship face to face. However, in the late summer of 1876 they spent some time together in the small town of Gossensass, near the Brenner Pass. Grieg had been attending the Bayreuth Festival with John Paulsen, a poet friend from Bergen, since he had been engaged to write about the Wagner performances for the newspapers back in Norway. On 4 August they received an invitation from Ibsen:

'You will be heartily welcome here, and I hope you don't make your visit too short. After the strenuous pleasures of Bayreuth you will certainly need some fresh mountain air, and you will certainly find that up here.'

Paulsen said of his first meeting with Ibsen that it was like standing *'in front of a solid rock wall – an impenetrable mystery'*.

Despite their long walks together (on which Ibsen uttered not a single word) and the few times in the evenings that Grieg managed to get Ibsen going, Paulsen concluded: *'I cannot recall Ibsen ever using an enthusiastic expression, a spontaneous word – anything that revealed a deep inner life. He was the soul of negation.'*

Grieg's close friend, the lyricist John Paulsen (1851–1924). (BOB)

Grieg wrote to Paulsen several years later: *'But the association with Ibsen is not giving you what you had expected. I can understand that. A person who has concerned himself so much with the concept of suspicion cannot come across as warm and pleasant in his personal contacts, even if he is genuine.'* (Letter to John Paulsen, 3 June 1881)

At a party in Rome in 1884, however, Ibsen surprised Grieg with his emotional reaction to Nina and Edvard's performance of most of Grieg's songs to texts by Ibsen:

'Just think, after Margaret's Cradle Song *and especially after* Album Lines *and* The Swan *the icy exterior melted, and with tears in his eyes he came over to the piano where we were, and pressed our hands, almost unable to speak. He mumbled something to the effect that this was true understanding ...'* (Letter to Frants Beyer, 19 March 1884)

Grieg dreamed of writing a lyric opera. He cherished an earnest hope that Ibsen would write him an opera libretto, and they did in fact make a couple of attempts to get a joint opera project off the ground. First Ibsen considered editing one of his earlier plays, *Olaf Liljekrans*, as the libretto for an opera. He told Grieg of his plans, but no text was ever forthcoming. Later on Ibsen decided to edit *The Vikings at Helgeland* for Grieg. The composer was thrilled, but when Ibsen sent him the draft of the first act he quickly rea-

Entry in Grieg's diary after receiving news of Ibsen's death: 'Poor, great Ibsen! He was not a happy man, for it is as if he carried within him a chunk of ice that would not melt. But under this chunk of ice lay a fervent love of mankind.' (BOB)

lised that this was not the kind of material he had hoped for, and they abandoned the project.

Despite their friendship, mutual admiration and respect, there was a wide gulf between the views of these two great artists on human nature and on art. Nevertheless, the unique bridge across this chasm, *Peer Gynt*, remains as a monument to the greatness of both men.

Grieg's warm feelings for Ibsen and his understanding of the great man are unmistakable in the words he wrote in his diary on receiving the news of Ibsen's death in 1906:

'Although I was prepared for it, the news came as a blow. How much I owe him! Poor, great Ibsen! He was not a happy man, for it is as if he carried within him a chunk of ice that would not melt. But under this chunk of ice lay a fervent love of mankind.' (Diary entry, 23 May 1906)

THE GOLDEN WORKS

Peer Gynt Suite no. 1, op. 46, 1888
Morning Mood and In the Hall of the Mountain King
– two of the greatest hits of classical music

The opening of act 4. The curtain rises and we are transported to the south-west coast of Morocco. Peer Gynt has been out in the big wide world, including America. He has made his fortune and has many international connections. He is now a wealthy man, thanks to dubious business ventures in many exotic climes, including trafficking slaves to Carolina and exporting idols to China. In this scene he is host to some of his shady friends, Master Cotton, Monsieur Ballon, Herr von Eberkopf and Hr Trumpeterstraale, with whom he has been smuggling weapons. His socalled friends slope off without him to the steamyacht anchored nearby, on the grounds that the profit will be greater with one fewer to share it.

The five black keys you can play 'Morning Mood' on (Grieg's grand piano at Troldhaugen).
(THG)

There has evidently been some heavy partying on the beach, for Peer Gynt is lying in the sand with a dreadful hangover. Out in the bay beyond, his magnificent yacht is ready to set sail on the azure Mediterranean. Peer Gynt has been left behind on the beach, and is too hung over to get himself to the boat. He watches helplessly as the fortune he has amassed and the potential profit on board the yacht disappears under full steam before his eyes. In his desperation he tries bargaining with God:

'Pssst! I've got rid of the nigger-plantation! I've sent missionaries to Asia! Doesn't one good turn deserve another? Get me on that boat!' [3]
Perhaps his prayer was answered, for his 'friends' do not get away with it. The ship is blown to smithereens, and when the cloud of smoke clears, there is nothing left of the yacht or its passengers.

This is the dramatic foreground of the scene. The music Grieg wrote for this scene is *Morning Mood*. In his letter to Hennum he

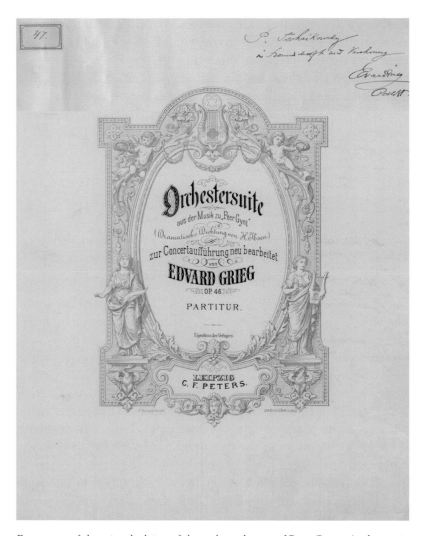

Front page of the printed edition of the orchestral score of Peer Gynt. *At the top is a handwritten greeting from Edvard Grieg to Peter Tchaikovsky: 'P Tchaikovsky in Freundschaft und Verehrung. Edvard Grieg'. Grieg gave the score to Tchaikovsky when they met in Leipzig in 1888. It is now in the Tchaikovsky Museum in Klin.*
(THG)

wrote: '*It is a morning scene where I think of the sun breaking through the clouds at the point in the score where the* forte *first appears.*'

How does this pure, romantic morning mood tally with what is happening on the stage? Grieg's music must be understood as being a counterpoint to the dramatic action. Peer Gynt is as far removed from his humble beginnings as he could be. Despite material success he has sunk to the lowest possible level of morality.

Peer Gynt and the Woman in Green at Den Nationale Scene in 1936. (Photo: Bøbak) (TUB)

Peer Gynt and Mother Aase at Den Nationale Scene in 1936. Hans Jacob Nilsen as Peer Gynt, Klara Dahl as Mother Aase. (Photo: Bøbak) (TUB)

TWO WOMEN – MOTHER AASE AND ANITRA

Between these two pieces we find two of the women in the drama. The first one is Mother Aase. Mother Aase's opening line: *'Peer, you're a liar!'* is similar to the opening chord of the *Piano Concerto in A minor*, in that it contains the essence of the entire drama in one short statement.

The Death of Aase is a moving piece, both with and without the text. The music is built around a very simple theme, with an ascending melodic line in the first part. The piece depicts how Aase, with the help of her son Peer's vivid imagination, attempts to escape the clutches of death. But death is too powerful. Not even Peer's optimistic flight from reality, intended to smooth the way for her through the pearly gates, can put off the inevitable.

Original manuscript of Anitra's Dance. (BOB)

The melody changes to a descending figure. Her life power ebbs away, and the music dies down until it is scarcely discernible, '... *so incredibly softly that one notices the music only as an indistinct sound.' (Letter to Johan Hennum, 14 December 1875)*

The other woman is Anitra. Grieg appears to have been very pleased with *Anitra's Dance*, for he wrote in his explanatory letter to Johan Hennum: '*I would be grateful if you would treat this piece with special affection.'*

Anitra, who appears at the sultan's tent in the desert, has many traits in common with The Woman in Green (the daughter of

Peer Gynt and Anitra at Den Nationale Scene in 1936. Hans Jacob Nilsen as Peer Gynt, Norma Balean as Anitra. (Photo: Bøbak) (TUB)

the Mountain King) when it comes to sensuality and wildness. Grieg shows this ambiguity in his masterful treatment of the opening theme, which is dancing, vivacious and seductive, yet in the minor key with 'trollish' harmonies. The simple surroundings (a tent and some cushions, and otherwise just sand as far as the eye can see) are portrayed using a thin string orchestration accompanied by light notes on a triangle.

Here, too, Grieg chooses to describe what is going on in Peer's mind. Ibsen's description of Anitra is quite at odds with the beauty portrayed by Grieg's music.

In Peer's eyes she is like this:

'Her feet move like the patter of drums. Hey! She is exquisite, this filly. Her build is on the generous side, not what beauty normally measures; but what is beauty? A pure convention [...] Her feet aren't altogether clean, nor her arms either, especially one. But that isn't a serious drawback. I'd rather say it was in her favour ...'

What Peer (and Ibsen) actually sees is one thing, while Grieg's music depicts Peer's innermost thoughts and dreams, at odds with reality.

PEER GYNT SUITE NO. 2, OP. 55
– A SEQUEL TO THE SUCCESS

Peer Gynt Suite no. 1 (1888) was an immediate success all over the world. Therefore it was only natural for Grieg to continue revising his music to *Peer Gynt* to compile another suite. This second suite was published by Edition Peters in 1893.

The mature Edvard Grieg (around 1880).
(EGM)

Peer Gynt Suite no. 2 opens with *The Abduction of the Bride. Ingrid's Lament.* This is the first musical and dramatic climax in the drama. Peer has gatecrashed the wedding celebrations at Haegstad Farm, and after drinking too much and getting into a fight, he goes so far as to abduct the bride, Ingrid. However, Peer's fickle and sick – almost demonic – nature soon loses interest in Ingrid.

At the start of the drama Peer Gynt was introduced with a merry *halling*-like motif. Now his true colours show through in a distorted, grotesque deformation of the same theme. But this piece is primarily about Ingrid and her sad fate. The character of the music is mournful and beseeching at first, until it starts to take on a threatening feel. This is in sharp contrast to Peer, who in *Allegro furioso* tells her to go to the devil.

Anitra features again in *Suite no. 2*. Peer Gynt has transformed himself from an abandoned drunkard on the north coast of Africa into a prophet in another country. The Bedouin girl, Anitra, and a number of slave girls entertain the prophet with exotic singing and dancing in *Arabian Dance*. The atmosphere Grieg creates in this piece through his use of oriental devices is quite brilliant. His use of percussion instruments and his harmonisation intensify the atmosphere. In his instructions to Johan Hennum, Grieg wrote the following about this dance:

'*A piece that I think will be effective […] I heard something similar this winter, and it sounded wonderful. […] The contrabassoons and bass drum must sound genuinely Turkish.*'

It is worth noting that this piece was composed fifteen years before Tchaikovsky's incidental music to the ballet *The Nutcracker*.

The third piece in this suite is a highly dramatic musical painting. We are at the introduction to the fifth act, and the time of reckoning is at hand. The style and intensity of *Peer Gynt's Homecoming. Stormy Evening on the Sea* is reminiscent of Wagner's *The Flying Dutchman*. Grieg uses the strongest possible effects, and demands '*a murderous noise!*' The music is wild, and the ship goes down with Peer clinging to the mast.

'*The presto and the outcry must sound absolutely frightening, and the following timpani solo depicts the expectant calm.*' (*Letter to Johan Hennum, 14 December 1875*)

However, as we know, Peer manages to get ashore at the expense of the ship's cook, for after all: '*… a fellow doesn't die in the middle of the fifth act*'.

The suite finishes with an absolute gem. Few songs have moved so many people all around the world as *Solveig's Song*. This song is perfectly in keeping with the very best in the Norwegian folk song tradition. The melody flows simply and effortlessly. Naturally, Grieg was conscious of the close relationship between this song and the folk songs of his native country, and the local colour was an important part of the role of this song in the drama. However, he took pains to make it quite clear to his biographer Henry T Finck that '*… this is perhaps the only one of my songs where an imitation of a folk song can be traced*'.

Duke Ellington plays Grieg: 'Swinging Suites by Edward E. and Edward G.' (THG)

Some people believe that Grieg had the Norwegian folk song *Jeg lagde mig så sildig* (I lay down so late) or the Swedish folk song *Ack, Värmeland, du sköna* (O Värmeland the beautiful) in mind when he composed *Solveig's Song*. Whether or not this is the case, this song stands as one of the most beautiful and most simplistic pieces of music ever written for the human voice. This is certainly true when it is performed well, although this song is not half as simple to sing as it may sound. It requires a light, high soprano voice with classical training, particularly in the coloratura passage towards the end. It always worried Grieg who was to play the role of Solveig when a new production was being put on. Would it be a good actor who could not sing, or a singer who could not act? Grieg was not alone in worrying about this; over the years many a theatre director has faced this very dilemma. It is interesting to note that Kirsten Flagstad first played Solveig at the age of fifteen. The songs commences with an introduction that paints an open atmosphere. This is followed by four double, slow notes beating time deep down. And out of this comes '*The winter may pass and the spring disappear …*' [4]

In the span between Mother Aase's opening '*Peer, you're a liar!*' and *Solveig's Song* at the end of the drama, Ibsen and Grieg not only laid bare the workings of Peer Gynt's mind, but the whole of human nature. The text and the music possess a power and depth capable of plucking the dark and the light strings and understrings of the human mind.

The young Nina Grieg. (BOB)

Hardanger – in the middle of Edvard Grieg's life

T HE VILLAGES of Børve and Lofthus in Hardanger occupy a special place in Norwegian music history, thanks to the short but important period of his life that Edvard Grieg spent there (from 1877 to 1879). The preceding decade had brought Nina and Edvard Grieg many successes, but also much frustration.

ARTIST COUPLE

From the time of their engagement, Nina and Edvard Grieg gave recitals together at which Nina performed Edvard's songs. Edvard said of his wife that *'she did exactly what I have striven for in my creative work: above all to interpret the poem.'* *(Letter to Henry T Finck, 17 July 1899)*

The couple were extremely successful and popular at home and abroad. Soon after their wedding they moved to Oslo, where they lived in an apartment in Øvre Voldgate 2 for almost nine years. Despite the fact that there was little tradition for classical concerts in Oslo, the young couple achieved much success and recognition through the recitals they gave together. Grieg's compositions, and those of his peers, were regarded as radical and new, but the audience was charmed by the charisma of these two young performers. Between 1869 and 1882 Edvard and Nina gave concerts in Drammen, Larvik, Arendal, Kristiansand, Stavanger and Haugesund, while in later years their only concerts in Norway were in Oslo and Bergen.

Edvard Grieg in autumn 1866, 23 years old, when he moved to Oslo. (BOB)

Øvre Voldgate in Oslo, where the Griegs rented rooms. Advertisement of Grieg's music teaching services in Morgenbladet, *26 September 1866. He had similar advertisements each autumn during the eight years the Griegs lived in Oslo.* (EGM)

Nina Grieg's mother, Adeline Falck Werligh Hagerup (1814–1907).
(BOB)

AT EDVARD'S SIDE

Nina Grieg made no attempt to forge an independent career for herself as a singer. Despite being a talented performer, she sang only at her husband's concerts, devoting the rest of her time to encouraging him and supporting his work in any way she could. She did her utmost to make Edvard's life, which was difficult at times, easier. However, audiences and fellow artists all over Europe were delighted by Nina Grieg's simplicity, her sincerity and her understanding of her husband's songs. One of the Griegs' friends in Leipzig, Frau Hedvig von Holstein, a personal friend of both Schumann and Mendelssohn, said of Nina that *'she sang with captivating abandon, dramatic vivacity, soulful treatment of the poem, and unaffected manner, unlike that of the typical prima donna.'* Nina received the same warm recommendations from Peter Tchaikovsky, who sent her signed copies of his songs with personal messages. Ibsen's reaction in Rome – *'true understanding'* – bears witness again to a true artist.

Nina Hagerup had ample opportunity to develop her talent when her family moved from Bergen to Copenhagen in 1853. Her mother, Adeline Falck Werligh Hagerup (1814–1907), had been an actor in the Danish-speaking groups at the theatre in Bergen,

Engagement picture of Nina Hagerup and Edvard Grieg in Copenhagen around 1866. Years later Grieg wrote: 'I don't think I have any greater talent for writing songs than for writing any other kind of music. Why, then, have songs played such a prominent role in my oeuvre? Quite simply because I, like other mortals, once in my life (to quote Goethe) had my moment of genius. And it was love that gave me this glory. I loved a girl with a wonderful voice and an equally wonderful gift as an interpreter. This woman became my wife and has been my companion through life down to the present day. I dare say that for me she has remained the only true interpreter of my songs.' (BOB)

St John's Church in 1870.
(EGM)

St John's Church was con-
secrated on 25 August
1861 in the presence of
King Frederik VII. (THG)

The interior of St John's Church at Nørrebro in Copenhagen, where Nina and Edvard
Grieg married on 11 June 1867. Neither his nor her parents were present. (THG)

and she continued to pursue her acting career in Copenhagen. Nina grew up in close contact with artistic circles in Copenhagen, she was well-versed in Scandinavian and European literature, played the piano extremely well and had a fantastic voice.

As we know, Nina and Edvard fell madly in love. Neither family was too pleased by this, and when the young couple made it clear that they were serious about each other, both sets of parents declared quite categorically that they were against the match. Edvard's father, Alexander Grieg, wrote his son long letters, in which he said that since Edvard had chosen to tread the thorny path of the artist, he must under no circumstances entertain the idea of marriage. Alexander also stated quite clearly that although he had agreed to support Edvard financially until such time as he had established a name for himself as an artist, this support did *not* extend to supporting a wife and family. Nina's mother was equally against the idea of the two marrying, telling her daughter in no uncertain terms that *'he is nothing and he has nothing and he writes music that nobody wants to listen to!'*

Nevertheless, Nina later wrote that around Christmas time in 1864 she and Edvard *'played Schumann's B major symphony in a four-hand arrangement for piano – and became engaged!'* Despite their parents' objections, the engagement was announced in June 1865, and two years later, on 11 June 1867, the young couple were married in St John's Church in Copenhagen. The only guests present were a few friends – neither set of parents was invited.

It is remarkable that Edvard's relationship with his parents was so strained in this period, for they had always been a tight-knit family. The explanation must lie in their objecting to his marrying a cousin. To make matters worse, she was the daughter of Herman Hagerup, who had a reputation for disastrous business deals. Uncle Herman had also married an artist, Adeline Werligh, and word was that she was a brazen woman. These concerns that his parents wrote about to Edvard were the last straw; he was indignant on behalf of his fiancée and came close to breaking off all contact with his family.

As the wedding date approached, his family in Bergen sent reconciliatory letters, assuring Edvard that they had come to terms with the idea of the marriage, and that the young couple were in their thoughts and would always be welcome at his parents' home. *'Let all of the old, unpleasant things be forgotten, and think only about the fact that we really are fond of you!'* wrote Edvard's sister

Herman Hagerup (1816–1900) was Nina's father and Edvard Grieg's uncle and father-in-law.
(BOB)

113

Frants Beyer (1851–1918), lawyer and passionate music lover. (BOB)

Hotel owner in Ullensvang, Brita Utne (1847–1941). The hotel is still run by the family. Brita Utne was a close friend of Edvard Grieg. (BOB)

Benedicte, adding dryly that she would no longer think of Nina as a *'drill sergeant'*. Edvard's resentment at his family's attitude, particularly to Nina, lasted for a long time, however, and his relationship with his parents only really improved after the news of Nina's pregnancy. On the birth of Alexandra on 10 April 1868, things took a decided turn for the better, and from this time onwards Nina and Edvard could really feel surrounded by family love.

PUTTING OSLO BEHIND HIM

The honeymoon period was soon over for Edvard and Nina. Immediately after the wedding they moved to Oslo, where they remained for the next eight years. Grieg composed a little, and conducted and taught a lot, but it was difficult gaining acceptance for artistic work in the capital, with the exception of their recital work. On the home front the young couple were never happier than after the birth of their daughter, Alexandra. Tragically, this happiness was short-lived, as little Alexandra died of meningitis just thirteen months old. Their new family unit had been shattered, and they were left with music and their performing career as their closest ties. When Edvard's parents both died within a short space of time in 1875, the feelings of emptiness, rootlessness and artistic stagnation were further intensified.

Their marriage went through a very rough patch at this time, although both Nina and Edvard did their best not to let things get on top of them. Nina's strategy for coping with illness and pain was to keep her spirits up and to pretend that she *'did not see it, and in that way it is bound to pass'*. Edvard, on the other hand, threw himself into his work and his friendships. He set weighty poems by Henrik Ibsen to music (*Six Songs*, op. 25) almost at the same time as light-hearted verse by his friend John Paulsen. Grieg also came across the ideas and poetry of Aasmund Olavsson Vinje at this time.

Grieg met Frants Beyer for the first time in 1871. This gifted lawyer and music lover came to mean a great deal to Grieg, and their friendship was quite exceptional. They did not only share the same musical interests; they also both had a huge love of the Norwegian mountains and landscape. Their many trips together to fjords and mountains helped Grieg find sorely needed peace of mind. These trips were a source of inspiration to him as an artist,

Lofthus in Hardanger with the Folgefonna glacier in the background. (THG)

Lofthus in Edvard Grieg's day. (BOB)

gave him an understanding of all that is distinctly Norwegian and helped open his eyes to the authenticity of Norwegian folk culture.

It was therefore hardly surprising that Grieg decided to go to live somewhere in rural Norway when he left Oslo for good in 1877. We do not know exactly why he chose Hardanger, but it turned out to be a blessing for him personally and for Norwegian music.

UNDER THE RADIANT YET HEAVY CAPE OF THE FOLGEFONNA GLACIER

Nina and Edvard went to live at Børve, a small mountain farm in the most stunning setting imaginable, with the Sørfjord below and the shining white slopes of the Folgefonna glacier opposite. In a letter to August Winding, a Danish friend, Grieg described the place with enthusiasm, although his words are tinged with melancholy:

115

MUSIC SOCIETY
'HARMONIEN'
The Music Society 'Har-
monien' was established in
1765, and one of its pri-
mary aims was to start up
an orchestra. It consisted
of members and invited
musicians, and it played at
the society's meetings. The
society's activities were in a
constant state of change,
like everything else at that
time. Ole Bull joined the
orchestra before his tenth
birthday, and his playing
impressed not only the
members of the society
but also the professional
musicians. Around 1850
Edvard Grieg's father,
Alexander Grieg, was
chairman of the society,
and Edvard's mother,
Gesine Hagerup Grieg,
was a prominent figure at
the society's musical events
as a pianist. At the start of
the twentieth century the
orchestra became profes-
sional and today the Bergen
Philharmonic Orchestra is
one of Norway's two national orchestras.

'It would be impossible for you not to get well if you were here!
The air is so light that one feels like a feather, or – that one could feel
that way if one didn't have to bear the burden that is an integral part
of the happiest and unhappiest lot on this earth – being an artist.'
(Letter to August Winding, 13 August 1877)

Nina and Edvard spent the winter of 1877–1878 in Hardanger,
but since it was not practical to live at Børve during the winter
months, they moved a few miles to Lofthus, to an inn run by Brita
and Hans Utne. Grieg borrowed a separate building where he spent
his days composing in peace and quiet. We do not know what Nina
found to occupy her time, but it must have been a trying time for
her, despite Brita and Hans's kind attempts to keep her company.

Life in Hardanger, the magnificent Norwegian landscape,
contact with local fiddlers, peace and quiet – all this was manna
to Grieg's soul. He had been through so much pain and turmoil
in his personal life; the deaths of first Alexandra then his parents, severe marital problems, and interminably long periods
devoid of creative ability. It is not hard to imagine how tough
this period must have been for Grieg – or how difficult he probably was to live with at this time.

In the course of the first winter, Grieg felt his creative powers
returning, and he composed some of his best and most personal
works. He himself referred to his String Quartet in G minor, op. 27
from this period as 'a piece of life's history'.

It was the synthesis of his personal experiences and the creative force of the Norwegian landscape and folk culture that was
expressed in the lofty works of this period. This is why the names of
Hardanger, and Børve and Lofthus in particular, will always have
a special place in Norwegian music history.

However, it did not take long for Grieg to grow tired of his
surroundings. The artistic surge he had experienced on arrival in
Hardanger died down almost as fast as it had appeared. From the
end of 1878 and until he moved to Bergen in 1880, Grieg did not
work on any new compositions. He was oppressed by feelings of
loneliness and isolation. 'The serenity of nature is too cold for me,'
he said. And he wrote to Gerhard Schjelderup in 1903: 'It finally
occurs to me that the mountains have nothing more to express. I was
getting empty-headed by looking at them, and found that it was time
to leave.' (Letter to Gerhard Schjelderup, 18. september 1903)

The city of Bergen and its harbour in the 1800s. The city lies like a horseshoe around the bay. (UBB)

FROM HARDANGER TO BERGEN

We can only imagine Nina's sense of dread when the self-willed Edvard announced his decision that they were moving to Hardanger, perhaps for good. Somewhere along the way Edvard and Nina had drifted apart. Once in Hardanger, Edvard shut himself off from everyone in the 'Compost' (Grieg's name for his composer's hut in Hardanger) all day long. He spent the evenings in the hotel drawing room, entertaining himself and his fellow guests with card games and music.

It must have been a relief to Nina when Grieg decided that Hardanger wasn't the right place for him to settle permanently. True enough, Bergen wasn't exactly Copenhagen, but it was a definite improvement from her point of view on the quiet, isolated existence she had led in Hardanger. Her contact with Edvard's brother, John, may have convinced her that they shared something of the same fate: he, too, was an artist at heart, but as the eldest son he had been obliged to take over the family business. He had studied the cello at the conservatory in Leipzig for three semesters and had hoped to pursue a career in music, but his father refused to support him. The family business had come on hard times, and he could not afford to pay for musical training for both his sons. After all, it was a waste of time and money: it was enough that he was supporting Edvard's musical career – the implication being that only Edvard was likely to be able to make a living as a musician. This unfairness, combined with his younger brother's success, was a bitter pill for John to swallow. His parents' devotion to Edvard and their financial support of Edvard's career triggered an acute case of sibling rivalry, not helped by the fact that the young Edvard had been overly critical of, and surly towards, his older brother in his youth. Their relationship was strained for many years by these events. When their parents died relations improved, but it is likely that John never really shook off the feeling that his little brother had been born with a silver spoon in his mouth.

Nina, who was also an artist in her own right, gradually came to feel that her husband put his art before anything else. In Oslo she had realised that they were growing further and further apart, and in Hardanger she was left to her own loneliness. She must have been heartily relieved when they moved to Bergen, even though life there would remind her of what they had left behind in Oslo. In Bergen she could let off steam to John, who could certainly identify with her feelings of being pushed aside. But the answer to the Griegs' marital problems did not lie in Nina's realising that other people could have strained relationships with Edvard, too, but rather in Edvard and Nina's close friendship with Marie and Frants Beyer.

BACK IN BERGEN

Grieg had been engaged to conduct the Harmonien Orchestra in Bergen for one season, and back in Bergen his creativity began to flow again. He completed the *Vinje Songs*, as well as composing the *Norwegian Dances*, op. 35 for four-handed piano and the

Cello Sonata in A minor, op. 36, dedicated to his brother John. Although they moved away from Lofthus, the Griegs did not lose touch with Hardanger and its magnificent landscape, or the friends they had made there. They continued to visit Brita and Hans Utne's hotel every summer, and over the years Grieg wrote several new compositions there.

Despite many artistic successes and being awarded the Knight's Grand Cross of the Royal Norwegian Order of St Olav, Grieg found working in his hometown extremely frustrating. One episode in particular caused quite a stir among the city's inhabitants and in the press. Grieg had planned a big concert for choir and orchestra, including Handel's *Coronation Anthem*. However, at the dress rehearsal half the ladies' choir was missing. It was the same evening as an important society ball, and despite a written agreement with Grieg, many of the choir members had gone to the ball. Grieg decided to make an example of them, and threw the absentees out of the choir. This led to a storm of protest, and a great many insults and much harsh criticism of Grieg. Surely he understood that *'those young ladies were looking forward with keen anticipation to a dance – who will blame them for that? And that it is obviously for this reason that they could not take part in the dress rehearsal.'* (A reader's letter printed in the local newspaper *Bergens Tidende, 11 December 1880*) But Grieg was unbending as ever in the cause of art. Honour was restored to a certain extent when sixty ladies from the choir sent Grieg a vote of confidence of their own free will. *'That was a nice gesture – in contrast to the city gossips and the press, all of whom have branded my course of action as rude.'* (Letter to Winding, 27 December 1880)

LIFE'S INSTITUTIONS

The whole of this period of Grieg's life was riddled with inner and outer turmoil. He just could not seem to get his private life or his professional life together. He had no home of his own, his marriage was on the rocks, he had no children to carry on the family name, and his parents were dead. To use a modern expression, Grieg was having a midlife crisis. He had expended all his energy on his career, and now he seemed to be facing an uncertain future both in his home life and artistically.

So what happened? Like many forty-year-olds of today, he ran off. In 1883 he abandoned Nina to the care of Marie and Frants

Franz von Lenbach (1836–1904).

Franz von Lenbach was one of Europe's most celebrated portrait painters. His subjects included Johann Strauss, Richard and Cosima Wagner, Pope Leo XIII, Franz Liszt, William Gladstone, Emperor Wilhelm I and Emperor Franz Joseph. Lenbach also painted Otto von Bismarck several times. Lenbach was an important cultural figure in Munich in the late 1800s and he was knighted in 1882.

There is an interesting story behind Franz von Lenbach's portrait of Nina Grieg. In a letter to his friend and fellow composer Niels Ravnkilde on 21 July 1884, Grieg wrote: 'I must not forget to tell you that the last evening in Rome proved to be fateful for Lenbach's picture of →

Franz von Lenbach's unfinished portrait of Edvard Grieg – painted during Grieg's visit to Rome in 1884. The portrait bears witness to the composer's personal troubles. It was never completed, since Grieg complained that it made him look 'so ill'. The picture is exhibited at the Edvard Grieg Museum. (EGM)

Beyer, and left town. His plan was to travel southwards to Paris to meet the young Norwegian painter Leis Schjelderup, sister of the composer Gerhard Schjelderup (Grieg's first Norwegian biographer). Leis lived in Paris in the 1880s. Grieg had met her in Hardanger, and his state of mind at that time had made him particularly susceptible to her considerable charms. In June 1883 he wrote to his publisher Max Abraham: *'I can't stand it in this cosy little place any longer. I must see and hear and talk about art'. (Letter to Max Abraham, 25 June 1883)*

Franz von Lenbach's colour pastel of Nina Grieg – painted during the Griegs' visit to Rome in 1884. This was one of the first pictures to be hung up at Troldhaugen on its completion in 1885. The picture still hangs in the living room at Troldhaugen today. (EGM)

Nina. You remember that it was taken out of the packing that Lenbach himself had prepared so that it could be admired – or more correctly, vilified – by the Scandinavians ... but alas! Upon arriving in Bergen it was discovered that the paints had run and smudged in several places in the face. The picture is now enclosed in glass and frame and from now on, fortunately, will not incur any further damage. But the damage is done and cannot be undone. He had promised to send us the oil painting [of Edvard Grieg], but whether he will do so is another question.' The portrait of Nina must have been sent to Lenbach in Munich for repairs at some later date. In a letter to the German conductor Hermann Levi, dated 30 October 1890, Grieg writes: 'My wife implied recently that the Lenbach portrait of her, once upon a time, might be sold at an auction along with his remaining works and bearing the title: "Unknown portrait". Luckily she was wrong, because before we left, the picture arrived and it is obvious that it has been given more attention by the creator. My sincere thanks to you for the successful commission. May I ask you to give my thanks to master Lenbach when you happen to see him again.'

It was on this pretext of artistic longing that he walked out on his marriage.

However, he did not travel straight to Paris, since he thought that he ought to learn a little French before arriving in France. So he went to stay with an American-Belgian friend, the musician Frank van der Stucken, in Rudolstadt for two months. His journey to Paris was postponed once again by an extremely hectic concert tour of central Europe. All this time, letters arrived for him almost daily from his friend Frants Beyer, begging Grieg

Georgia Elise (Leis)
Schjelderup
(1856–1933). (EGM)

Frank van der Stucken
(1858–1929). (EGM)

Detail of another portrait
of Edvard Grieg painted
by Franz von Lenbach
during Grieg's visit to
Rome in 1884. (Private-
ly owned)(PRIVAT EIE)

to reconsider and to return home. But Grieg steadily declined to do so, explaining that *'to come home now would be a disaster for me. It would be to go back to school, to tear myself out of my development – the fermentation that I can undergo only out here'*. (Letter to Frants Beyer, 29 July 1883)

But in the end he had to come to a decision. The whole situation was untenable – a devastated Nina was staying with their friend Frants Beyer, who in turn was attempting to console Nina at the same time as trying to bring Edvard to his senses. And all the while Grieg became more and more unsure as to whether he really could find happiness in Paris. Finally he reached a decision: he would stick by Nina. The bonds that bound them together were too strong to be severed, and he – and she – would have to be willing to rebuild the marriage.

It was as if a heavy load lifted from Grieg's shoulders once he had finally made this decision. He expressed his gratitude in a moving New Year greeting to his friend Frants Beyer from Amsterdam.

'Dear, dear friend! I really must have a couple of words with you before the old year comes to an end. I cannot thank you for the year. I can only tell you that without you I probably would not have got through it, that you are my best friend, and that I will care for you in a different way than I care for all other people as long as this heart of mine continues to beat [...] I open my arms to you, to the new year, to spring, the new spring of the spirit and of nature, to joy, to peace. I could embrace the whole of humankind in gratitude for the bright star that – despite everything, and through the fog – shines over my existence.' (Letter to Frants Beyer, 29 December 1883)

Grieg's life and work could have taken a dramatic turn if it hadn't been for the intervention of Frants Beyer. What Beyer understood was that if Grieg was to be capable of productive work again, he needed a fixed framework for his existence, certain fixed institutions of life. That was why it was vital for him to go back to Nina and attempt to rebuild his marriage. The next step was to find them a home of their own. Most of us need certain institutions in our lives, even if at times we rebel against them – nevertheless they need to be there.

With characteristic humour and warmth Beyer helped Grieg build these institutions. In the spring of 1884 Marie and Frants Beyer set off southwards with Nina, met Grieg in Amsterdam and accompanied the couple to Italy on a trip of reconciliation. The trip proved successful and we can see Nina's delight in the famous portrait Franz von Lenbach painted of her in Rome that spring. The portrait now hangs in the sitting room at Troldhaugen.

The first stage of Beyer's plan had succeeded, and he now turned to the issue of creating a home for the Griegs, and the building of Troldhaugen provided this next institution in Grieg's life. He recovered from his midlife crisis thanks to his friend's understanding and help.

It is easy to see from the correspondence between Grieg and Beyer that Beyer was an exceptional friend. One small, curious example of his kindness illustrates this point nicely. Grieg and Beyer often went walking together in the mountains, frequently to Mount Løvstakken, Grieg's favourite mountain in Bergen. Sometimes when they had planned a trip up there together, Beyer would nip up the day before, and hide some little surprise such as a couple of dark beers, or a bottle of port. Friends like that don't grow on trees!

Nevertheless, we may be forgiven for wondering what might have happened had Grieg resisted his friend's advice. Would he have fallen to pieces? Or might he have continued on that new artistic surge that his six-month solo tour of central Europe showed that he was still capable of? Would he have returned to work almost exclusively in the small genres as Frants Beyer encouraged him to, since they both knew he mastered the small form, or might he have mustered up the courage to tackle the larger musical forms once more?

Franz von Lenbach painted this portrait of Edvard Grieg in 1890.

MAJOR WORK IN G MINOR

'… with my life's blood in days of sorrow and despair'

The period of 1875 to 1885 was, as we have seen, a turbulent period in Grieg's life, but although he did not write many new works in this period, those he did produce were among his finest. Two works from this period deserve particular attention: the *Ballade in G minor*, op. 24 and the *String Quartet in G minor*, op. 27. Both are in the key of G minor, the key chosen by Grieg and many other composers to express their strongest emotions.

Ballade in G minor, op. 24

Through hard work Grieg eventually overcame his grief, his marital problems and his sense of artistic stagnation. He expressed his feelings at the loss of his parents in his finest piano work, the

Nina and Edvard Grieg in Rome, 1884. (BOB)

Eugene d'Albert (1864–1932). (BOB)

Gottfred Matthison-Hansen (1832–1909), Danish organist and composer. (BOB)

Ballade in G minor, op. 24 (*Ballade in the Form of Variations on a Norwegian Melody*). Once again he turned to folk music in search of thematic material, and it was in LM Lindeman's *Older and Newer Norwegian Mountain Melodies*, that he found a folk song from Valdres called *The Northland Peasantry*. This melody had all the qualities he was looking for, not least a tendency towards a minor key and an accented leading note. This gave Grieg plenty of scope for bold, imaginative harmonisation, which he exploited to the full.

In fourteen variations Grieg leads us through a wide range of emotion and expression. He alternates between heavy, sombre variations (nos. 1, 3, 5 and 8), bouncy, energetic ones (nos. 2, 6 and 7) and variations that sound almost like folk dances (nos. 4 and 10). After the slow, contemplative variation in no. 9 Grieg breaks free of the strict variation form. The following variations are longer, the thematic material is developed and the tension mounts, and the whole piece concludes with a frenetic display of energy reminiscent of the style of Bartók, and others in the early 1900s, known as barbarism. At a wild pace he moves up the keyboard, higher and higher, before leaping right down to a low E flat, a long note that lasts for what feels like an eternity, before gliding down *pianissimo* to the dominant D – and the simplicity of the first eight bars of the folk tune ends the battle, dying away to nothing in resignation.

Ballade is extremely demanding technically. Grieg himself never played it in public, but that was mainly because this work contained so many strong emotions for him that he could not bear the idea of performing it in front of an audience. However, he played it through for his publisher in Leipzig, Max Abraham at Edition Peters, with the composer Iver Holter present, and Holter later described this performance:

'Grieg put his entire soul into the interpretation; and when he was finished, not only was he so physically exhausted that he was bathed in sweat: he was also so agitated and shaken that he could not say a word for a long time. Grieg was convinced that his publisher would not want to publish this piece, but to his great delight Max Abraham was not only willing to publish it, he was clearly taken with it, remarking that this work would "add even greater lustre to Grieg's name".'

In 1898 Grieg heard his work performed at a concert in the Gewandhaus in Leipzig by Eugène d'Albert, who in Grieg's words played *'so brilliantly that it took people by storm. Just think what that means! He had more or less all the qualifications: elegance and grand*

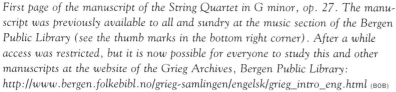

First page of the manuscript of the String Quartet in G minor, op. 27. The manuscript was previously available to all and sundry at the music section of the Bergen Public Library (see the thumb marks in the bottom right corner). After a while access was restricted, but it is now possible for everyone to study this and other manuscripts at the website of the Grieg Archives, Bergen Public Library: http://www.bergen.folkebibl.no/grieg-samlingen/engelsk/grieg_intro_eng.html (BOB)

Recent photo of the composer's hut at Ullensvang Hotel. (THG)

From my window in Utne. *Grieg's sketch of the view from his composer's hut.* (BOB)

style, mighty crescendos culminating in utter fury. And then after this you should have heard the daringly long fermata on the deep E flat. I think he held it for half a minute! But the effect was colossal. And then he concluded that old, sad song so slowly, so quietly and simply that I myself was completely enthralled.' (Letter to Frants Beyer, 27 March 1898)

'A PIECE OF LIFE'S HISTORY'

Grieg's next composition in G minor was no less dramatic. The *String Quartet*, op. 27 is not just one of the most intense pieces of Norwegian chamber music ever, it was unique in contemporary European music. Franz Liszt remarked, after hearing the quartet performed in Wiesbaden, that this work was one of *the* most exciting pieces of European chamber music of the 1870s and 1880s.

Soon after his arrival in Hardanger in 1877, Grieg started work on a new string quartet. He wrote to his friend Gottfred Matthison-Hansen:

Edvard Grieg's 53rd birthday was celebrated in Lofthus on 15 June 1896. From top left: Chistian Smith, Tonny Hagerup, Marie Grieg and Johan Halvorsen. Second row: Frants Beyer, John Grieg, Brita Utne, Edvard and Nina Grieg, Adeline Hagerup, Ludvig Müller. In front: Annie Halvorsen, Børre Giertsen, Nancy Giertsen, Alexandra Bjerke and (standing) Herman Hagerup. (BOB)

'The next composition that you will see from me will be a work for string instruments. I'm in the middle of it, but God knows when I will finish. Just now I am once again experiencing a numbing incompetence that must be violently attacked.' (Letter to Gottfred Matthison-Hansen, 13 August 1877)

On completing the quartet in 1878, he wrote to Matthison-Hansen once more, fully aware of the stature of the work he had just finished: 'It is not intended to deal in trivialities for petty minds. It aims at breadth, flight of imagination, and above all sonority for the instruments for which it is written.'

Nor did Grieg attempt to hide the emotions and turmoil behind this dramatic music. He wrote to his biographer Aimar Grønvold in 1883: 'For I feel that in this work are hidden traces of that life's blood of which the future will hopefully see more than mere drops ...'

The quartet opens with a dramatic musical statement, an imperative. But this is followed by a transition via a chord devoid of hope to an open solution.

The entire composition is built around this opening motif, which is finely woven into each of the movements. Liszt had started using this kind of unifying technique, but Grieg was the first to do so consistently throughout a large-scale work. It would be another fifteen years before Debussy made use of a similar principle in his *String Quartet in G minor*.

In order to achieve the dramatic expression he was after, Grieg used a dense, almost orchestral instrumentation, with extensive use of double stopping and closely interwoven parts. This was quite far removed from the techniques traditionally used in chamber music, and Grieg was criticised by some of his contemporaries (and some modern-day critics) for the 'thick, syrupy' orchestral sound of his quartet. Grieg's response to this criticism was that in a performance in accordance with his intentions, the tightly knit parts would cloud neither the melodic line nor the musical form.

When he had finished this work, Grieg contacted one of the leading chamber musicians in Europe, the violinist Robert Heckmann in Cologne, who provided invaluable assistance with respect to various technical questions Grieg had. Grieg went to Germany in the autumn of 1878 to attend the Heckmann Quartet's rehearsals for the premiere of this work, and he was present at the first performance, which took place in Cologne on 29 October. Grieg dedicated the quartet to Heckmann as thanks for his help. A few weeks later the quartet was performed in Leipzig. It was well received by the audience, but Eduard Bernsdorf, who had almost without fail given Grieg's music very negative write-ups, wrote a mean-spirited critique in *Signale*.

The Heckmann Quartet from Cologne performed Grieg's quartet at its first performance. (EGM)

'The Heckmann Quartet from Cologne gave a concert in the Gewandhaus on 30 November championing a composer of our own time, Mr Edvard Grieg from Oslo. Thus it was a purely propagandistic concert and Mr Grieg has every reason to be grateful to Mr Heckmann and his colleagues. Would that we could have been as grateful to the gentlemen from Cologne as Mr Grieg! That, unfortunately, we could not be. For the Griegian products have given us no joy or pleasure at all – not the G minor sonata [sic] for Violin and Piano (opus 13), not the still unpublished String Quartet (also in G minor), and not the many songs or the little piano pieces from opuses 6, 19 and 28. Quite the opposite. We have felt only displeasure and repugnance toward all the boorish and absurd stuff that is gathered together under the guise of a Norwegian national stamp, toward the mediocrity of the compositional inventiveness that lurks behind the rough-hewn and exaggerated Norwegian exterior (something non-Norwegians must accept in good faith), and toward the lack of any talent for structure and development*

The String Quartet in EW Fritsch's edition, Leipzig Quartet. (THG)

– indeed the lack of any ability whatsoever to create – adequately, without patchwork – a continuous whole in a movement (as here in the sonata and the quartet).

'Finally we must acknowledge that – no matter how curious it may appear from our standpoint – performers and compositions at the concert were almost without exception received with great enthusiasm. Indeed, Mr Grieg even had to repeat Bridal Procession.*'*

Grieg was despondent at these crass insults, and admitted later that he had been tempted to burn the manuscript. Luckily he did not do so, and the *String Quartet* went on to become a firm favourite with performers and audiences alike. It must have been balm to Grieg's socialist and anti-snobbish soul that the same quartet enjoyed a huge success at a family concert at the Copenhagen Labour Union just before Christmas 1899. He wrote to Julius Röntgen:

'My old view was confirmed: Here is where one finds the best audiences! To hell with the blasé, bejewelled, so-called fashionable audiences, be they in the Gewandhaus in Leipzig or the Music Society in Copenhagen! No, the unspoiled people are capable of enthusiasm; the others, with rare exceptions, are not.' (Letter to Julius Röntgen, 22 December 1899)

It is interesting to study the thematic material on which the quartet is based. After completing the score of the incidental music to *Peer Gynt*, Grieg was so inspired by Ibsen's powerful poems that he also set six of them to music in his *Six Songs*, op. 25. One of the songs, *Fiddlers*, is about the conflict between love and the call of the artist. The poem opens with the lines:

My dreams were of my beloved
Through the warm summer night,
But by the river I wander'd
In an eerie and pale moonlight.
Heigh, do you know song and terror?
Can you dazzle the heart of the fair,
That in mighty halls and cathedrals
She'll covet to follow you there? [5]

But the struggle to reach the inner voice of art comes at a high price, and the poet continues:

Edvard Grieg's older brother, John, had musical ambitions too, but as the elder son he had to take over his father's business. He and his German-born wife, Marie, had seven children, and they lived in the old Grieg family home in Strandgaten. Edvard wrote his Cello Sonata *op. 36 for John.*

(EGM)

I conjur'd the sprite of the waters;
He lur'd me to regions wide,
But when that dread sprite I had master'd,
She was my brother's bride!
In mighty halls and cathedrals
I fiddled tunes refin'd,
But evil songs and horror
Were ever in my mind.

This poem may help us understand why Grieg chose this particular song as the starting point for his quartet, reflecting as it does the whole of his crisis-ridden situation. Somehow he managed to give this conflict a voice through his *String Quartet*.

A number of letters to and from Grieg confirm beyond a doubt that clashes with Nina were one of the main ingredients in the drama expressed in the *String Quartet*. Nevertheless, it is going too far to draw the conclusion that Nina was in any literal sense his 'brother's bride', that is, having an affair with Edvard's brother John.

Grieg's sketchbooks show that he had difficulty getting going on this quartet. It wasn't until he hit upon using the *Fiddlers* motif as a sort of *idée fixe* that things began to fall into place. To emphasise the dramatic element in the work, he uses the theme in the minor key, and it is not until the same motif occurs in the second theme that it is played in the major, as we know it from *Fiddlers*.

This motif occurs again and again throughout the quartet, at times only hinted at in the thick instrumental texture, and at other times developed into sweeping melodic phrases. At the close of the last movement the motif rings out in a grandiose theme where the note values are twice as long. The theme soars through a chaotic cascade of notes towards what might have been the final resolution of the thematic development.

Instead, the work closes in the same way in which it started: just as we start to feel that we are close to a happy ending, the opening bars of the first movement sound once more with their chord devoid of all hope. There is no end to the struggle, Grieg merely brings the music to a halt in G major, before the quartet ends on a final unison G.

In this *String Quartet* Grieg acknowledges and processes the huge personal dilemmas he was facing. The material is too full of conflicts and harrowing emotions to be able to reach any kind of resolution. The conflicts, like the music, live on in us.

ABA FORM
The ABA form is a widely used form of composition where a piece is in three parts. Grieg often used this form in his songs and piano pieces. Put simply, it consists of two themes, the first theme is used at the beginning, followed by the second theme – usually contrasting – in the middle, and then the first theme is repeated at the end. This form is very common in folk music (*Twinkle, twinkle, little star*), pop music (*Yesterday*) and other genres.

Between the dramatic first and last movements, Grieg deals with these conflicts in different ways in the second and third movements. In the second movement, *Romanze*, he allows two completely different themes to collide with each other. The cello starts with a poignant, lyrical melody, which is interrupted by a frenetic middle section in which the first violin rages round in jerks and bounds. Underneath these themes the accompaniment wanders restlessly from key to key, with fragments of the motif woven into the complex texture. The movement closes with a variation on the first section, and the last word in this argument is one of resigned calm.

The slow movement, which almost has the character of an intermezzo, is followed by an actual *Intermezzo*. This movement is constructed around the same basic ABA form as much of Grieg's music. The A section is full of high drama. Grieg uses the motif in a different rhythmic setting, with strong syncopation (2 against 3) creating a feeling of stubbornness and resistance. This is followed by the B section with a dashing but heavy *halling*-like theme in the cello. The theme passes to the other instruments with acrobatic leaps. Then the A section returns, before Grieg adds a humoristic touch to the *Intermezzo* in the coda.

A GOOD DEED

While in Hardanger, Grieg also composed *The Mountain Thrall*, op. 32. This work was one of his compositions which Grieg was most pleased with, and it was written during Edvard and Nina's first winter in Hardanger. Grieg later wrote about this period: '*It was an important period in my life, filled with significant events and emotional upheavals.*' (Letter to Gerhard Schjelderup, 18 September 1903)

The text of *The Mountain Thrall* is a short epic poem from Magnus Brostrup Landstad's *Norwegian Folk Poetry* (1853). It is the story of a young man lost in a haunted forest, who, after being bewitched by an elfin maid, can never again have a normal love life. This was a theme close to Grieg's heart at that time. He felt that he had expressed some of his innermost feelings through this work, and he quoted Bjørnson, saying: '*God knows it was written with devotion!*' adding that, '*It is as if with this piece I have done one of the few good deeds of my life.*'

The Holberg statue in Bergen was unveiled in connection with the 200th anniversary of the poet's birth. 'There were umbrellas, naturally – it wouldn't have been Bergen without them,' wrote Grieg after the ceremony on 3 December 1884. (EGM)

Statue of Ludvig Holberg, by the Swedish sculptor Johan Börjeson. (THG)

Although Grieg composed just a handful of works in this period of his life, those few compositions are a central part of his output, and through these works we find the clue to understanding much of Grieg's life and music.

DELIGHTFUL DIGRESSION

After leaving Hardanger for Bergen, Nina and Edvard visited Brita and Hans Utne in Ullensvang as regular as clockwork each year in the summertime, and Grieg nearly always produced new compositions in these beautiful summery surroundings.

One summer he composed *Norwegian Dances*, op. 35 for four-handed piano. The Griegs loved playing these pieces together, at home and in the concert hall. Another summer he composed the opening of his *Cello Sonata in A minor*, op. 36. In this setting he often returned to folk music as a source of inspiration.

Grieg spent the late summer and autumn of 1884 in Hardanger, working on a number of compositions, although his mind was also very much taken up with his *'best opus'* – the building of Troldhaugen. Countless letters were sent back and forth between Grieg and the young architect Schak Bull, containing sketches of house plans, questions, budgets and the like.

Announcements in the local newspaper Bergens Tidende *for the Holberg Anniversary, December 1884.* (BOB)

However, Grieg was also kept busy with a commission he had received in connection with the celebrations in Bergen to mark the bicentennial of the birth of the Norwegian-Danish playwright Ludvig Holberg. A monument was to be unveiled, and that meant a cantata was needed. This task went to Nordahl Rolfsen, the writer and educationalist, and Edvard Grieg.

This was not at all the type of work that Grieg enjoyed, as we can see in a letter from Grieg to Frants Beyer in October 1884: *'I am bored by having to write a piece for male chorus for the Holberg celebration. Well, I may be writing poor music, but on the other hand I'm doing all right as a fisherman. Yesterday I pulled in seventy of them.'* (Letter to Frants Beyer, 9 October 1884)

As the date approached, he became less and less keen on the whole project, and he saw in his mind's eye what the event would be like:

'Moreover, so far as music is concerned I've been bored silly because I've had to spend my time writing a cantata for male chorus a cappella. I have to conduct the thing on 3 December on the main square in Bergen, where the monument is to be unveiled. I can see it now: snow, hail, storm and thunder, a large male chorus with open mouths into which the rain pours, and me conducting with a rain coat, winter coat, galoshes and umbrella! Then, of course, a cold or God knows what other kind of illness! Ah well, that is one way to die for one's country!' (Letter to Julius Röntgen, 30 October 1884)

However, even though he was bored by having to work on the cantata, he applied himself diligently to the task, reading extensively about Holberg, his writings and his philosophy. After the event, he wrote to his Danish friend Niels Ravnkilde in Rome:

'Father Holberg cost me two months of strenuous work. But he deserves it, too, splendid fellow that he is – he more than any other Norwegian, I say in this moment. The truth is that I really haven't known him until now. His views on history, on mortality, on life's biggest questions were foreign to me. Now I have learned that his horizon was one of the widest we have encountered in all history.' (Letter to Niels Ravnkilde, 17 December 1884)

The cantata was duly performed by a male voice choir of 250 in the pouring rain (what else in Bergen in December?!) to an enthusiastic crowd.

While working on these two opuses – the house and the cantata – Grieg digressed delightfully in writing a piano suite in an old style that he named *Holberg Suite*, op. 40. It was his encounter with Holberg's multifaceted genius, his humour, satire and sober philosophy that inspired Grieg to compose the *Holberg Suite*, which is based on the old French dance suite forms favoured by Couperin, Rameau and Bach. At Grieg's hand these old dance movements received a new, personal garb. He completed the suite and the cantata in August and October 1884, respectively.

It is clear that Grieg derived much pleasure from working on this suite, both from how quickly he completed it and his own comments. When he had finished, he wrote to Julius Röntgen: '*Once in a great while it really is a good exercise to conceal one's own individuality.*' (*Letter to Julius Röntgen, 26 August 1884*)

The suite was performed in the Workers' Union Hall in Bergen a few days after the unveiling of the monument, and it was an immediate success. However, Grieg scoffed when a Danish critic wrote that Mr Grieg had struck out in a new direction. '*Stuff and nonsense!*' he protested.

The Workers' Union Hall in Bergen. (EGM)

Some time later Grieg arranged his *Holberg Suite* for string orchestra, and it is in this version that the piece has won worldwide acclaim.

The suite opens with a firework display of a *Preludium*. In the version for string orchestra, Grieg literally lets the music work its way around the room by starting the galloping theme off in the first violins at the left-hand side of the stage, via the second violins and violas, and across to the cellos and double basses on the right-hand side. He finishes up with all the riders amassed in a magnificent parade.

The same intensity is to be found in the last movement, *Rigaudon*, which starts off as a race between the solo violin and the solo viola, while the rest of the orchestra provides eager support. After a more lyrical middle section, somewhat reminiscent of the middle section of *March of the Dwarfs*, op. 54 no. 3, the riders return, before Grieg once again gathers the dancers together in a solemn coda.

The two dances in the middle of the suite, *Gavotte* and *Musette*, run into one another. The *Gavotte*, with the typical accent on the third beat, is an elegant piece. Grieg makes the French *Musette* more like a Norwegian folkdance on a Hardanger fiddle in the first section, while the second half soars on the sonorous wings of the cello.

In the two slow movements *Sarabande* (second movement) and *Air* (fourth movement) Grieg demonstrates his mastery of melody and harmony. The mood in *Sarabande* is thick and dark, like in a shaded Spanish garden, but Grieg emerges from this uncompromising, florid background with a typically light, lyrical touch.

Lyric Pieces 1

A FRIEZE OF LIFE

FROM EARLY CHILDHOOD, the piano was the cornerstone of Edvard Grieg's music. It was while tinkering at the piano keyboard that he carried out his first experiments in harmony and produced his earliest compositions, and what success he enjoyed as a student at the Leipzig Conservatory was as a pianist and a composer of piano music. Later, as an acknowledged 'wizard in the kingdom of music', he continued to compose for the piano. His *Four Piano Pieces*, op. 1 (1861–63) and *Poetic Tone Pictures*, op. 3 (1863) are clearly grounded in the Leipzig tradition – it is not until *Humoresques*, op. 6 (1865) that we find the unmistakable hallmark of Edvard Grieg. After meeting Rikard Nordraak in Copenhagen, he felt convinced that in order to succeed as a composer, that is to say *as a Norwegian composer*, he would have to rid himself of '*all the* idées fixes *he had learned in Leipzig*'. Now he knew that his inspiration was to be found in the authenticity of Norwegian folk music. That was without a doubt where his future lay.

By the time *Lyric Pieces I*, op. 12 was published in 1867, Grieg had very much found his own unique style and musical form. Over the years his creative genius produced nine more volumes of *Lyric Pieces*, a genre for ever to be associated with the name of Edvard Grieg.

From the opening *Arietta* in *Lyric Pieces I* (1867) to the final *Remembrances* in *Lyric Pieces* X (1901), these 66 lyric pieces span the entire spectrum of Grieg's personality, his artistic experience and development. These romantic pieces are a cut above the general run of album leaves and miniatures so popular in his day.

The official picture of Bjørnstjerne Bjørnson and Edvard Grieg on the bridge in front of the villa at Troldhaugen. It was taken on Grieg's 60th birthday, 15 June 1903. The figures of Karoline Bjørnson and Nina Grieg have been removed from the photo. (EGM)

The ten volumes of *Lyric Pieces* are not merely a random selection of individual musical poems – Edvard Grieg masterfully compiled each set in such a way that the pieces in each volume form a natural musical whole.

The very last piece, *Remembrances*, is a melancholy variant in waltz time of the very first *Arietta*. The way in which Grieg rounds off the series like this is a wonderful illustration of his mastery of the small form, with his neatly balanced but unexpected harmonic turns at the end of each phrase. The ring is complete, a frieze of life that ends almost as it started, but on a new plane.

A NATIONAL SONG IS BORN

The eight pieces in the first volume (*Arietta, Waltz, Watchman's Song, Fairy Dance, Folk Song, Norwegian, Album Leaf* and *National Song*) contain the full range of moods to be found throughout the entire series of *Lyric Pieces*.

The following year Grieg arranged *National Song* for male voice choir. Nina and Edvard Grieg spent Christmas 1867 in Oslo, and were invited to celebrate Christmas at the home of Bjørnstjerne Bjørnson and his family in Rosenkrantzgaten. Everyone was in high spirits and, characteristically, Bjørnson insisted on Grieg accompanying all 32 verses of one of his favourite hymns by Grundtvig. Afterwards Bjørnson recited the entire hymn by heart. *'I was deeply impressed!'* Grieg recorded in his diary.

Bjørnson gave Grieg a copy of his *Short Pieces* in return for Grieg's book of *Lyric Pieces* – hot off the press – which Grieg had presented him with earlier that day.

The title of the last piece, *National Song*, had caught Bjørnson's eye in particular, and he insisted on Grieg playing it at the party. Bjørnson was fired up with enthusiasm by the power and solemnity of the music, and declared there and then his intention of writing words to Grieg's melody. He would dedicate the song to the youth of Norway, he proclaimed!

Grieg did not take this too seriously, putting it down to the high spirits of the Christmas party, but the very next day Bjørnson announced joyfully that his text was well underway, although he had yet to find just the right words at the beginning – it needed to be something catchy.

Detail from Leis Schjelderup's portrait of Edvard Grieg (1885).
(BERGEN ART MUSEUM)

The following day Grieg was giving one of his many piano lessons in the attic studio in the Griegs' apartment in Øvre Voldgate, when he suddenly heard:

'... the doorbell ringing as if it were going to ring right off the door. Then there was a racket as of invading wild hordes and a roar, "Forward, forward! Hurrah! Now I've got it! Forward!"

'My pupil trembled like an aspen leaf. My wife, who was in the next room, was scared out of her wits. But when the door flew open and Bjørnson stood there, happy and glowing like the sun, everybody joined in the excitement. Then we heard the beautiful poem, which was nearly completed:

'"Forward!" was our fathers' battle cry.

'"Forward!" We shall raise the banner high!' [6]

The song was first performed in the arrangement for male voice choir when students in Oslo held a torchlight procession in honour of Norwegian poet Johan Sebastian Welhaven in 1868.

The first volume of *Lyric Pieces* would later be followed by a further nine volumes, the last eight of which were closely linked to life at Troldhaugen.

Edvard Grieg's 60th birthday on 15 June 1903. The photo was taken in the garden at Troldhaugen, where well-wishers swarmed around Grieg as he thanked the mayor of Bergen for his kind speech. (BOB)

Troldhaugen
– 'my very best opus!'

EDVARD GRIEG was only fifteen years old when he left his parents' home in Bergen in 1858 and travelled to Leipzig to *'become an artist'*. From that day and right up to 16 April 1885, when he moved into Troldhaugen, he had no permanent home of his own. During their years in Oslo, Edvard and Nina lived in rented accommodation, and on their travels they either stayed with friends and family in Bergen, Copenhagen and Leipzig, or enjoyed a life of relative luxury at various hotels and health spas around Europe. Nevertheless, we see from Grieg's extensive correspondence that they longed for a place of their own, somewhere where Edvard could find the necessary silence and peace of mind he needed to compose his music.

This yearning became even stronger after the deaths of his parents in autumn 1875, since this meant that he and Nina no longer had a home to return to in Bergen. Staying with Edvard's brother or sisters was simply not the same as going home to his parents. Edvard's brother, John, had a large family of his own, so there was little space for guests.

Grieg became restless and depressed after his parents' deaths. He spent two winters in Bergen from 1880 to 1882 as the conductor of the Harmonien Orchestra (the forerunner of the Bergen Philharmonic Orchestra), but he did not want to settle there. The music scene was too small, Bergen was too provincial, and he felt cut off from the impressions and stimulation of Europe's major centres of art. However, during his time in Bergen and Hardanger, he and Nina developed a close friendship with Frants Beyer, a lawyer and keen music lover, and his wife Marie. The Griegs and the

Neighbours and best friends Marie and Frants Beyer. They called their property Næsset. (BOB)

139

Salomon Monsen Hop owned the farmland (Hestetræet) where Grieg purchased the rocky headland overlooking Lake Nordåsvannet. (EGM)

Old picture of Troldhaugen and Lake Nordåsvannet. (EGM)

Beyers became firm friends, and it seems that they started playing with the idea of building houses next door to each other quite early on in the friendship.

After Grieg left Bergen, Beyer bought a plot of land at Hop by Lake Nordåsvannet in Fana. They called their place Næsset and Beyer kept Grieg informed about every stage of the building process. When Nina and Edvard returned from Italy around Whitsun in 1884, they were the first guests to stay at Næsset.

Frants Beyer had hoped that a second house could be built on the site, but despite their close friendship, the two couples had to admit, though deeply disappointed, that there simply wasn't enough space for two houses there. However, there was an overgrown knoll just across the cove owned by a farmer named Salomon Monsen Hop, who was willing to sell a piece of his land to the Griegs. They paid 2300 Norwegian kroner for the plot. Frants Beyer helped draw up the contract, which included a clause stating that the adjoining plot of land (where the Troldsalen concert hall and the Edvard

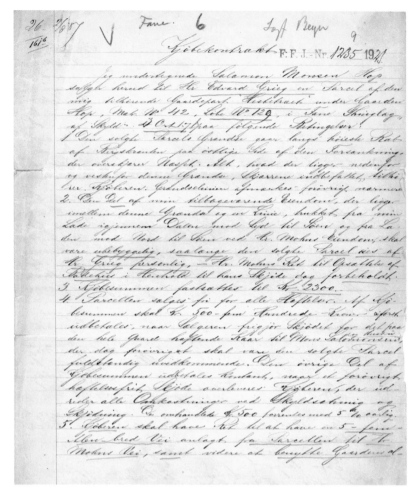

Grieg's title deed for Troldhaugen. (EGM)

The contract of purchase between Salomon Monsen Hop and Edvard Grieg. (EGM)

Grieg Museum now stand) could not be sold without Grieg's knowledge. There would be no grazing rights on the land either.

From this time on Grieg described the place as his new opus, with great enthusiasm:

'Before leaving, however, I made preparations for a new opus, the best one I have ever produced: I bought a plot of land a few miles from Bergen, and this autumn I intend to realise my old dream to build my own cabin and get my own home. It may look like madness from an artistic standpoint. But the die is now cast, and so far, at least, I do not regret it. On the contrary: I am as happy as a child about it. No opus has filled me with more enthusiasm than this one. I spend half the day painting and drawing: rooms, basements, attic rooms –

The architect Schak August Steenberg Bull (1858–1956) was a young cousin of Edvard Grieg. In his later years he grew more and more like Edvard Grieg in appearance. (BOB)

Troldhaugen in spring. (THG)

including one in which you shall rest on soft cushions when you come.' (Letter to Niels Ravnkilde, 21 July 1884)

But what was the new opus to be called? Every property had to have an official name, and it was important to find a name with the right ring to it.

Detail of the fence, as it still is today. (THG)

Grieg's sketches of details for his new home. (BOB)

Edvard Grieg sketched this plan of the villa on the back of an envelope (letter to architect Schak Bull).(BOB)

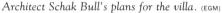

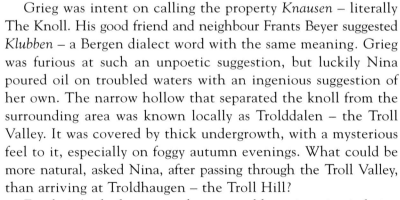

Architect Schak Bull's plans for the villa. (EGM)

Architect Schak Bull's plans for the villa. (EGM)

Grieg was intent on calling the property *Knausen* – literally The Knoll. His good friend and neighbour Frants Beyer suggested *Klubben* – a Bergen dialect word with the same meaning. Grieg was furious at such an unpoetic suggestion, but luckily Nina poured oil on troubled waters with an ingenious suggestion of her own. The narrow hollow that separated the knoll from the surrounding area was known locally as Trolddalen – the Troll Valley. It was covered by thick undergrowth, with a mysterious feel to it, especially on foggy autumn evenings. What could be more natural, asked Nina, after passing through the Troll Valley, than arriving at Troldhaugen – the Troll Hill?

Eureka! And of course today we could not imagine it being called anything but Troldhaugen.

The Griegs spent the summer of 1884 in Hardanger. During this stay Grieg completed a cantata commissioned for the Holberg Anniversary to be celebrated in December that year in Bergen, and his famous *Holberg Suite*. At the same time he was full of plans

THE VILLA

The villa has a base area of about 100 m². The basement contains a pantry, a wine cellar, the so-called flower room and storage rooms. There are two entrances to the ground floor, both on the east face of the building: a kitchen entrance to the north east (no longer in use) and the main entrance at the south east corner. There is a flight of stone steps leading up to the front door. There is a small porch outside the kitchen. The kitchen has a larder to the north and a small maid's room to the south. The kitchen leads into the dining room, and there are folding doors between the dining room and the sitting room, which can also be accessed from the hall. There are French windows which open out on to the veranda beyond.

Landscape views flood in through the large south-facing window. (EGM)

for the new house. What he really wanted was more or less a replica of the Beyers' villa, at least as far as the interior went. But this plan was eventually abandoned and instead Grieg hired his cousin Schak Bull, a promising young architect just twenty-six years old, to design the house and to supervise the building work.

The original plan was to build a 'simple, Norwegian farmhouse', but the end result was a Victorian country house in the style typical of the time, with a tower and an open, richly ornamented veranda on the west face. The veranda around the tower room ran the entire width of the house, to show their neighbours that they had style and money. The windowsills and cornices were ornately carved and at the top of the tower was a terrace with a flagpole, where Nina Grieg had a small vegetable garden.

One of the distinguishing features of Troldhaugen is the many large windows. Even the basement, half submerged below ground level, has relatively large windows, since Grieg wanted plenty of light and air in the pantry and wine cellar. The largest room in the cellar was known as the flower room.

The building project was a huge financial undertaking for Grieg, costing him 12,500 Norwegian kroner – roughly equivalent to ten years' income for most people. The Griegs' financial situation was far from secure, but Grieg was always careful with money, and he was helped out financially by his publisher, Max Abraham of Edition Peters in Leipzig. He also worked hard to earn extra income. After a concert in Bergen he wrote: *'If I make any money on this, I'll put it in my wallet and bury it at Troldhaugen.'* On another occasion he expressed the hope that a new volume of songs (opus 39) would *'… scrape up at least enough money for the basement windows'*.

The Griegs managed to finance the building project, despite the constant additions and alterations underway, without risk of financial ruin.

In Grieg's day the house had no running water or indoor toilet. The tiny building just outside the front door housed the outdoor toilet, and they drew water from the well and then pumped it to the kitchen.

One of Grieg's main priorities in the design of Troldhaugen was ensuring that there was as much daylight as possible in the various rooms. He was keen to be able to enjoy the beautiful natural surroundings to the full from inside the house. However, this

The interior of the sitting room took visitors to Nina and Edvard's home by surprise, with its eclectic mix of styles – traditional Norwegian peasant style side by side with the Victorian taste for plush and lace. The room was bathed in beautiful natural light from the huge windows. The overall effect was both charming and personal. This mixture of a European urban style and a traditional rustic Norwegian style reflects Grieg's personality and expression very well. And so the interior feels 'right'. (THG)

The bare timber walls give the room a golden glow. (THG)

made furnishing the rooms quite tricky, as we see from the following question in a letter from Grieg to Schak Bull:

'It is regrettable that there is so little room between the two windows of the dining room that no space can be found for our sideboard. Is there anything to be done?'

Grieg designed the dining room with three large windows and seven doors. By opening the folding doors between the dining room and the sitting room it was possible to create a huge music room with four-metre high ceilings and daylight flooding in through the huge south-facing window, with its magnificent view. It was beautiful, but dreadfully cold, given the house's exposed location. Grieg's idea was that the house would serve many different functions – artistic work, large gatherings and as a base for experiencing the wonderful natural surroundings. But the house was actually too small and impractical for this, although paradoxically it was almost too large and roomy for Nina and Edvard on their own.

In the middle of the sitting room is a plush sofa from the 1880s. Over the sofa is a mirror, with family pictures either side. The candelabrum (with real candles) was a 60th birthday gift to Edvard Grieg from the 'Ladies of Bergen'. (THG)

THE TROLDSALEN CONCERT HALL AT TROLDHAUGEN

The architects Peter Helland-Hansen and Sverre Lied were extremely successful in realising the vision of the first director of the museum, Sigmund Torsteinson, to build a concert hall in Trolddalen. The design is in keeping with its surroundings and the building has scarcely altered the terrain. The building is situated in such a way that when you walk across the bridge to the house, the concert hall is only visible if you actually turn round and look for it. The grass roof also contributes to the discreet, secluded impression, as well as creating a romantic period feeling. The concert hall was completed in the spring of 1985 and was officially opened during the Bergen International Festival by King Olav V. It is unusual in that the back wall of the stage is made of glass, so the audience has an overview of Grieg's composer's hut and Lake Nordåsvannet. This view is so breathtaking that it is sure to create a good atmosphere. The audiences here are always extremely positive, which is no doubt one of the reasons that so many artists find it so enjoyable and inspiring performing here. When *Lyric Pieces V*, op. 54 is performed here, the audience can actually see the place where the music was composed, while listening to a live performance.

Nina and Edvard in the sitting room. (EGM)

It is interesting to study the overall design of the house and the many details inside and out, as they give us some insight into Grieg's thinking. Reflecting on Grieg's decisions and choices, just like studying his music, can bring us to a deeper understanding of his personality and help us grasp the special atmosphere of the place.

A small example of this is the furnishing of the living room. It has the bare timbered walls of a Norwegian farmhouse, while a plush sofa stands in front of a wall hung with decorative mirrors and family pictures, typical of the European bourgeoisie of the 1880s. This is characteristic of Grieg – he was Norwegian through and through, and yet at the same time thoroughly continental.

A HOME OF THEIR OWN

1885 was a watershed in Nina and Edvard Grieg's life. After several years of marital problems, Nina and Edvard had made a fresh start in Rome in 1884. This was when they started on their plans for Troldhaugen. Grieg wrote to his publisher Max Abraham in March 1885:

Troldsalen is adapted to the landscape in a way which makes it almost invisible when you arrive at Troldhaugen.

The composer's hut at Troldhaugen, built in 1891. (THG)

'I really don't know these days whether I am a musician or a builder. Every single day I take the train back and forth to the house. All my ideas are used up there, and masses of unborn compositions are smothered by the newly excavated soil. When you come for a visit some time, all you have to do is dig around and Norwegian chorus, orchestra and piano pieces will gush up from the bowels of the earth! We must not be confused by the fact that these works will look like peas and potatoes and radishes – for there really is music in them.'

Having a home of his own was meant to fulfil Edvard Grieg's innermost longings and dreams, but things did not turn out quite as he had hoped. He had confidently hoped for a steady stream of visitors from all over Europe, but the journey to this northerly outpost was as good as insurmountable for those living on the continent. On the home front Grieg soon discovered that Bergen was a city full of 'extreme lethargy and materialism'. He often felt isolated at Troldhaugen, with its 'good and evil trolls', and cut off from important events of the day. It was nigh on impossible to combine the unmitigated peace he needed to be able to compose with his insatiable thirst for new experiences. In the summer of 1885 he wrote to John Paulsen: *'This autumn I must invent some devilry to get away again.'*

When you go to a concert in Troldsalen, the concert hall's ideal design and position serve to intensify the musical experience.

Desk with writing implements. (THG)

Grieg's desk in his composer's hut. In the background is his piano (made by Brødrene Hals) and on the wall a Hardanger fiddle. (THG)

Someone has put a pile of stones in front of the window on the lake side; it is said that it was local boys from Hop who put them there, so they could peep into this strange building with its enticing music.

THE COMPOSER'S HUT

When Troldhaugen was completed in 1885, Grieg thought that he would now have sufficient space for composing, for entertaining and for collaboration with other artists. However, the house was not really any bigger than any other house; it simply had higher ceilings and was more ornately decorated. When the house was full of people, sound carried easily from one room to the next. The tower room, which was supposed to be Grieg's study, simply wasn't quiet enough for him, and it was impossible to work in the living room, while the kitchen was always full of women. What made matters worse was that the house was forever full of guests, both invited and uninvited. By the turn of the previous century Bergen had already gained a reputation as 'The Gateway to the Fjords', attracting a large number of foreign visitors. This became something of a nuisance, for many of these tourists had an interest in Norwegian culture as well as nature, and naturally they took the opportunity to take the train from Bergen to Hop, from where it was a pleasant walk to the home of the famous composer. But Grieg could not stand having people around him while he was composing. He preferred

The artist at work on the picture. (EGM)

Erik Werenskiold: Edvard Grieg in a Norwegian landscape (1902). Today the picture is on display at the Grieghallen concert hall in Bergen. (EGM)

The veranda with the rose window. (THG)

In My Native Country (no. 3) and *Erotikon* (no. 5) are beautiful, atmospheric pieces from his new home. The titles speak for them-selves. Between these two we find *Little Bird*, another brilliant piece of poetry on nature.

The volume ends with Grieg's attractive ode *To Spring*, full of the joys of new life. This piece sums up the whole opus with its many impressions and emotions to do with the miracle of spring, as well as the 'new spring' which the completion of Troldhaugen represented. *To Spring* is one of the musical highlights of Grieg's *Lyric Pieces* and a wonderful example of his ability to grapple with a huge concept in a highly concentrated form.

While *Lyric Pieces III* is very much a description of life in Grieg's new home, the next album, *Volume IV* from 1888, contains seven studies of musical concepts and genres – *Waltz-Impromptu*, *Album Leaf*, *Melody*, *Halling*, *Melancholy*, *Springar* and *Elegy* – each of which paints a picture of some aspect of Grieg's musical person-ality.

Edvard Grieg at the piano, photograhped by Emil Bieber in Berlin, 1905. (EGM)

A PLACE FOR AND OF MUSIC

It would be no exaggeration to say that Grieg's composer's hut at Troldhaugen started a new era in his output. While *Lyric Pieces III* was written in the villa, most of Grieg's works from *Lyric Pieces V* (opus 54) onwards first saw the light of day in his composer's hut.

Lyric Pieces V contains six pieces which show Grieg at his broadest and best. He starts with a lyrical picture of Norwegian nature in *Shepherd's Boy*. The style here is clear and pure; the harmonies are advanced and the melody lyrical, but there is not a hint of sentimentality.

The next piece is *Gangar*. Although in the style of a Norwegian folk dance, this is nevertheless entirely Grieg's own composition. The way in which he treats and repeats the themes provides the piece with both solidity and excitement. From its firm, simple opening note the piece billows to and fro from the quietest *piano* to full pedal and *forte*, before falling slowly back to nothing.

March of the Trolls is one of Grieg's three pieces that depict the trolls of Norwegian folklore. The two others are *In the Hall of*

Another of Erik Werenskiold's drawings of Grieg in his composer's hut (1895).
(EGM)

View across the Gulf of Naples. Village on the island of Ischia. (ED)

the Mountain King – featuring huge, wicked trolls – and *Puck, Lyric Pieces* X, op. 71 no. 3, with its reasonably harmless small trolls that float round in clouds of fog at the twilight hour. As long as these trolls are left to their own devices, they generally get up to more good than mischief. Grieg is on record as saying that there were both 'good and evil trolls' at Troldhaugen. These small trolls that frolic around must surely be of the harmless, basically benevolent kind. Admittedly they point a warning finger at us here and there, but for the most part they mind their own business.

What Grieg thought about the trolls in *In the Hall of the Mountain King*, we know from his description made while he was working with *Peer Gynt*. (This is quoted in the chapter 'Peer Gynt'.)

March of the Trolls describes the medium-sized trolls. They can be all right too – provided they get what they want – but they are certainly not as harmless as the trolls in *Puck*. Grieg describes them as they come marching out of the mountain after sunset, any number of them. More and more of them appear and they become really rather pompous. But according to Norwegian folklore, all trolls must return into the mountain before the rising of

The Peters building in Thalstrasse 10, Leipzig in Grieg's day. (EGM)

Dr Max Abraham (1831–1900), director of Edition Peters in Leipzig. In 1889 Edvard Grieg signed a contract with Edition Peters giving them the exclusive publishing rights to his music. This proved to be a favourable deal for both parties and Grieg became a wealthy man. Max Abraham was not just a good friend, but also Grieg's trusted advisor and impresario. Grieg had a small studio apartment in the Peters building in Thalstrasse in Leipzig. (BOB)

the sun. Woe betide the troll who returns too late – for he will be turned into stone!

We hear the sound of the trolls slinking back into the mountain before the sun rises and an idyllic pastoral morning scene takes over. But then night falls again and the trolls appear once more. Do they all make it back in time? Just listen to Grieg to find out!

Looking round the rocky Norwegian countryside, it is apparent that there must have been a great many latecomers among the trolls, for the countryside is full of mysteriously shaped boulders!

Sitting in the composer's hut that first summer must have been a rather cold and damp experience. Perhaps the next piece was by way of compensation for the clammy dampness. Grieg's one and only *Nocturne* (or *Notturno* as he entitled it) may well be a manifestation of musical daydreams of his beloved Sorrento and the velvety warm summer evenings spent gazing across the azure Mediterranean towards Naples, Ischia, Procida and Capri. How strange that Claude Debussy composed his *Clair de Lune* at almost exactly the same time, although the two composers knew nothing about each other at this stage. Great minds think alike!

Dr Henri Hinrichsen (1868–1942). Dr Abraham's son-in-law and successor in the publishing business. (BOB)

Edvard Grieg at the top of his favourite mountain near Bergen, Mount Løvstakken. (EGM)

The next piece is Grieg's only *Scherzo*. Grieg really shows his mastery of a continental style here. Grieg was constantly being censured by German music critics for composing nothing but Norwegian folk music. This accusation irritated Grieg, who knew better. The *Scherzo's* playful, carefree introduction and closing section embrace a tender middle section full of reflection.

The final piece in *Lyric Pieces* V is one of the strangest of all of Grieg's works. *Bell Ringing* is unique in that it is one long tonal study. It has been called the first impressionistic experiment. There is no melody – instead the piece centres around the different tonal effects. Nevertheless Grieg succeeded in creating a very special atmosphere and excitement in this piece. He was very much aware that *Bell Ringing* was an experiment, and he joked that it was a piece of madness. Even though he made no further ventures into pure impressionism, he later returned to this piece.

Grieg himself was extremely pleased with this new volume. He wrote to his publisher, Max Abraham at Edition Peters in Leipzig, that he was sending him '... *a new volume of* Lyric Pieces, *about which I am unreservedly excited!*' (1891)

In 1903 Grieg received a version of *Gangar, March of the Dwarfs, Nocturne* and *Bell Ringing* arranged for orchestra eight years earlier by the American conductor Anton Seidl. After studying this version, Grieg decided to produce his own orchestration, since he felt that his intentions had not been fully realised in Seidl's score.

And so in 1905 *Lyric Suite for Orchestra* was published, containing four of the pieces from *Lyric Pieces V*, although Grieg replaced *Bell Ringing* with *Shepherd's Boy*. This suite shows that Grieg undoubtedly had a flair for orchestration, despite his frequent remarks that his student days in Leipzig were a waste of time and far from satisfactory in this area.

Lyric Pieces III (opus 43) and *Lyric Pieces V* (opus 54) are without a doubt the mainstays of the series of lyric pieces. But every piece in the entire series is worth dwelling on, for Grieg has something important to say in each and every one. Even in the periods when he struggled most to find inspiration, he managed to come up with new lyric pieces. He wrote in a letter to his friend C F Emil Hornemann, a Danish composer, in 1896: '*My silence is unforgivable, for I have, so to speak, done nothing except for the so-called* Lyric Pieces *that swarm around me like lice and fleas out in the country.*'

A SIMPLE ALPINE SYMPHONY

Evening in the Mountains, Lyric Pieces IX, op. 68 no. 4, is an interesting parallel to Richard Strauss's magnificent *Alpine Symphony*. While Strauss allows the impressive sight of the huge, majestic mountains to suffuse us with colossal cascades of orchestral refinement, falling sixths, fifths and fourths, Grieg's starting point could hardly be more different. The entire wild, massive landscape with the sharp outline of the mountains against the sky, peak upon peak, majestic and silent – all this is sketched for us by a simple unaccompanied melodic line throughout the first section of the piece. And then the impressions slowly start to sink in. Contemplation – daring – the deepest abysses against the highest summits. '*To the mountains, to the mountains! For that is where truth is to be found!*'

GRIEG PLAYS GRIEG

Between 1903 and 1906 Grieg made recordings of some of his piano pieces, some on traditional gramophone and some on Welte Mignon (pianola). The CD *Grieg plays Grieg* consists of nine gramophone recordings from Paris, 1903, and three Welte Mignon recordings from Leipzig, 1906. One of these, *Bridal Procession*, is also available in a version transferred to gramophone in 1934. It is hard to assess Grieg's style of playing or technical skill from these recordings, which were made towards the end of his life when old age and poor health affected his playing. Nevertheless, they give us a clear impression of his pianistic style, full of charm and impulsiveness, with a uniquely romantic expression and beautiful mastery of tonal colour. This is particularly clear in the lyrical pieces *Butterfly* and *Little Bird*, where we hear the composer's voice clearly. Thanks to the wonders of modern technology in the form of a digital system called NoNoise, it has been possible to remove much of the surface noise from the recordings without affecting the timbre of the instrument.

Edvard Grieg in 1887 just after completing his third violin sonata. Drawn at Troldhaugen by August Johannessen. This picture can be seen in the Grieghallen concert hall in Bergen. (EGM)

YEARNING

Edvard Grieg was a restless soul. He seems to have yearned constantly to be somewhere else. It is almost as if one of the most
important reasons for building and living at Troldhaugen was that
at least then he would have a home to be homesick for. It is clear
from his letters and comments that whenever he was away from
Troldhaugen he longed to return there, for it was only there that
he could really find the peace and quiet he needed to be able to
work. But as soon as he was home, he ached to be away again. 'It
is so quiet here …' he wrote to his friend John Paulsen. Nothing
interesting ever happened in Bergen. The weather was terrible
and his friends from abroad never came to visit him there. No,
he had to get away, however beautiful it was at Troldhaugen.

These feelings are expressed poetically in several of his *Lyric
Pieces*. *In My Native Country* from opus 43 is full of harmony,
peace and satisfaction. In *Homesickness*, *Lyric Pieces VI*, op. 57
no. 6, we feel the onset of homesickness, while in *Homeward*,
Lyric Pieces VII, op. 62 no. 6, he can hardly wait to get home.

Whenever Grieg arrived home at Troldhaugen after a long
winter's travelling, he would jump out of the carriage, rush into
the house and sit at the piano. And there he would stay, breathing
in the sweet smell of home and playing and playing – until the
others had taken off their winter boots, brought in the luggage
and got the fires going.

Reflection, and what we somewhat imprecisely refer to as nos-
talgia, were key concepts in romanticism. In pieces such as *Once
Upon a Time, From Early Years* and *Vanished Days* Grieg draws on
the rich palette of reflection. But with Grieg it is always more than
a yearning for something which has passed.

This frieze of life also contains lullabies, descriptions of nature
and pieces in the style of folk tunes. Each and every one of them is
a fine poem, and together they provide us with a fantastically rich
documentation of Grieg's breadth and depth. A lifetime of impressions and experiences has been captured in the common language
of music.

Brooklet, Lyric Pieces VII, op. 62 no. 4 is a fabulous virtuoso
jewel. I would thoroughly recommend listening to the rock guitarist
Mads Eriksen's version of this piece. He recorded an entire album of
Grieg pieces for the 150th anniversary of Grieg's birth in 1993. In
my opinion this is one of the very best transcriptions of its kind.

WEDDING DAY AT TROLDHAUGEN

Among the many gems of lyric pieces that stemmed from Grieg's hand, *Wedding Day at Troldhaugen* is the icing on the cake. This piece contains the whole of Grieg's rhythmic and melodic exuberance, coupled with a contemplative, romantic atmosphere only he could achieve. The piece opens with the plink of a fork against a wineglass forcefully calling us to attention:

ta, ta, taa   ta, ta, taa   ta, ta, taa   ta, ta, taa

From this opening the music races along with bravura. Although it gives the impression of being an extremely virtuoso piece, it is so well written for the instrument that it does not require extreme technical ability.

The piece is in traditional ABA form. The middle section contains a calm passage with a pastoral feel. Simple descending themes are tried out first high up then lower down, with a variety of harmonic colouring, reflecting twenty-five years of artistic and marital partnership. Then the A section returns and the whole piece ends in triumph.

Music dealer and concert arranger Carl Rabe (1829–1897) in Bergen.
(BOB)

Wedding Day at Troldhaugen was composed in the summer of 1896, and was originally a musical greeting to Nancy Giertsen, a dear friend of the Griegs in Bergen, to mark her 37th birthday. They had a special book made with a birthday greeting, with the opening bars of the piece on the front page. The original title was *The Well-wishers are Coming*. Inside the book, the whole piece was written out in the composer's own hand.

When the piece was to be published the following year as the final piece in *Lyric Pieces VIII*, op. 65, Grieg and his publishers agreed to give it the appealing title *Wedding Day at Troldhaugen*. This referred of course to Nina and Edvard's silver wedding anniversary on 11 June 1892.

Nina and Edvard had arranged a silver wedding celebration, but it looked set to be a chilly affair. The spring and early summer of 1892 were, not uncommonly for Bergen, extremely wet and cold. But on 10 June the weather changed; the cold, damp period gave way to mild summer warmth and brightness.

On the morning of their anniversary, Nina and Edvard awoke to the sounds of a beautiful chorale playing. The Bergen Military Band had taken their places just below the veranda at Troldhaugen, and at 6 am sharp they opened with *Ein' feste Burg* and a serenade composed especially for the occasion.

Grieg jumped out of bed, grabbed a dressing gown and rushed downstairs to greet the musicians. When he got to the sitting room, a strange sight met his eyes. Frants Beyer was standing smiling in the midst of a sea of flowers. Somebody was placing a brand-new Steinway grand in the room. Grieg's friend, Carl Rabe, the music dealer, and his associates had ordered the

Grieg's Steinway grand was a present from friends in Bergen to mark Nina and Edvard's silver wedding on 11 June 1892.

(EGM)

instrument from Steinway & Sons in Hamburg, and here it was, in Nina and Edvard's sitting room. For a moment Grieg was torn – should he try out the new Steinway, or should he run out to the musicians on the lawn? He did both, of course, but we do not know in which order!

Later that morning a large delegation of citizens arrived from Bergen. They had come by train to the nearby station at Hop, and there was much speechmaking and presentation of gifts, large and small. There was a festive atmosphere, the sun was shining and all was well with the world. But unfortunately, like all good things, the party had to draw to a close, as the guests had to catch the next train back to town. Edvard Grieg became quite upset as everyone said their goodbyes – he had not had time to talk to everyone yet, and here they were saying goodbye!

Just then, he had a wild idea. He jumped onto the stone table in the garden and issued a spontaneous invitation to everyone to come back that evening for a dinner party! This was rather a rash thing to do, even though the Griegs had planned a party.

'What about food?! We were expecting 50 guests, but that number had just increased to 130!' It was generally known that housekeeping was not Nina's forte, and in any case they did not have enough plates or cutlery, nor food enough in the larders for so many people. But luckily Marie Beyer, Frants's wife, was a genius in the kitchen. And the Beyers had a telegraph and a telephone and were able to contact the hotels in town. Food, drink, plates, tables, chairs and waiters were duly ordered, and since the weather had suddenly turned summery, they could lay tables outside in the garden.

It was a magical evening. *'… when the evening came, it was just like a fairy tale – everything was ready! […] Between (the courses) speeches were made, there was piano playing (me), singing (my wife) and, not least, much drinking – indeed the punch flowed as freely as Rhine wine in Heine's poetry.' (Letter to August Winding, 26 June 1892)*

At 9 pm the evening train from Bergen shunted in to Hop Station with a 230-man strong male voice choir. They sang as they marched, banners flying, to Troldhaugen. The locals had been joined at Lake Nordåsvannet by people from the city centre, in their thousands it was said, to sit outside and enjoy the first real summer evening, and to celebrate their famous neighbours, Nina

Grieg's port glass can be seen at Troldhaugen.
(THG)

Edvard Grieg raises his glass of port in the garden at Troldhaugen (1906). (EGM)

and Edvard Grieg. *'Salutes were fired from the nearby islands, while the reflection of beautiful Bengalese lights and midsummer bonfires glistened in the lake.'*

There is no record of how long the party went on, but there is no doubt that those present never forgot that evening. Grieg's genius captured the celebrations and the feelings of joy and gratitude, seen through a veil of reflection, in *Wedding Day at Troldhaugen*, allowing present-day listeners a glimpse of the place, the time and the atmosphere.

'We met in the songs [...] and the common understanding was there. Otherwise there could be all kinds of disagreements. [...] With Grieg's music, it was strange. I had it within me. When he came with something new, I never had to learn it, it was there.'
(NINA GRIEG)

Nina Grieg dressed for a concert. (EGM)

The songs – Grieg's second frieze of life

J UST LIKE THE TEN volumes of *Lyric Pieces*, Edvard Grieg's songs span his entire career from start to finish. His passion for literature and his acquaintance with the great authors of the day stimulated him to devote much of his creativity to this genre. But beyond a doubt the most important factor behind many of the 180 songs he composed was Nina Hagerup Grieg, whom he acknowledged as his greatest inspiration and his finest interpreter.

In a letter to the American musicologist Henry T Finck, Grieg wrote a lengthy account of his work as a composer. A large portion of this letter deals with his songs:

Nina Grieg at her desk.
(BOB)

'I do not think I have any greater talent for writing songs than for writing any other kind of music. Why, then, have songs played such a prominent role in my life's work? Quite simply because I, like other mortals, once in my life (to quote Goethe) had my moment of genius. And it was love that gave me this glory. I loved a girl with a wonderful voice and an equally wonderful gift as an interpreter. This woman became my wife and has been my companion through life down to the present day. I dare say that for me she has remained the only true interpreter of my songs.' (Letter to Henry T Finck, 17 July 1899)

AN EXTRAORDINARY ENGAGEMENT PRESENT

Nina Hagerup was involved in Grieg's songs as early as his second album, *Six Songs*, op. 4, which he completed in 1864 and dedicated to her. These six German poems are not love songs, so Grieg kept his feelings for his cousin pretty much under wraps at this stage.

His next set of songs, on the other hand, *Melodies of the Heart*, op. 5, published in April 1865, consisted of four love poems by Hans Christian Andersen, the great poet and fairy tale author.

Nina Grieg. (BOB)

Nina Grieg survived her husband by 28 years. On her 90th birthday, 24 November 1935, she was celebrated throughout Scandinavia. She was not simply the wife of the famous composer, but a remarkable singer in her own right. Nina Grieg was a thoroughly modern woman, with great insight into literature, music and art. She spoke several languages, conducted herself pleasantly and unpretentiously in all situations and had an easy manner with everyone around her.

Nina Hagerup at the time of her engagement to Edvard Grieg (1865). (BOB)

These songs were Edvard's engagement present to Nina. What finer expression of love could anyone hope for?

The two best-known songs in this album, *Two Brown Eyes* and *I Love But Thee*, are real gems of the love song genre. *I Love But Thee* is one of the few Grieg songs to have gained worldwide popularity, and has been performed and recorded in countless versions and arrangements.

The musicologist Per Dahl collected all the recordings made of *I Love But Thee* throughout the twentieth century, over 300

Front page of the manuscript of Melodies of the Heart – *Edvard's engagement present to Nina.* (BOB)

The author of Melodies of the Heart, *Hans Christian Andersen (1805–1875).* (BOB)

Manuscript of Two Brown Eyes *and the opening of* I Love But Thee. (BOB)

in all. In 1993 he published a discography and bibliography of all the material available at that date, entitled *I Love But Thee in 252 Ways.* In November 2006 he wrote a doctoral dissertation called *I Love But Thee. The Listener's Argument*. Singers of all kinds have sung this song, including Bing Crosby, who performed it in a version for baritone and string orchestra arranged for the musical *Song of Norway* (New York, 1944). This version is a real Hollywood croon, with Crosby's inimitable warm tones. (His articulation is also streets ahead of that of many other performers.)

WITH BJØRNSON INTO NATIONAL ROMANTICISM

Grieg's cooperation with Bjørnstjerne Bjørnson would prove to be his salvation and inspiration in the difficult Oslo period which lasted from 1867 until the Griegs moved to Hardanger ten years later. It was nigh on impossible to make a living as a composer in Oslo; in fact he could only just scrape a living conducting and teaching. Promising pupils were few and far between, and the orchestra and concert-going public were not taken with the modern music Grieg tried to add to the orchestral repertoire. In Bjørnson's poetry he found a national romantic spirit that he could identify with, and this gave him the courage and strength to continue his efforts to further the cause of art, and his political and social conscience found a practical outlet.

These years of fruitful cooperation resulted in a great many compositions. Thanks to both men's commitment to political and cultural causes, they produced a host of songs dedicated to the honour of the nation and of various public figures, such as *Norwegian Sailors' Song*, EG 163, from 1870, for male voice choir. This song gained instant popularity and remained part of the standard repertoire in Norway throughout the twentieth century.

Before the two men started planning their major opera project *Olav Trygvason* in 1873, Grieg had already set several of Bjørnson's poems to music, including *Four Songs*, op. 21, completed in 1872.

The First Meeting embraces a universe of emotions, but in a concise, introverted form, which poses quite a challenge for the performer.

In the other three songs Bjørnson is more as we are used to thinking of him: lively and powerful, yet devoted and generous. Grieg captured the whole spectrum of Bjørnson's poetry in these songs. The titles speak for themselves: *Good Morning!* could not be marked anything but *extremely lively*. *To Springtime my Song*

to double the vocal line, but at Grieg's hand this 'shadow' is not merely an accompaniment to the melody, but seems to hint at the water lily's secret underwater world. It is firmly rooted in the depths, and cannot easily be pulled up. The deceptively simple beauty runs deeper than is seen at first sight, although the song concludes with the hopefulness of innocence.

Opus 25 closes with *A Bird-Song*, a lyric pastoral which on the face of it may seem so simplistic as to be rather uninteresting. The key to unlocking the potential in this song lies in the performer's timing and presentation, capturing the whole atmosphere in just a few bars. Then, and only then, does the performer do Grieg justice.

The most remarkable song in this album is *A Swan*, which is poetry of the highest order from both Ibsen and Grieg. The silent swan, whose voice is unlocked only in death, was for Grieg a symbol of the fate of the artist, since it is only through art that life's greatest challenges and troubles can be overcome.

The condensed form of the poem is reflected in the music. There is no clear melodic line. The motif is painted in pastel in a transparent tonal landscape, while the harmonies underneath are fluid and move unexpectedly through different keys. It is not until the closing chord that the harmonies resolve to the supernatural overtones of:

'True swan, in death winging your song came, so splendid!'
How still, my white swan,
Your silence unbroken;
Ne'er a sound to foretoken
Your bright voice, my mute one.
Anxious guardian o'er elves,
Which lie sleeping,
Always list'ning,
O'er deep waters sweeping.
At our last meeting,
Your guise of white beauty
Belied this last duty:
To trumpet your song, then!
In birth, your singing
Marked life's journey ended.
True swan, in death winging
Your song came, so splendid! 9

*This drawing of Edvard Grieg and Aasmund Olavsson Vinje by Christian Skreds-
vig was used on the cover of the Vinje Songs. The 1974 winner of the Grieg Prize,
the singer Olav Eriksen, found this picture in an antique shop in Oslo shortly after
receiving the prize in Bergen (NOK 5000 plus a diploma and plaque). The picture
cost NOK 5000, and he bought it there and then, and donated it to Troldhaugen,
where it now hangs over Grieg's grand piano in the sitting room.* (BOB)

*Johannes Brahms
(1833–1897).* (BOB)

'MORE I RECEIVED THAN I EVER HAD DESERVED'

In the autumn of 1878 Grieg left Hardanger for a concert tour of
central Europe. His *String Quartet* had a baptism by fire in Cologne
and Leipzig. From there he journeyed to Copenhagen where he
held a number of concerts for audiences that included royalty.
He did not arrive back in Hardanger until the spring of 1879.

On his return he discovered that the surroundings which just
two years previously had made such a profound impression on
him and triggered such a spate of creativity no longer seemed to
inspire him. His European tour had provided him with quite different sorts of stimulation, including meeting Johannes Brahms
and hearing Joseph Joachim give the first performance of Brahms's
Violin Concerto. He had received plenty of encouragement through
the success of his own compositions, too, with the exception of the
harsh critiques by Bernsdorf in *Signale*. After all this, the maje-stic
scenery of Hardanger seemed to him too quiet and cold. He had
hoped to get straight back to composing, but these surroundings
no longer kindled his creative spark.

When Grieg had first arrived in Børve in 1877, he had written
about some 'golden nuggets' of poetry he had come across. Among
these were the first poems he had encountered by Aasmund Olavsson Vinje. The idealism of this multifaceted poet, philosopher and
promoter of universal enlightenment gave a new lease of life to

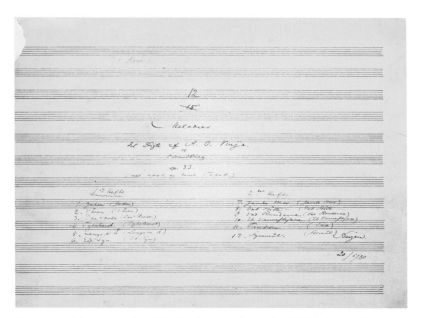

Front page of the manuscript of Twelve Songs to Poems by AO Vinje, op. 33. (BOB)

Manuscript of Last Spring. (BOB)

Aasmund Olavsson Vinje.(1818–1870). (EGM)

Grieg's troubled mind. He realised that there were no quick fixes or shortcuts open to him; the only way out of the crisis he found himself in was through trials and suffering.

Ola Mosafinn
(1828–1912). (EGM)

Manuscript of Last Spring. (BOB)

Now stand upon the ruins you've made,
of your own life's hope.
Then first to view, with eyes grown wise,
the wider scope. 10
(From *The Youth*, by AO Vinje)

In 1874 Grieg had set to music a poem by Vinje called *The Old Mother*, a simple and beautiful tribute dedicated by Edvard to his mother Gesine, who *'with boundless energy and an unbending sense of duty toiled and suffered until she dropped'*. Many a son or daughter has felt that this song expresses in words and music the feelings they have for their own mother.

The first song Grieg composed to a text by Vinje in his Hardanger period was *Beside the Stream*, a life drama that many people can identify with. External forces tear away at us, tugging at our heartstrings. And it is in our youth that we are most likely to sustain the deepest wounds.

Still woods, which o'er the black brook bend
To stroke its sheen with leafy kiss,
Beware, deep currents dig and wend
To draw you down in its abyss.
Like you, I many a time would see

And best in life's fair spring should be
The one who kiss'd with gallantry
That hand which struck most hurtfully,
Struck most hurtfully! [11]

Grieg ends the song with a moving epilogue:

Still woods! Still woods -! Still woods —! Still woods —-!

It was not until the Griegs had moved to Bergen that Edvard turned once more to these profound poems. On Grieg's birthday on 15 June 1879, while Edvard and Nina were still in Hardanger, they were visited by Ole Bull. Bull brought with him several fiddlers, including Ola Mosafinn, who delighted both Grieg and Bull with their playing.

Aasmund Olavsson Vinje. (EGM)

Grieg spent the following winter on tour as usual, starting off with two concerts in his hometown of Bergen. From there they travelled to his 'second home' Leipzig, where his *Piano Concerto in A minor* was very well received. From Leipzig they continued via Copenhagen – and more concerts and visits to his musical 'family' – to Oslo (which Grieg never referred to as home) where he held four chamber music recitals. At the end of April 1880 Grieg returned to his native town to take up his new post as conductor of the Harmonien Orchestra.

By 28 April he had already started composing again, inspired anew by Vinje's poems. He wrote *The Berry* in a dark attic room in his childhood home in Strandgaten, but the contrast between his physical surroundings and the kaleidoscope of autumnal colours and gem-like berries in the song could not be greater. The theme of this song is simple: the greatest joy in the colourful world of autumn, whether a ripened berry or a mature human being, is to give oneself to others.

After this followed a steady stream of songs, fifteen in all, twelve of which were published under the title *Twelve Songs to Poems by AO Vinje*, op. 33.

Grieg's understandable fear that his creative vein had dried up for good (he had, after all, composed nothing for two whole years) was swept away by the power of Vinje's poetry. It was with great joy and satisfaction that Grieg submitted this set of songs to his publishers.

The Vinje songs contain strong ties between nature and human nature. In *Last Spring* it is not the new spring that is being cele-

At Rondane *is the most obvious encore at festival concerts in the Villa at Troldhaugen. In the time before the concert hall, Troldsalen, was built (1985), all the concerts took place in the Villa. A large group of people followed the concerts sitting in the garden, because the concerts were played outdoors through loudspeakers. After the concert, the singer stands in the doorway to the garden and sings this beautiful encore to the garden audience.* (FIB)

brated, but the privilege of being allowed to experience the miracle of nature '*yet once again*' before our life ebbs away. This must surely be one of the most beautiful melodies Grieg ever composed. Despite the seriousness and melancholy of the subject matter, Grieg's tune is in the major. The very title lends itself to a special kind of musical treatment, and Grieg chose quite dissonant harmonies which do not resolve until the very end of the song.

Two songs were later published in an arrangement for string orchestra, under the title *Two Elegiac Melodies. The Wounded Heart* and *Last Spring* op. 34. These became two of the most popular pieces on Grieg's many European tours. Grieg spoke warmly on several occasions of the success these pieces enjoyed, for instance in a letter to Frants Beyer after the German premiere in Weimar in 1883:

'*Oh, you should have heard* The Wounded Heart *and* Last Spring *last evening. It was absolutely wonderful to hear how they played it. […] And then the fact that the German audience was caught up in it! In addition to the applause of the audience, at the best places I heard from the orchestra, "Bravo, bravo." And from the box to my left (I was conducting on the stage) I heard Liszt's grunt, this familiar sound that he makes only when something pleases him.' (Letter to Frants Beyer, 17 October 1883)*

Grieg wrote even more solemnly to Johan Andreas Budtz Christie, a Norwegian priest and friend:

'I do not remember many times in my life when I have been so moved. I hardly knew where I was, in the palace theatre in Weimar or out in the sombre, brooding Norwegian mountains. The truth is that I was in neither of those places but rather on the ethereal wings of harmony in outer space.' (Letter to Johan Andreas Budtz Christie, 28 December 1883)

Last Spring and *At Rondane* are two of the finest pieces in the Norwegian song literature, and they share something of the same special atmosphere. In both songs the sunset lights up the beautiful natural surroundings in a way that makes us melancholy and glad at the same time. The effect is so overwhelming that it can *'dispel fear'*. When we come face to face with such natural magnificence, all pettiness and meanness is forgotten as we feel *'sunset's magic power'*. All worries about tomorrow are brushed aside. *'I trust night warm, safe shelter will provide me, and trust the sun's last golden rays to guide me'*.[12]

Vinje's texts ranged from the exquisite to biting irony: there is little warmth to be found in *A Piece on Friendship* or *Faith*. Grieg, who was no stranger to irony, be it good-natured or deadly serious, matched Vinje's irony in his musical treatment of these two texts. In *Faith*, for instance, he sets Vinje's mocking criticism of the hypocrisy of many Christians to what appears to be a hymn tune.

A Vision and *The First Thing* deal with different aspects of the gift and necessity of love. *A Vision* describes the poet's fleeting glimpse of a woman he could never win, while the opening of *The First Thing* spells out the imperative of love:

The first thing, man, you're called upon to do is simply die,
When you wish no more the maid to woo that's caught your eye.[13]

Grieg's interpretation of the last poem in the cycle, *The Goal*, was quite at odds with the author's intentions. This is, as far as we know, the only deviation from Grieg's strict adherence to his self-imposed rule of being totally faithful to the intentions of the author of any words he set to music. Vinje had written this poem as a contribution to the impassioned language debate in Norway at that time, but Grieg was not aware of this and interpreted it as being addressed *'to a friend, or perhaps even to the poet's wife!'* *(Letter to Henry T Finck, 17 July 1899)*. As such Grieg believed this song had a universal appeal that would be perfectly suited for rounding off this song cycle. *The Goal* is far more extrovert and dramatic than the other songs in the cycle. In Grieg's version it is both Norwegian and typically Griegian, with the Grieg motif, *halling* rhythms, and harmonies and motifs inspired by Norwegian folk music.

The first song in this cycle, *The Youth*, is in strong contrast to this magnificent close. The text of *The Youth* deals with the enormous yet real demands made on the youth who dreams of becoming a man. Grieg draws this text over a huge melodic and dynamic arch to great effect. As Johan Svendsen put it, much to Grieg's delight: *'Here music and poetry have been sensitively united to create passion of such magnitude, that I know of no equal in the whole of song literature.' (Letter from Johan Svendsen to Grieg, 22 June 1882)*

TO GERMAN POETRY IN HIS MATURITY

Johann Wolfgang von Goethe (1749–1832).
(EGM)

When Grieg started out on the path of creating national music, he naturally turned to Nordic literature for texts for his songs. However, as a performer and composer he quickly won repute throughout Europe. This posed something of a dilemma for him, since his songs did not receive the acclaim they deserved outside Scandinavia. It was extremely difficult to get hold of good translations and of course this ruined the impression made by his songs on audiences unfamiliar with a Scandinavian language. What's more, there was a group of critics on the continent, most notably Eduard Bernsdorf of *Signale*, who refused to regard Grieg as a genuine composer. They referred to him sneeringly as a producer of exotic romanticisations of somewhat dubious Norwegian folk music – *'Er norwegert,'* they scoffed. This became a source of increasing concern to Grieg, although it never caused him to doubt the task he had set himself:

'To depict Norwegian nature, Norwegian folk life, Norwegian history and Norwegian folk poetry in music stands for me as the area in which I think I can achieve something.' (Letter to Bjørnstjerne Bjørnson, 21 February 1875)

However, this task was not synonymous with being exclusively national (or hyper-Norwegian as Grieg called it). He simply wanted

Erik Werenskiold: The Composer Edvard Grieg *(1892).* (National Museum, Stockholm)

*Heinrich Heine
(1797–1856).*

*Ludwig Uhland
(1787–1862).*

to be true to himself. When he found his personal artistic calling, through the catalysts Bull and Nordraak, it lay *'a thousand miles away from Leipzig and its atmosphere'*. Grieg's inspiration would forever lie in his love for his country and his appreciation of the magnificent melancholy of the fjords and mountains of Western Norway.

From 1889 onwards we see from Grieg's speeches, writing and compositions that he was becoming more cosmopolitan in style, with a 'wider horizon'. He submitted a letter to the periodical *Musikbladet* in Copenhagen in response to an article published by the chief editor, Wilhelm Hansen, on the subject of national compositions. In this letter, which Grieg entitled '*A Cosmopolitan Credo*' (14 September 1889), he emphatically refuted certain assertions in the article, and argued that it was absolutely possible to have a universal vision of individuality and be influenced by cosmopolitan currents, at the same time as having clearly national roots.

This more universal view of his own individuality shows in Grieg's song writing, for instance *Six Songs*, op. 48. Grieg chose some of the very finest poems in the German language, by Heine, Geibel, Uhland, von der Vogelweide, Goethe and Bodenstedt. This album was dedicated to Ellen Nordgren Gulbranson, a Norwegian-Swedish singer who was generally regarded as the finest soprano in Europe in her day. Nordahl Rolfsen produced fine Norwegian translations of the poems. At times these songs have sunk almost into obscurity, particularly in Norway after the Second World War, but they are now experiencing a well-deserved renaissance.

Once again Grieg shows his genius for entering the world of the poet and allowing the atmosphere of the poem to determine the music he wrote. In *The Way of the World* and *The Nightingale's Secret* we notice an affinity to German folk tunes, and all these songs are very clearly in the Lieder tradition, while still bearing the obvious hallmark of Grieg.

The Time of Roses is one of the favourites of the author of this book, both in the original version and in the arrangement for cello and piano, which is a real *Song Without Words*. The album closes with the love song *A Dream*, in which Grieg laced this German *Lied* with delightful small Griegian folk music-like embellishments in between the phrases. The song finishes with a heady rush of love. There is a world of emotion between the first two songs –

The Griegs in concert garb, London 1888. (EGM)

The Swedish-Norwegian singer Ellen Nordgren Gulbranson (1863–1947) was an acclaimed singer in her day. She often performed at Grieg's many concerts all across Europe.
(EGM)

the light-hearted, springy *Greeting* and the brief, introverted *One Day, O Heart of Mine* – and *A Dream*, in which the joyful vision turns into a beautiful day.

SONGS TO CONTEMPORARY NORDIC LYRICS

Given the formative impressions on Grieg of his years as a student in Leipzig, he naturally looked to the rich sources of German poetry when writing his earliest albums of songs (opus 2 and 4). However, he soon turned to Nordic poets, and it was first and foremost contemporary Nordic poetry he set to music throughout most of his career. First came *Melodies of the Heart*, op. 5 to texts by Hans Christian Andersen, and this was followed by an album of songs and ballads by Andreas Munch (opus 9), whom Grieg met for the first time in Rome in 1865.

Andreas Munch (1811–1884). (EGM)

In addition to these, and the two great writers Bjørnson and Ibsen, Grieg was very taken with the poems of John Paulsen, a fellow Bergener. Paulsen and Grieg became close friends, and although Paulsen's poems were not of the most profound, Grieg composed some excellent songs to romantic texts by Paulsen. It was perhaps typical of Grieg that he was willing to forego a certain degree of substance in Paulsen's texts for the sake of his human qualities. Grieg was, as we know, a true philanthropist, whose philosophy was: 'One must first be a human being!'

Immediately after he had finished *Six Songs*, op. 25, to texts by Ibsen, Grieg turned to Paulsen's light, spring-like lyricism. On completing the five songs in opus 26, Grieg wrote a letter to Paulsen in which he stated quite unambiguously, yet fondly, the importance of drawing on one's personal experience if one was to create genuine art.

'In you I see much of myself as I was in former days. Therefore I can tell you: get steel, steel, steel! And when you ask, "Where do I get it?" there is only this one, terrible answer: you buy it with your heart's blood! God knows I speak from experience. Believe me, my friend, I am not sure that I should wish steel for you, it is so costly!! May God give you strength!' (Letter to John Paulsen, 27 June 1876)

The five songs in opus 26 are in sharp contrast to Ibsen's poetry, but Grieg's ability to give the text new dimensions raises Paulsen's verse to a new level. This is most obvious in the rather ingratiating *I Walked One Balmy Summer Eve* and the strikingly attractive *The First Primrose*. The latter shows new sides of Grieg's skill at writing songs, as he manages to weave a catchy, graceful melody from the chromaticism of the melody and the accompaniment.

Many years later, in the autumn of 1893, Grieg composed two new albums of songs to texts by John Paulsen, while Nina was being treated for a serious kidney disease in hospital in Copenhagen. Grieg's prescription for his wife was *'a new song almost every day'*. The songs he wrote to aid her recovery were all settings of poems by Paulsen. After six weeks in hospital Nina *'got out of the cage'* and Grieg had to rent an extra room at the hotel in order to continue his frenzy of composing in peace.

Peters edition of Two Elegiac Melodies, *op. 34*. (BOB)

John Paulsen. (BOB)

Nordahl Rolfsen (1848–1928), author and educationalist.

'So now I have also recovered sufficiently that I can receive visits from elegant ladies. There is one marvellous girl, believe it or not, who has visited me almost daily of late, and she gives me many new songs, some of which do her honour. Yes, long live lyricism and eroticism. Why deny oneself a love affair! I don't go searching for one, but when it comes walking in the door I'm not just going to stand there.' (Letter to Frants Beyer, 29 December 1893)

Who was this marvellous girl that visited the 50-year-old Grieg while his wife was confined to bed? None other than the muse of inspiration. And these visits resulted in 'a bunch of new songs with texts by Norwegian poets' – Five Songs, op. 58 and Six

PETER TCHAI-
KOVSKY WROTE
OF HIS FIRST
MEETING WITH
EDVARD GRIEG:
'As they were playing
through Brahms' new trio,
a man walked into the
room – very small of
stature, middle-aged,
extremely sickly in appearance, shoulders of uneven
height, head covered with
long, blond, tousled locks.
His beard and moustache
were most unusual ...
indeed almost youthful.
The facial features of this
man, whose appearance
for some reason immedi-
ately appealed to me, are
not especially noteworthy;
one cannot call them
either handsome or unusu-
al. But on the other hand,
he has unusually attrac-
tive, medium-sized, sky-
blue eyes of irresistibly
charming character, eyes
that remind one of an
innocent, adorable child.
I was glad in the very
depths of my soul when,
upon being introduced to
one another, it was revealed that the bearer of this
inexplicably attractive
exterior was a musician
whose deeply felt music
had long since secured for
him a place in my heart.
It was Edvard Grieg.'
(From Peter Tchaikovsky's
*Autobiographical Descrip-
tions of a Journey Abroad
in 1888*)

*Edvard Grieg: 'On the top of a tiny, little body is a head that has an aura of deter-
mination, nobles and goodness. His hair is white and puffed up, falling backwards.
The short moustache covers the determined mouth. The round – childish – eyes may
have a sharp and penetrating look.'* (Berliner Lokalanzeiger, 4 April 1907) (EGM)

Elegiac Songs, op. 59 to texts by John Paulsen and *Five Songs*, op. 60
to texts by Vilhelm Krag.

Krag's poetry is rather more lush and challenging than Paulsen's, and as such it inspired Grieg to exciting harmonic and
melodic displays. The mood of these songs ranges from mournful-
ness in *The Mother's Lament* to some of Grieg's greatest bravura
in *Midsummer Eve*.

In contrast, the style in *A Bird Cried Out*, which is just fourteen
bars long, is almost minimalistic. The action talks place against the
direction of the melody, and the vocal line and harmonisation

have an illustrative function far beyond traditional harmonic thinking. The theme is taken from an entry Grieg made in his sketchbook on a visit to Hardanger, under which he noted: *'Seagull cry heard in the Hardanger fjord'*.

The first song in the album, *Little Kirsten*, is one of the most delightful songs Grieg composed; it has the simplicity of a folk song and it conjures up the wistful idyll of a southern Norwegian summer.

In 1894, the year in which this album was published, Grieg was approached by the educationalist OA Grøndahl who asked him to write music to seven poems in Nordahl Rolfsen's primary reader. This resulted in *Seven Children's Songs*, op. 61, some of the best songs ever to be written for children.

For anyone who had anything to do with horses as a child, *Good-night Song for Dobbin* is bound to awaken fond memories and bring a tear to the eye. And the smile and good humour of the kidling, the calf and the other young animals in Bjørnson's *Farmyard Song* are as enchanting today as ever.

The Norwegian Mountains remained one of the most popular songs in Norwegian classrooms until the 1970s, when pop songs and ballads replaced traditional school songbooks.

Grieg's *The Christmas Tree* to a text by Johan Krohn stands tall as a tree, although it has not enjoyed the popularity it deserves.

Hymn of the Fatherland (Runeberg/Rolfsen) is played on the morning of 17 May (Norway's national day) each year, by Nina and Edvard Grieg's grave at Troldhaugen.

The two songs Grieg himself was most pleased with in this album were *The Ocean* (Rolfsen) and *Fisherman's Song* (Petter Dass), but these are probably more suited to the concert hall than the classroom. The melodies are far from simple, including the use of an unusual interval – the augmented fourth (C# instead of C in G major) – in *The Ocean*. It was supposed to *'sound like sea salt'*.

Grieg wrote two albums of songs to texts by the Danish poet, painter and hedonist Holger Drachmann. The first album was *Reminiscences from Mountain and Fjord*, op. 44, published in 1886, based on a trip they took together during Grieg's second summer at Troldhaugen. They had planned to start work on a requiem, and it had been agreed that Drachmann should stay at Næsset (the home of Grieg's friend and closest neighbour Frants Beyer) so that both men could work in peace and quiet. Marie Beyer described this visit in her memoirs:

'In 1886 Holger Drachmann came to visit the Griegs at Troldhaugen for a couple of weeks. The long summer days continued long into the short summer nights, filled with high spirits and, of course, the clinking of glasses.'

It appears from Marie Beyer's account that any idea of working on the planned requiem simply petered out. Instead the two men took themselves off on a walking trip in the Jotunheimen mountains, where they came across all sorts of animals and people. The company of the cheerful Drachmann was like a tonic for Grieg.

'Am completely rejuvenated! And eager to get to work!' (Postcard to Frants Beyer, 1886)

Grieg asked Drachmann to write some memorable, *'but brief!'* poems from their trip. Drachmann was not known for his brevity or moderation in any aspect of his life! The result was four poems, each describing a young lady they had met on their walking trip who had caught the fancy of Drachmann (and perhaps Grieg). He framed these musical portraits between two mood paintings from the Jotunheimen mountains entitled *Prologue* and *Epilogue*.

The poems in *Six Songs*, op. 49 (1889) are also by Drachmann. This album contains both hearty bravura and poems about nature. *Tell Me Now, Did You See the Lad* and *Kind Greetings, Fair Ladies* are overflowing with the same Danish-Norwegian merriment we recognise from the paintings of the Skagen school of painters. In the last song in the album, *Spring Showers*, Grieg and Drachmann touch on the misty landscape of the dawning impressionism.

For his last two albums, *Five Songs*, op. 69 and *Five Songs*, op. 70, Grieg turned once more to Denmark, this time to poems written by his friend Otto Benzon, a physician. Neither of these albums was the success Grieg had hoped they would be. Some of the songs have a certain charm, including the energetic *Eros* (which is somewhat reminiscent of the more stately style of Richard Strauss's songs) and the simpler, more intimate *Summer Night*.

The most striking thing about Grieg's entire song output is the utmost respect with which he treats the poem, irrespective of its literary quality or subject matter. Grieg wrote to his biographer Henry T Finck in 1899:

'When I compose songs, my principal goal is not to write music but first of all to do justice to the poet's most secret intentions. To let the poem come to the fore as strongly as possible – that is my task. If this task is performed well, then the music is successful too. Otherwise it is

'The Trolls of The Native Norwegian language are attacking Christiania.'
Garborg, Sivle and Garborg caricatured by Olaf Gulbransson. (EGM)

not, even if in and of itself it is ethereally beautiful.' (Letter to Henry T Finck, 17 July 1899)

A WORLD OF UNBORN MUSIC

Edvard Grieg lived at a time when Norway was undergoing a cultural and political thaw of massive proportions. It was not merely the dissolution of the union with Sweden; there were all sorts of political and cultural issues that led to heated debate and deep divisions in the population. One of the most impassioned debates in the late 1800s was the language question in Norway. After 400 years under Danish rule, Norway had no written language of its own, but used Danish as the official language of schools, the church and government. During the nineteenth century, various steps were taken to reinstate a specifically Norwegian language. In 1850 Ole Bull had founded the first Norwegian-language theatre. Radical artists and politicians began 'Norwegianising' their Danish (both Ibsen and Grieg were in favour of this approach). However, some linguists and writers took a far more radical approach, particularly the philologist

Hulda and Arne Garborg. (EGM)

*Ivar Aasen
(1813–1896).* (EGM)

*Arne Garborg
(1851–1924) in his
garden at Labråten in
Eastern Norway.* (EGM)

Ivar Aasen. Aasen travelled round Norway making systematic studies of rural Norwegian dialects, and he laid the foundations for a new written Norwegian standard based on common elements from many of these dialects. This new standard was referred to as *Landsmaal* (literally: national language, now known as New Norwegian), and authors such as Kristofer Janson and Aasmund Olavsson Vinje started to write in *Landsmaal*.

The highly intelligent and talented writer Arne Garborg threw himself into this debate in the late 1890s. He had already made a name for himself in Norway and throughout Europe as a gifted writer, philosopher and public speaker.

The conflict became more and more impassioned, and in 1899 Bjørnstjerne Bjørnson joined the public debate. He was on the opposite side of the fence from Ibsen and Grieg, and passionately defended his own written language as the one true national language. And once Bjørnson had joined the debate, he used fair means and foul to attack his opponents. They, for their part, answered at least as vehemently and the conflict escalated. The language debate in Norway still lives on today, although not half as fervently as in Grieg's day.

Edvard Grieg had always viewed *Landsmaal* with interest, and as early as 1866 he had set a poem written in *Landsmaal* – *Little Lad*, by Kristofer Janson – to music. While living in Hardanger Grieg lived in close contact with the sonorous, rich local dialect there, and it was during this period that he became an avid reader of the poems of Aasmund Olavsson Vinje. This stood him in good stead when he began his work on Garborg's fantastic poetry in *The Mountain Maid*.

Grieg's love of *Landsmaal* continued for the rest of his life, but he despaired at the way in which the language debate developed, particularly as he felt that it led to an increasing level of narrow-mindedness and fanaticism on the part of the proponents of *Landsmaal*. He was particularly critical of Garborg's *Knudahei Letters* (1904), which he referred to as a *'rural mood with pleasing descriptions of nature'*. By this stage Garborg could no longer be regarded as a European, as he definitely had been in the 1890s. He maintained that city dwellers were a completely different breed from him. Grieg, on the other hand, felt strongly that just because he did not come from a rural area or speak a dialect close to *Landsmaal*, he was every bit as capable of national feeling as Garborg.

Knudaheio, Garborg's summer house at his ancestral Jæren, built in 1899. (BOB)

Knudaheio is now a museum. (THG)

Grieg was so disappointed at the way in which the language issue became an instrument of political machinations that he distanced himself from the entire debate. He had a keen interest in linguistic form and language development, but he did not believe that such issues lent themselves to coercion. Unfortunately this balanced kind of standpoint tended to be drowned out in the power struggle that carried on throughout the twentieth century in the language debate. The language issue has been used – and abused – in many conflicts of interest, between urban and rural factions, and between national and international interests.

It is safe to say that Grieg's use of New Norwegian poetry helped open people's eyes to the inherent qualities of *Landsmaal*. *The Mountain Maid* and the *Vinje Songs* were therefore extremely important in giving the Norwegian language its own distinct melody.

'THE BEST SONGS I HAVE WRITTEN'

The enthusiasm Grieg expressed in his letters when working on Arne Garborg's *The Mountain Maid* is without equal elsewhere in his correspondence. He received a copy of Garborg's epic about the young girl Veslemøy early in 1895, and he was immediately drawn into a world of nature mysticism and poesy that triggered exceptional creativity. The book consists of 71 poems and Grieg recognised at once that these texts could form the starting point

Picture on front cover of The Mountain Maid.
(BOB)

The atmosphere of The Mountain Maid *is coloured by the unique landscape at* Høgjæren. (THG)

First page of the manuscript of The Mountain Maid *op. 67.*(BOB)

for some truly great music. In the course of just a few weeks he not only composed a large number of songs, but he also found the time to write enthusiastic letters to friends and colleagues about this project that had so fuelled his imagination.

When he wrote to Julius Röntgen on 12 June, he had already completed twelve of the songs. The first song was finished on 14 May.

'During the past few days I have been buried in a most remarkable collection of lyric poetry; it is The Mountain Maid *by Arne Garborg that has just been published. It is an absolutely brilliant book in which the music really has already been composed: one has only to write it down.' (Letter to Julius Röntgen, 12 June 1898)*

It is not surprising that Grieg found Garborg's poetry highly musical, for Garborg was a proficient musician and, like Grieg, extremely interested in folk music. There is no doubt that the two men's shared interest and talent struck a deep chord in *The Mountain Maid*. Grieg described the lyrics of *The Mountain Maid* as *'a masterpiece, full of originality, simplicity and depth and of an absolutely indescribable richness of colour'. (Letter to Oscar Meyer, 7 June 1898)*

Grieg worked at a feverish pitch on the material all through that spring at Troldhaugen, without any clear idea of the precise form his composition would take. He simply wrote and wrote, completing twelve songs in under a month, as well as sketches for

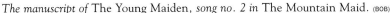

The manuscript of The Young Maiden, *song no. 2 in* The Mountain Maid. (BOB)

Agathe Backer Grøndahl (1847–1907), pianist, composer and close friend of Grieg. (BOB)

Eva Sars Nansen (1858–1907). A singer, married to Fridtjof Nansen. (BOB)

at least four more. But he was not yet sure how to combine these songs, or how to expand on them. He wrote to Gottfred Matthison-Hansen and Iver Holter that his new work *The Mountain Maid* would be '*something for voice and orchestra*'. He had not yet decided on the exact form of the finished product, but he was utterly con-vinced that the material in this book was a stroke of genius.

In the autumn of 1895 Grieg travelled to Leipzig again, and he wrote to his friend Beyer that he was hoping to continue work on *The Mountain Maid* there. But the same thing happened that had occurred before – the creative process had been interrupted and he was unable to pick up the thread where he had left off.

(EGM)

Peter Tchaikovsky
(1840–1893) also
described Nina Grieg:

'Now I had the opportunity
of learning to appreciate
Madame Grieg's many and
valuable qualities. In the
first place, she proved to be
an excellent though not
very finished singer; sec-
ondly, I have never met a
better-informed or more
highly cultivated woman,
and she is, among other
things, an excellent judge
of literature, in which
Grieg himself was also
deeply interested; and
thirdly, I was soon convinced that Madame Grieg
was as amiable, as gentle,
as childishly simple and
without guile as her celebrated husband.'
(From Peter Tchaikovsky's
Autobiographical
Descriptions of a Journey
Abroad in 1888)

'*... all of that lies hundreds of miles away. I can no longer revive*
the former moods. Yes, indeed, one's surroundings are a delicate spider
web, more delicate than one realises oneself.' *(Letter to Frants Beyer,*
27 October 1895)

So it was that *The Mountain Maid* fell into an enchanted sleep
that lasted for nearly three years, without any attempt on Grieg's
part to get these songs published. He had tested the material out
on Nina and close friends, and yet the material lay untouched
and unfinished. He wrote to Julius Röntgen in 1896:

'*The Mountain Maid slumbers on. I haven't touched it since*
Christmas when it was sung for you. Of late I have unfortunately
been lyrical, or perhaps I should say bestial (opus 65 including Wedding
Day at Troldhaugen). *Can't you cure me of this illness? What I want*
to compose doesn't get composed, and what I don't want to compose
does. A dreadful illness.' *(Letter to Julius Röntgen, 20 June 1896)*

Nevertheless, Grieg's subconscious never quite let the material
in *The Mountain Maid* go, and in 1898 he selected eight of the
songs to form the cycle in opus 67, and put the finishing touches
to them. They were published in two versions: in New Norwegian
and Danish by Wilhelm Hansen in Copenhagen, and in German
and English by Edition Peters in Leipzig.

Grieg was a little anxious about how these songs would be
received. He was worried that some people would be prejudiced
simply because the lyrics were written in the much debated New
Norwegian. He was also concerned whether audiences would
appreciate the breadth and depth of these songs, which were so
different from the popular light songs of the day. He need not have
worried, however, for the cycle became an immediate success, particularly in the Nordic countries. To Grieg's great satisfaction, a
number of performers interpreted *The Mountain Maid* in an excellent manner.

The complete cycle was performed for the first time on 2 November 1899 in Oslo by the soprano Eva Nansen (wife of Fridtjof
Nansen) and Grieg's dear friend Agathe Backer Grøndahl. Grieg
himself was not able to be present, as he and the Norwegian-born
Swedish singer Dagmar Möller were giving a recital in Stockholm
later that week, including four of the songs from *The Mountain*
Maid.

Arne Garborg sat down straight after the concert in Oslo to
write an animated letter to Grieg, thanking him for his enchanting treatment of the texts. '*Yes, now I am happy and proud – abso-*

The 'small trolls' Nina and Edvard Grieg, drawn by O Hartman. (EGM)

Pet names: Nina called Edvard 'Vardo'. Edvard called Nina 'Nisk'.

Nina and Edvard strolling down Oslo's main street, Karl Johan. (EGM)

lutely disgracefully proud – that you were able to use these verses. Thank you!'

During the three years it took Grieg to complete this song cycle, he wrestled with how to arrive at the best possible form. He was determined to create a coherent entity of the sixteen un-completed songs, in a way that would present Garborg's book *The Mountain Maid* in its entirety, yet concisely. Using just a few care-fully selected poems, Grieg managed to write music that painted a complete picture and created a new whole.

In the selection of eight songs he finished up with, he man-aged to achieve this aim. The song cycle depicts the whole of *The Mountain Maid*. This opus is one of the very best examples of Grieg's mastery of the somewhat larger forms. Although the songs are relatively short, they make up a whole, stretched out in a wide-sweeping arch.

The top of the arch in this song cycle consists of the middle two songs *The Tryst* and *Love*. These songs describe the attraction between two young people and the consummation of their love, spanning the entire process from the thrill of anticipation, ecstasy and love-making, to the fetters of love, fear and a nagging premonition of betrayal and doom.

On either side of these love songs Grieg placed light-hearted pastoral depictions of Veslemøy's surroundings and everyday life. *Blueberry Slope* and *Kidlings' Dance* portray the young Veslemøy at one with nature. All her concerns are dispelled by her joy at the good humour of nature.

In the pair of songs either side of these pastoral songs, Grieg placed two portraits of this remarkable young herd girl in *Veslemøy, The Young Maiden* and *Hurtful Day*. Veslemøy has extraordinary powers that set her aside from her peers in the rural community she comes from. And so she turns to nature to satisfy her longings and her questioning. Veslemøy has visions in which she communes with nature and with supernatural powers in a way that we mere mortals cannot fully understand. '*She is lovely, so lissome, so lithe,*'[14] says Garborg's text, but in Grieg's accompaniment to the simple melody that describes Veslemøy, we glimpse the complexity of her spiritual life. There is much more to her personality hidden below her '*manner impassive and calm*'.

Veslemøy also experiences human love when '*her handsome lover*' visits her. But after their momentous meeting her lover returns no more, and she is left like a wild animal trapped in a snare. We sense Veslemøy's premonition at the close of *Love*, and when this nagging doubt is confirmed and she realises that she has been betrayed, there is no escape for the young girl. '*Hot tears again stream down, her cheeks to sear. Now must she die; she's lost her love so dear.*' *The Tryst* has turned into a *Hurtful Day*.

The cycle finishes with *At the Brook*. Veslemøy turns once more to nature mysticism and finds her only possible escape – into nature. This song brings to mind Franz Schubert's spurned young miller in *Die schöne Müllerin*. He, too, seeks escape and solace in the brook. In a masterly fashion Grieg uses an apparently strophic form, following the unbroken gurgling of the brook, and yet at the end of each of the five verses, when Veslemøy '*rests, dreams,*

Edvard Grieg photographed in 1905 by Nicola Perscheid in Leipzig. (EGM)

In the course of the summer Grieg produced two sonatas, which clearly combine his own distinctly Norwegian style with traditional European music forms. The first to be completed was his *Piano Sonata in E minor*. His choice of key for this sonata was no coincidence; Gade's *Sonata*, op. 28 (1840) was also in E minor, and Grieg dedicated his sonata to Gade. Shortly after this, Grieg also finished his first *Violin Sonata*. Grieg took his sonatas to Professor Gade's home in Klampenborg, to go through them with him. Grieg recalled this inspiring occasion in an interview in *Dannebrog* (26 December 1893).

'*Whether it was the charming surroundings or the refreshing air that inspired me I shall not attempt to say. It is enough to say that my piano sonata was composed in the space of just eleven days, and soon thereafter I also finished my first violin sonata. I took them both to Gade at Klampenborg. He looked through them with pleasure, nodded, clapped me on the shoulder and said, "That's pretty darn good. Now let's go and look at them more closely." We then crept up a steep, narrow ladder to Gade's study, where he sat down at the piano and became completely enthralled. It has been said that when Gade was inspired he drank huge quantities of water. That day the professor emptied four large carafes.*'

The four-movement *Piano Sonata* is extremely fresh and vigorous, and a fine example of Grieg's special talent for combining good tunes with tough harmonies. The sonata is highly pianistic, exploiting the instrument to the full. There is little use of special effects, but it encompasses a huge range of expression. The *Piano Sonata* heralds the genius of the *Piano Concerto in A minor* three years later, with its mastery of the capabilities of the instrument.

In this same giddy atmosphere, yet filled with even more light and warmth, came his *Violin Sonata in F major*, op. 8 only a matter of weeks after the *Piano Sonata*. F major is often referred to as the key of springtime, and indeed Beethoven's *Violin Sonata in F major* is often called the *Spring Sonata*.

In this sonata Grieg goes even further in incorporating motifs and themes from Norwegian folk music. The sonata opens with an unanswered question on the piano: a series of long, vague minor chords. Where is this leading to? The ice melts and fresh bubbling spring water trickles out of the instruments in a thrilling rhythmic melody that flows over crevasses and stones until it widens out in a pure, clear F major roughly twenty bars into the piece.

Købmagergade in Copenhagen in Grieg's day. (EGM)

With a second theme in the minor, Grieg develops the first movement in perfect sonata form, demonstrating a masterful command of the form, particularly in his imaginative development of the thematic material. Thanks to his natural inclination to try out all themes and motifs in both the major and the minor, he renews the material time and time again, and the result is much richer and more authentic music.

Edvard's Grieg's elder brother, John, was a talented cellist, but he had to sacrifice his hopes of a career as a musician to take care of the family business.(EGM)

In the second movement, which is almost a minuet, the opening motif is loud and bold. The typical Grieg 'A–A–G#–E' motif is at the heart of this whole movement. In the trio section (the middle section) Grieg conjures up the Hardanger fiddle; as the tempo quickens we are back in the major key, and the *springar* (a Norwegian folk dance) trips gleefully over the strings. The contrast to the first section is huge, even though this section too is built around the Grieg motif.

The last movement is in the same form as the first. It is clear that Grieg was overflowing with melodic material when he composed this sonata and indeed some critics have accused him of not developing his material adequately. And yet there is an unbroken line throughout the movement, indeed throughout the entire work. There is a strong sense of coherence and broad utilisation of the thematic material. The resilient opening and clear tonality of the final movement are developed very imaginatively. The whole work is typically Grieg, with its constant unexpected shifts between the brash, almost aggressive elements and the emotional, almost melancholy minor passages.

In this sonata Grieg shows a deep understanding of the range of expression the violin is capable of. The piece is well written for both instruments, and devoid of all unnecessary virtuosity, yet it requires considerable technique and insight.

The *Violin Sonata* represented something of an international breakthrough for Norwegian chamber music. It was first performed at a concert in the Gewandhaus in Leipzig in November 1865, with Grieg at the keyboard. The programme included his *Piano Sonata* and this *Violin Sonata*, with the Swedish violinist Anders Petterson as soloist. Grieg had stopped off at Leipzig en route to Rome, in the hope that his travelling companion, Rikard Nord-raak, who was ill in Berlin, would recover in time to join him there. The concert was a success, with a positive critique in the music journal *Signale*, and it provided Grieg with extra funding for his trip to Italy.

'Mr Edvard H Grieg from Bergen, Norway, who was once a student at the Leipzig Conservatory, and who is making a stop here on his way to Italy, in the last two weeks performed two of his own new compositions at evening concerts at the Conservatory. One was a solo sonata for piano, the other a violin sonata that he performed together with a Swedish fellow artist, Mr Petterson from Stockholm. Both works were such as to awaken more than ordinary interest, thanks to their

time. For a start, we know that with the completion of Trold-haugen he finally had somewhere where he could concentrate over a long period, which of course was especially important when working on something as substantial as a violin sonata. In addition, in the autumn of 1886 Grieg received a visit from the Italian violinist Teresina Tua, whose presence and playing no doubt helped progress on the sonata that Grieg had just started writing.

Grieg complained bitterly on many occasions about his lack of firsthand knowledge of the violin. For instance, he would dearly have liked to be able to write down the many intricate folk dances he heard the great Norwegian fiddlers play. In 1901, when he was working on the folk music passed on by Myllar-guten to Johannes Dahle, he wrote to Johan Halvorsen *'I have fretted and fumed about not being a fiddle player.'* He also made pejorative remarks about the shortcomings of the training he received in Leipzig, for he claimed that he had not gained a deep understanding of writing for stringed instruments in his time there.

However, when we see how deftly Grieg treats the string instruments in his sonatas, string quartets and orchestral pieces, we can be in no doubt that he produced impressively idiomatic writing for these instruments, perfectly suited to their possibilities and character. This was no doubt due in part to his close contact and collaboration with the top performers of his day. The 'god-father' of the European violin tradition was Giovanni Battista Viotti (1755–1824), whose credo to his students *'Listen to all talented musicians; profit from them all, but do not imitate any of them!'* Grieg took to heart right from the start of his career.

As a student and throughout his adult life Grieg met all the great European violinists of the day. Ole Bull was an early influence who had a huge impact on Grieg. The legendary Ferdinand David was a professor at the Leipzig Conservatory, and later on Grieg came into contact with Joseph Joachim, Henri Wieniawski and Eugène Ysaÿe. He also worked closely with other foreign violinists such as Robert Heckmann, Adolf Brodsky, Wilhelmina-Norman Neruda, Johannes Wolff and Tor Aulin. So throughout his life Grieg was surrounded by people who could give him valuable advice on writing for the violin, and in addition it is clear that he had an intuitive feel for the timbre of string instruments. All of this produced extremely good results.

Holger Drachmann's painting of Troldhaugen. (EGM)

*Holger Drachmann
(1846–1908).* (EGM)

Another likely reason why Grieg turned once more to the traditional Classical form of the sonata was his despair over the reception his music by certain European critics, who claimed that Grieg was a purely national composer whose work consisted of no more than striking small arrangements of the exotic folk music of his native country. In addition to this, as a respected artist of worldwide acclaim, he felt the need to express himself *'on a wider horizon'*.

Grieg set to work on the sonata in the summer of 1886, but he was constantly interrupted by uninvited visitors to Troldhaugen. Things took a turn for the better after Grieg and his friend Holger Drachmann had been on a high-spirited hiking trip in the Jotunheimen mountains, and in the course of the autumn many details fell into place. But Grieg was not satisfied with his composition and he put it to one side until the following autumn, when he took it with him to Leipzig and put the finishing touches to it there. During the final stages of this composition Grieg collaborated closely with the young Norwegian violinist Johan Halvorsen, a pupil of the Russian virtuoso Adolf Brodsky. It was Brodsky who performed the piece for the first time in public, together with Grieg. Right from their first rehearsal, Grieg was overwhelmed,

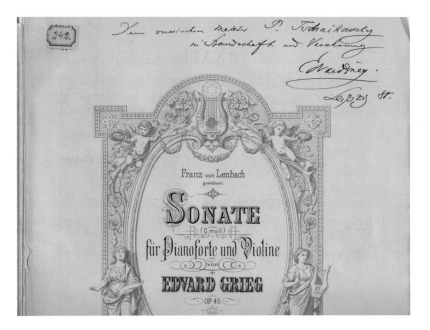

Sonata for Violin and Piano in C minor, *op. 45, dedicated to Franz von Lenbach. In writing a personal greeting to Tchaikovsky from Grieg.* (THG)

Adolf Brodsky (1851–1928). (EGM)

for here at last was a musician who fully understood every single one of the composer's intentions. The piece was transformed out of all recognition, Grieg wrote enthusiastically to his friend Beyer. The first performance was on 10 December 1887 at the Neues Gewandhaus in Leipzig, and Grieg and Brodsky remained close friends for the rest of their lives.

On the day of the premiere Brodsky and Grieg had something of a disagreement, since Brodsky wanted Grieg to play with the lid of the grand piano down, whereas Grieg felt it should be right up. The norm at that time was for the solo part to ring out clear and unhampered, with a dampened accompaniment. However, Grieg maintained that in his sonata both parts were of equal importance, and that the timbre of his piano was far better with the lid up, and he promised to play more softly. Brodsky still felt the piano was too loud in relation to the violin, and Grieg had to give him 'ein norwegisches Versprechen!' (a Norwegian promise). Brodsky trusted his word, and they played the concert in accordance with Grieg's wishes.

'And how he played! After each movement there was prolonged applause, and two curtain calls after the finale ...' (Letter to Frants Beyer, 11 December 1887)

Once again Eduard Bernsdorf of *Signale*, always strongly oriented towards German music, wrote a damning critique of Grieg's work, although he spoke warmly of both Brodsky's and Grieg's playing. This time he was very much alone in his criticism: the sonata was an instant success and became immensely popular. Within a year Peters had sold 1,500 copies of the sonata, an astonishing number *'even compared with Brahms'*. (*Letter from Max Abraham to Grieg, 1887*)

The sonata drew much praise and positive critiques from all sides, and the Belgian musicologist Ernest Closson went so far as to say that this sonata must be one of the most inspired works ever written. From start to finish it was a revelation of inspiration, intelligence and independence. The work soon made its way into the repertoire of violinists everywhere, from Brodsky, Wieniawski and Ysaÿe in the nineteenth century to Kreisler, Heifetz, Menuhin and Stern in the twentieth century and into the new millennium with the artists who will be the great names of our own century.

Grieg composed his *Violin Sonata no. 3 in C minor*, op. 45 at the same time that Cesar Franck wrote his *Violin Sonata in A major* and shortly before Brahms's *D minor Sonata*. Together these form a unique collection of the noblest expressivity and intensity of romanticism, while each of the three points forwards in its own way to a new era and a new mode of expression.

The violinists who performed this work with Grieg at the piano, even in his later years when his health was failing, all reported that Grieg played the piano part quite brilliantly. His tempo in the first movement was invariably fast and wild, and he requested (with gentle insistence) that the violinist give everything he had. His lyrical expression was said to be overwhelmingly *cantabile*.

This sonata shows no obvious sign of Grieg's making use of specific sources of folk music, rather it appears to be more the result of many years in close contact with folk music, which Grieg had internalised. It is not a work in which we hear Grieg combined with Norwegian folk music, it is thoroughly Griegian through and through. Although careful analysis of the score reveals the same motifs and compositional techniques as in his earlier sonatas, here the process is carried out with greater refinement and finely balanced control.

The second movement is not just an ode to music, but more specifically to his friend and colleague Johan Svendsen. The tempo

as a solo and chamber music instrument. He was also highly influential in his native country. Spain was subject to extremely difficult, volatile political circumstances throughout the century, but Casals always held the red banner and the banner of music high. All the major cellists of the 20th century had some sort of contact with Casals and were influenced by him in some way. When his pupils play the Grieg Cello Sonata, there is an unbroken line between performer and composer through Casals. In the world of music, the passing of the generations cannot be counted in the usual way, since the master–pupil principle allows direct lines of connection to span several generations. Just think of the time span represented by Yehudi Menuhin, one of the greatest 20th-century legends. In his childhood he met and played with the old masters, and right up until his death he was deeply committed to the development of talent in the very young. Just like Casals, he was a living link between artists born in the mid-1800s and those whose careers will continue far into the 21st century.

The building Grieg stayed in at Karlsbad, and Grieg's name on the guest list. (EGM)

In other words, Grieg was not altogether satisfied with his new work. He was always his own harshest critic. Admittedly we recognise much of the thematic material in the *Cello Sonata* from earlier works, as well as certain structural similarities, particularly with the *Piano Concerto in A minor*, the *Homage March* from *Sigurd Jorsalfar* and the well-known Grieg motif. In the introduction to the second movement there is a passage in the piano part taken more or less straight from his setting of Bjørnson's poem *From Monte Pincio*. Since he had quoted his own works so much in this sonata, Grieg did not see the *Cello Sonata* as marking '*a forward step in my development*'. However, there is no doubt that this is an extremely well-written sonata for a beautiful instrument that does not have a particularly large chamber music repertoire.

Grieg dedicated the *Cello Sonata* to his brother John Grieg, and the brothers performed it together several times. The premiere performance was in Dresden in October 1883 by Grieg and the German cellist Ludwig Grützmacher. A few days later Grieg played it with one of the greatest cellists of the nineteenth century, Julius Klengel, in Leipzig. As usual Eduard Bernsdorf was fairly damning in his assessment in *Signale*, although once again he had to admit that the composer had held the audience spellbound.

Despite Grieg's concerns about the quality of the sonata, it has stood the test of time and is now part of the standard repertoire for cellists. In the first movement the jittery, powerful first theme alternates in a typically Griegian way with lyrical, pastoral passages. The second movement is a pure idyll – a *cantabile* version of the *Homage March* from *Sigurd Jorsalfar*. The third movement opens with a lingering cello solo followed by an energetic theme like a *halling* (a Norwegian folk dance), which hurls the instruments into a long exciting chase.

Once more Grieg excels in his masterly exploitation of the potential of the instruments. The piano part is technically demanding but extremely well written, as it really makes the most of the tonal properties of the instrument without stealing the cello's thunder. Grieg blends the cello with the piano, but allows the cello to soar alone at just the right places.

'... LIKE A NORWEGIAN OLD CHEESE YET TO MATURE'

Grieg spent the winter of 1891 in Copenhagen. He had fully intended to get down to composing again, but he could not settle, and spent much of his time fretting over his inability to be creative. In letters to his friend Frants Beyer he writes:

'It is a period of decadence and decline. There is nothing inspiring or stimulating. No, give me peaceful nature instead! It speaks more and better than these prattling, petty people ...' (Letter to Frants Beyer, 20 January 1891)

'The music that I come up with one day I tear out of my heart the next – because it isn't genuine. My ideas are bloodless just like me, and I am beginning to lose faith in myself.' (Letter to Frants Beyer, 9 February 1891)

But in late March, Grieg wrote to Beyer again: *'I have written two movements of a string quartet. Of course, it was supposed to have been completely finished down here. But it isn't. And I'm going to Oslo in April ...' (Letter to Frants Beyer, 26 March 1891)*

However, it was disastrous for the quartet that Grieg did not manage to complete it in Copenhagen. He never managed to pick up the thread, and for the rest of his life it gnawed at his conscience. In December 1895 he wrote to his friend Adolf Brodsky:

'Your idea about playing violin pieces by me is brilliant, for as a matter of fact I haven't written any. But make me healthy again and I will shake something out of my sleeve. But then you must go along with the idea that either these as yet unborn pieces or that damned String Quartet, *that constantly lies there unfinished like a piece of Norwegian "old cheese", be adorned with your name ...' (Letter to Adolf Brodsky, 25 December 1895)*

In 1903 Grieg wrote to his publisher Henri Hinrichsen, the new director of Edition Peters:

'Perhaps you remember my mentioning an unfinished string quartet? I had also intended to get it done. But these last years have brought so much misery, both physically and spiritually, that I wasn't in the mood to proceed with this cheerful work – quite the opposite of opus 27 (String Quartet in G minor). But I hope to find the long-sought tranquillity and inclination this summer.' (Letter to Henri Hinrichsen, 7 February 1903)

Unfortunately he did not find the long-sought tranquillity and inclination. The last time he mentioned the quartet in writing was in a letter to Adolf Brodsky in August 1906: '*I should at least have finished the* String Quartet *for you!*'

At the time of his death there were only two movements in manuscript plus a number of sketches for the last two movements. At the request of Nina Grieg the Dutch pianist and composer Julius Röntgen, a close friend of Grieg, went through all of Grieg's manuscripts after his death, including the *Quartet in F major*. Röntgen decided to get Peters to publish the first two movements. This was in 1908.

Röntgen also had a rather unusual 'premiere' of the quartet in his home. He and some of his musician friends played it through, as described in a letter from Röntgen to Nina Grieg:

'*But now you must hear who made up the quartet. It was unusual: Harold Bauer, the great pianist, played first violin and really did a fine job. Pablo Casals played second violin and held the violin between his legs just like a cello. I played the viola, and Mrs Casals played cello in a remarkable way. All four of us were filled with the greatest excitement – with my wife as the only audience!*'

Despite its publication, the unfinished quartet has rarely been performed in public. In the summer of 1996 The Chilingirian Quartet visited Norway, with the *Quartet in F major* as part of their repertoire. Before their concert at Troldhaugen Levon Chilingirian, the leader, asked if he might see Grieg's original manuscripts, since he wanted to check whether the printed version was the same as Grieg's manuscript at various points. The Edvard Grieg Archives at the Bergen Public Library were happy to let him see the manuscript, and it soon became clear that Julius Röntgen had made a number of changes that were not in keeping with Grieg's manuscript or intentions.

Levon Chilingirian was keen to study this in greater detail and was allowed to borrow a copy of the manuscripts, including what there was of the third and fourth movements. In the period leading up to autumn 1998 he went through the manuscripts with a fine toothcomb and as far as possible reconstructed Edvard Grieg's original version. This version was performed for the first time at the Bergen International Festival, in Grieg's villa at Troldhaugen, on 28 May 1998.

This new edition of the quartet has been published and has given rise to renewed interest in performing this work.

The character of this quartet is quite different from the quartet in G minor. While the G minor quartet is a dramatic, dense piece dripping with lifeblood, the F major quartet is in a completely different mood. It shares the typical Grieg sound, but here it is the lyrical, tuneful and expressive side of Grieg that comes to the fore.

Grieg virtually completed the first and second movements, although the manuscripts show that he had various alternative ideas for certain phrases and cadenzas. If we compare Julius Röntgen's edition from 1908 with the manuscript version, we see that Röntgen did not simply choose between Grieg's suggestions, he also added some ideas of his own.

The slow movement is melodic and beautiful, and when the cello sums up the melodic material towards the end of the movement, Grieg reiterates and underlines the themes in a masterful way, but unfortunately he ends without a coda, leaving the movement feeling somewhat amputated.

There are only a few sketches for the last movement. At first sight the lively main theme looks promising and with a typically Grieg feel to it, but as soon as Grieg tries to develop the material, we see that he encountered insurmountable problems – the thematic material is not substantial enough to be developed and transformed, and the whole things peters out into nothing.

This was a great loss for the string quartet literature, but as we know, Grieg was simply incapable of producing music that he did not feel was excellent or genuine.

Levon Chilingirian. (EGM)

'The sunny key of the F major quartet provides an unexpected vehicle for exploring extremes in expression. The first movement is relaxed in mood until a turbulent and chromatically challenging development section literally whips us off our feet! The mysterious and oriental-sounding scherzo is seemingly complemented by a faster dance in the trio until a frenzied passage of brutal energy interrupts. The adagio is a beautiful song followed by a quiet, prayer-like passage leading to recitatives accompanied by dramatic tremolos. The finale sets a happy mood, contrasted by a passage of Nordic beauty. We can only wonder what an effective climax this movement would have made had Edvard Grieg found the inspiration and time to complete it.'

Lindeman's Older
and Newer Norwegian
Mountain Melodies.
(BOB)

Sjur Helgeland (1858–1924). (EGM)

Folk music

NORWEGIAN FOLK MUSIC runs like a life nerve throughout Grieg's entire output, from *Humoresques*, op. 6 to his final work, *Four Psalms*, op. 74.

'I have found that the obscure depth in our folk melodies has its foundations in their undreamed-of harmonic possibilities. In my arrangements in opus 66 and elsewhere I have tried to give expression to my sense of the hidden harmonies in our folk tunes.' (Letter to Henry T Finck, 17 July 1899)

Grieg's first major project involving the rich heritage of folk tunes came on the heels of his hugely successful *Piano Concerto in A minor* and the great personal tragedy of the death of his young daughter, Alexandra. In the difficult months after Alexandra's death Grieg found comfort and inspiration in arranging some of the folk melodies collected by Ludvig Matthias Lindeman, and he completed his first major arrangement of folk tunes, *Twenty-five Norwegian Folk Songs and Dances*, op. 17.

Grieg kept the simplicity of the melodies, never trying to add special effects or technical sophistication, and yet these pieces are far more than a traditional reproduction of the material. It is particularly his choice of chords that gives rise to the excitement, and notably the fact that he uses different harmonisations each time a part of the melody is repeated, giving the tunes greater depth of content and different faces.

The twenty-five pieces form a huge arch around the central *Solfager and the Snake King* (no. 12). This piece, which has roots right back to mediaeval times, possesses a magnificent dignity in Grieg's arrangement, full of rhythmic tension and rich harmonies.

Another of these pieces that Grieg often performed at recitals was *Dance from Jølster* (no. 5), which combines two folk tunes from

Ludvig Mathias Lindeman (1812–1887). (BOB)

Ludvig Matthias Lindeman's (1812–1887) transcriptions were like a treasure trove for Grieg, although he also found inspiration and material elsewhere at times. Ludvig Mathias Lindeman was the first person in Norway to undertake systematic collection of Norwegian folk tunes, in the 1840s. On his travels through rural Norway he collected several hundred tunes. The first collection, *Norwegian Mountain Melodies*, caused quite a stir. This volume was later followed by *Older and Newer Norwegian Mountain Melodies*, (1853–67). Together they constitute a firm foundation of much Norwegian art music.

Jølster in Sunnfjord, Western Norway. The first tune is an upbeat, powerful tune, almost like a rock song, while the other is calm and contemplative. Grieg opens the piece with a riff, and then the *halling*-like dance tune trips around in the right hand, while the left hand plays violent chromatic chords with accents on the off-beat. The pensive melancholy of the middle section is chased away by the return of the *halling*, which hurls itself around and ends with a traditional 'hallingkast'.

Grieg's *Twenty-five Norwegian Folk Songs and Dances*, op. 17 set the standard for his treatment of folk tunes. Throughout his many works based on raw materials from Lindeman's collection (op. 17, 24, 29, 30, 35, 51, 63, 64 and 74) and those based on other folk music sources (op. 66 and 72), Grieg handles this material with the understanding and insight of a true artist. Opus 17 was his first major attempt at this type of composition. His compositions evolved in step with his artistic development and he plumbed unimagined depths in Norway's musical heritage.

Grieg regarded Lindeman's collections of folk tunes, along with Asbjørnsen and Moe's collections of folktales and legends, Magnus Brostrup Landstad's collection of folk songs and Ivar Aasen's dialect studies, as important 'stones in that building which is Norway'.

As far as music was concerned, it was Ole Bull that really set the ball going. At his concerts at home and abroad Bull performed and improvised Norwegian folk tunes and dance melodies, as well as composing important works in which Norwegian folk music came to expression in all its simplicity combined with his unique virtuosity. *Visit to a Summer Farm* and *In Lonely Moments* are two gems on a different scale, but in the same noble vein.

Others also made important contributions in this field. As early as 1825 Waldemar Thrane (1790–1828) had composed the first Norwegian opera, *The Mountain Adventure*, in which *Aagot's Mountain Song* overflows with the atmosphere of Norwegian mountain pastures. A more prolific composer, who made more consistent use of folk music in his works, was Halfdan Kjerulf, a central figure in Norwegian music in the mid-1800s. His songs and choral pieces, with unmistakable roots in folk music, are of particularly high artistic quality. Kjerulf also made use of a great many melodies from Lindeman's collections in his piano pieces.

Grieg was very much aware of this heritage and the seed of new growth that his predecessors had planted. In his eulogy at Ole Bull's funeral in 1880, Grieg said:

The good friends Julius Röntgen, Frants Beyer and Edvard Grieg hiking in the mountains. This picture was taken on Mount Løvstakken near Bergen. (BOB)

Photo from Ole Bull's funeral. The coffin is carried ashore from D/S Kong Sverre at Holbergs-allmenningen in Bergen, 27 August 1880. The funeral was attended by thousands of people from Norway and abroad. (BOB)

'Because you brought honour to our country like none other, because you lifted our people up with you towards art's shining heights like none other, because you were a faithful, warm-hearted pioneer for our young national music – one who conquered the hearts of everyone – like none other, because you have planted a seed that will sprout and grow in the future, and for which coming generations will bless your name – with thousands upon thousands of thanks for all this, in the name of Norwegian music I lay this wreath on your casket. Peace be with you.'

Grieg certainly fulfilled Ole Bull's wish. He realised that through a synthesis of his own musicality and Norwegian folk music he could help build Norway as an independent nation.

Frants Beyer (with his typical 'Frants smile'). (EGM)

Lindeman's collections provided Grieg with an almost inexhaustible source of raw material, but he never felt in any way bound by Lindeman's harmonisations or arrangements. Grieg went straight to the core of the material, and fused this with his own musicality. He detected a whole realm of previously unimagined harmonic possibilities behind the beautiful tunes, and his childhood fascination with the magical world of harmonies was triggered once more.

INSPIRATION AND CONCENTRATION

On a walking trip with Julius Röntgen and Frants Beyer on the Hardangervidda plateau in 1886, Grieg harmonised a folk tune that Beyer gave him. It was a bout of foul weather that brought this about; a heavy downpour and thick fog prevented the men from going out. To while away the time in the tiny, damp cabin,

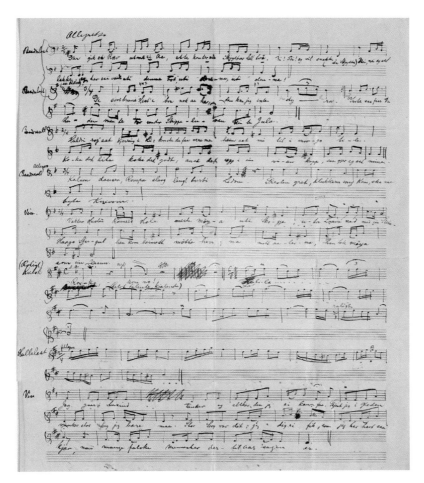

Frants Beyer, who was a lawyer, travelled a lot in Western-Norway. He met all kinds of people from whom he learned local songs and tunes. He usually wrote them down. Here is one of the melodies that Grieg used in his opus 66. (BOB)

Beyer suggested that Röntgen and Grieg should both produce a composition on a given theme. The two men agreed, and Beyer wrote out a folk tune he had heard at the age of fourteen, *It is the Greatest Folly*, and handed it to Grieg.

'Grieg tore at his hair, and muttered a pianissimo "The devil take it!" Then he fell silent, grabbed a pencil and scribbled and scribbled, until he had finished harmonising the melody. It really was a fine example of inspiration and concentration.' (Letter from Frants Beyer to Grieg's biographer Henry T Finck after Grieg's death)

This effort, without the aid of a composer's hut or a piano, was so successful that he asked Beyer to send him a new batch of folk

GJENDINE SLAALIEN (1871–1972)

Gjendine Slaalien was a true daughter of the mountain. She was actually born in the mountains, when her mother went into labour seven weeks prematurely, while working at the summer pastures at Gjende. Gjendine was born in the tourist cabin there, a very primitive stone building. A priest happened to pass through during the summer, and he insisted on christening the tiny baby who lay swaddled under the table where she was sheltered from the leaking roof. The priest took Gjendine, her family and the tourists who were staying there down to Lake Gjendin, and baptised her in the clear mountain water. 'I baptise you Kaia Gjendine, a true daughter of the mountain,' said the priest. And that is just what she was.

Gjendine Slaalien photographed at Bøverdalen just after her 100th birthday. This picture, taken on 2 October 1971, is probably the last one ever taken of her. (EGM)

tunes for him to work on during the two weeks he and Nina were planning on staying at the Fossli Hotel by the Vøringsfossen waterfall.

Frants Beyer was not only a trusted and thoughtful friend, he was also an avid and skilful collector of folk tunes. In connection with his work as a lawyer in Bergen he did a good deal of travelling around the fjords of Western Norway, and he made a point of never travelling without a notebook in his pocket. He was a man who found it easy to connect with people of all ages and backgrounds, and wherever he went, he always asked to hear the old folk songs, verses and poems. As a result he had collected any number of folk tunes that had never been written down before. He also spent his summer holidays each year in the mountains and this provided him with another source of traditional folk tunes. Beyer collected nearly all the melodies Grieg used in opus 66 in Sunnfjord and the Jotunheimen mountains. He had heard them sung by milkmaids, farmers and old women. Some of the songs he heard were really a form of broadside ballads, but they had assimilated the melodic and harmonic forms of the folk music tradition.

While staying at Fossli, Grieg received fourteen melodies from Beyer, all of which fired Grieg's imagination to such a degree that he harmonised all fourteen in his head with no piano or other aids.

'When one has the Vøringsfossen waterfall nearby, one feels more independent and is more daring than down in the valley.' (Letter to Julius Röntgen, 22 August 1896)

Back at Troldhaugen, Beyer produced even more folk songs and in September 1896 Grieg was able to tell his publisher, Max Abraham at Edition Peters, that his Nineteen Norwegian Folk Songs, op. 66 had been completed.

'This summer when I was in the mountains, I got a large number of previously unpublished and unknown folk tunes which are so beautiful that I found it a real joy to arrange them for piano.' (Letter to Max Abraham, 22 September 1896)

With the exception of the final song, Gjendine's Lullaby, all of the songs in this opus were collected and transcribed by Frants Beyer, to whom, naturally enough, the work is dedicated.

While working on these arrangements, Grieg wrote something in a letter to Julius Röntgen that gives us an important key to understanding Grieg's life and art:

'How strange life is! It is like folk songs; one doesn't know whether they were conceived in the major or the minor.' (Letter to Julius Röntgen, 15 August 1896)

This duality, the many nuances and multiple layers are the hallmark of Grieg's music and personality. When he came across musical or literary material that contained this same duality, it kindled his creativity as nothing else could.

Grieg used twenty of the melodies collected by Beyer, although in two cases he combined two melodies in a single arrangement, so these twenty tunes became eighteen separate pieces. The prevailing mood in this opus is '... the deepest melancholy, interrupted only here and there by a momentary ray of light.' (Letter to Agathe Backer Grøndahl, 28 May 1897)

Composer friends Julius Röntgen and Edvard Grieg in high spirits – enjoying a cigar in the open air. (BOB)

Although the atmosphere in most of these pieces is melancholy, this work is far from monotonous or drab. Grieg really did show daring up there at the top of the Vøringsfossen waterfall. He expresses himself on many levels through his rich colouring and varied use of the melodies, from the almost dormant *Cow Call* (no. 1) and the miniature form of *Ranveig* (no. 12) (with a duration of just 20 seconds) to the almost symphonic variation of *I Wander Deep in Thought* (no. 18).

The opus contains simple cow calls, lullabies and ballads, but Grieg manages to maintain the simplicity and authenticity of each of these small pieces at the same time as creating an independent character piece of each and every one. As a whole they make up an epic of folk music.

The impressionistic tone poem *In Ola Valley, in Ola Lake* (no. 14) is a bold tonal experiment, rather like *Bell Ringing, Lyric Pieces V*, op. 54 no. 6. The poem tells the story of a distraught mother who tries in vain to use the church bell to get the sea to surrender the body of her drowned son. The tolling of the bell and the untold secrets of the waves hover eerily throughout the piece, and the melody weaves in and out of this supernatural loom.

The final piece of this opus is, as far as we know, the only folk tune ever collected by Grieg in person. In the summer of 1891 Grieg was on a walking holiday with his friends Röntgen and Beyer in the Jotunheimen mountains, and they came to a place called Skogadalsbøen. Here they met the beautiful young Gjendine Slaalien from Bøverdalen, along with several other young local girls working in the summer pastures. Gjendine was an attractive girl of twenty who sang all day as she worked, and she seemed to have an endless store of songs and tunes. The three men were quite taken with her.

Gjendine was greatly amused when 'little Grieg' came to her, paper and pen at the ready, and asked her to sing. To start with she found it difficult to keep a straight face, and constantly burst out laughing and was unable to carry on, but when they agreed to stand either side of a doorway, things went much more smoothly. However, for the most part it was Frants Beyer who persuaded the girls to sing. His method of breaking the ice was simple: he sang along with them.

Stalheim Hotel. This fantastic hotel has been a cornerstone of Norwegian tourism for many generations. (EGM)

One evening the three men walked with the girls to a tiny mountain farmhouse, where they spent the night. The girls hummed and sang for all they were worth, and Beyer was kept busy noting everything down. Gjendine later recollected, *'We got through a few bottles that night, but my goodness, how we sang!'*

Since it was Beyer who noted down most of the melodies and songs, it is hardly surprising that Gjendine thought it was he who was the composer. In 1905 Gjendine sent a letter to Edvard Grieg in which she recalled the fun she had had with him, Beyer and Röntgen in Jotunheimen, and she said that she had followed his career as an actor [sic] with great interest in the newspapers over the years.

There is no doubt that these surroundings brought out a different side of the composer's otherwise rather serious personality. The fresh air and uplifting landscape made Grieg, who could be extremely lively in the company of friends, even more playful. He hit upon the funniest pranks and practical jokes, so it was hardly surprising that Gjendine thought he was an actor.

Gjendine was not just kept busy tending the animals turned out to graze at summer pasture. She also helped look after her sister's baby that summer. One day as she minded the baby while she was milking, she started singing a lullaby. Grieg was nearby, and he was immediately transfixed by this beautiful melody. Using the back of the cow as a writing table, he noted the lullaby down as Gjendine sang. No wonder Grieg wrote to his publisher, Max Abraham in Leipzig, that this opus was 'fresh from the cow'. This song has a typically Griegian sound; with its twisting and turning around the leading note it is reminiscent of the tune he used in *Ballade in G minor*, op. 24.

Grieg and his friends visited Skogadalsbøen several more times after 1891, and both *A Little Grey Man*, no. 13 and *Tomorrow You Shall Marry Her*, no. 10 were songs he first heard sung by Gjendine Slaalien. Gjendine lived to the grand old age of 100. In 1961 she made a recording of various songs, including these two, and her performance was remarkably similar to Beyer's transcription made 70 years previously.

Julius Röntgen was not only taken with Gjendine's songs, he was taken with her personality. He had been widowed a few years earlier, and he actually proposed to Gjendine and asked her to set up home with him in Amsterdam. She refused his proposal, despite her liking for him, because she simply could not imagine leaving behind the animals and the beautiful countryside of her childhood.

Röntgen was a gentleman and he respected Gjendine's decision. Some years later he did remarry, and he took his new Dutch bride to Jotunheimen, where they met Gjendine, who in the meantime had married a local man from Bøverdalen. Julius Röntgen was a prominent figure in the Netherlands, and when Crown Princess Juliana was planning a walking holiday in the Jotunheimen mountains, Röntgen recommended Gjendine Slaalien as a local guide for the royal guest.

The Norwegian Broadcasting Corporation (NRK) made a recording of Gjendine Slaalien, and she visited Troldhaugen and the Bergen International Festival a couple of times as an honorary guest. These meetings with a living legend were extremely moving occasions.

Opus 66 was probably not conceived first and foremost as concert music, but Grieg crafted the nineteen pieces together into a natural whole. This opus was not just pioneering work in the presentation of previously unrecorded folk tunes, it has also become part of the standard concert repertoire.

'A SIN I WILL COMMIT!'

Ole Bull had introduced the young Grieg to the tradition of Norwegian folk fiddlers, and it was a kind of music which he enjoyed greatly. Grieg never let the chance to hear good fiddlers pass him by; he sought them out actively on his travels and he attended the first fiddler contests that took place towards the end of the nineteenth century, sometimes as a judge and at other times as an enthusiastic observer.

There is a story that Grieg, on returning to Norway after one of his extremely tiring European concert tours, was to spend some days relaxing with Nina at the popular Stalheim Hotel between Voss and Gudvangen. From Voss they had to travel the last leg of the journey by horse-drawn carriage, and Grieg had invited the master fiddler Sjur Helgeland to accompany them. The journey passed with much music making and a good few drams, so the party arrived at the hotel in high spirits. As the hotel owner, Mrs Patterson, and her staff received the eminent guests at the front steps, she announced proudly that she had hired the services of a German trio to provide some highbrow entertainment. She asked Grieg what he thought of this ensemble, whereupon Grieg replied, 'Oh, that kind of thing is two a penny; but I have brought a first-rate fiddler with me today.' 'Oh yes, Sjur,' his hostess replied, visibly disappointed. Grieg and Sjur Helgeland went out onto the terrace, had a few drinks, and then Grieg asked Sjur to play again. Soon the other hotel guests joined them, and it is said that they sat there until the small hours.

It was folk dances of this sort that provided the material for what would prove to be Grieg's greatest piano work. Back in 1888 he had received a letter from the master fiddler Knut Johannessen Dahle (1834–1921) from Tinn in Telemark, who wrote that he had a huge repertoire of folk dances that he had '… carefully learned to play like the good old fiddlers Myllarguten, Haavard Gibøen and Hans Helaas (Hellos) from Bøe.' (Letter from Knut Dahle to Grieg, 8 April 1888)

Grieg was excited at the prospect and replied immediately that he was very keen to undertake a project of this sort. He invited Dahle to visit him at Troldhaugen if they could find a mutually convenient time. This proved difficult, so Grieg made plans to travel to Telemark with Frants Beyer, but their trip had to be cancelled at the last minute. Dahle then suggested that they meet

Knut Johannessen Dahle travelled to Oslo and stayed with Johan Halvorsen for two or three weeks, during which time the old slaatter (folk dances) from Myllarguten were passed on from Dahle to Halvorsen. He transcribed them, learned to play them and subsequently sent them to Grieg.

Knut Johannessen Dahle. (EGM)

Johan Halvorsen. (EGM)

Ole Bull. Illustration by A.B. Crosby. (BOB)

This picture of 'Myllarguten' hangs in the composer's hut at Troldhaugen. (EGM)

up in Oslo, provided that Grieg paid for his travelling and living expenses since, as he wrote, 'I am, as usual, short of money.' However, for some reason the project came to a standstill and it would be another twelve years before the two men made contact again. In the meantime Dahle had spent a few years in America, where he had made his living as a fiddler in the Midwest, but in 1900 he returned to Norway. On his return he contacted Grieg for a second time, telling him about his time in America, and he also told Grieg that some of the dances he had learned from Myllarguten in his youth had been transcribed there. But he was keen that Grieg, great composer as he was, should carry on this task. He felt that time was running out, for he was now an old man, and he feared that his music would be buried with him, especially since the younger generation had a different style of playing than that which he had been taught.

This time Grieg reacted without delay. No sooner had he received the letter from Dahle in October 1901 than he wrote to his friend, colleague and relation Johan Halvorsen (married to Annie, John Grieg's daughter) in Oslo. He was a fine violinist who Grieg felt sure would be capable of transcribing the small details in the

Torgeir Augundsson, known as
'Myllarguten'. (EGM)

Ole Bull. (EGM)

Advertisement for concert by 'Myllarguten' and Ole Bull in January 1849. When Ole Bull presented Torgeir Augundsson at their joint concerts in Oslo, it was as if a piece of rural Norway was being put on show. 'Myllarguten' fascinated the urban Oslo dwellers, who were deeply impressed by his playing. The applause was loud and long, but 'Myllarguten' was not used to this method of showing appreciation, so instead of bowing, he put down his fiddle and applauded with them.

dances that other people might miss. In his letter to Halvorsen, Grieg expressed his commitment to the preservation of traditional folk music, and he pointed out the necessity of using professional violinists when collecting the material. He could not resist thumbing his nose at the authorities at the end of his letter: *'Just imagine, if you did this, and if I then set the slaatter for piano, and if in this way we made them world-famous through Peters – right under the noses of our un-national National Parliament'.* Halvorsen replied at once, accepting the task, and asking Grieg to send Dahle to him immediately.

Dahle came, and he played and played – with the odd beer as refreshment in between dances – for fourteen days on end. Halvorsen and Dahle got on extremely well together, and in a letter to Grieg Dahle wrote, *'Halvorsen is a master violinist, I haven't heard his equal.'* Halvorsen was so enthusiastic after this visit that he concluded his letter to Grieg with the words: *'I should certainly get hold of Sjur Helgeland, Ole Moe and all the others now that I have begun with this.'* He had bought himself a Hardanger fiddle and was practising day and night to produce the right sounds and the right 'oomph' to his playing.

PREFACE

'These Norwegian "Slåtter" (Norwegian peasant dances) that for the first time are written down from the traditional Hardanger fiddle tunes given by an old fiddler from Telemark, and given a free transcription for the piano, I hereby give to the public. Those of you who have an affinity to folk tones will be taken by the originality, the mixture of pure beauty, bold power and untamed wildness both in melodies and rhythm. It is as if the music is from a bold and bizarre fantasy – reminiscences from a time where the Norwegian peasant culture in the mountain valleys was isolated from the world. It has kept both origin and originality. My object in arranging the music for the piano was to raise these works of the people to an artistic level, by giving them what I might call a style of musical concord, or bringing them under a system of harmony. Naturally, many of the little embellishments, characteristic of the peasant's fiddle and of their peculiar manner of bowing, cannot be reproduced on the piano and were accordingly omitted. On the other hand, by virtue of its manifold dynamic and rhythmic qualities, the piano affords the great advantage of enabling us to avoid a monotonous uniformity, by varying the harmony of repeated passages or parts. I have endeavoured to make myself clear in the lines set forth, in →

Grieg's preface in the printed edition of Norwegian Peasant Dances, *op. 72.* (BOB)

In the course of these two weeks Halvorsen transcribed seventeen dance tunes, and it was no mean early Christmas present Grieg received at the beginning of December 1901. On Saturday 6 December he wrote the following letter of thanks:

'*This is quite some Saturday night, dear Halvorsen. Outdoors there is raging a southerly gale that shakes the house, not to mention a veritable deluge pouring down from the heavens. But here in the house it is cosy and comfortable. I have just received your dance tunes and finished reading through them, and I am absolutely chortling with delight. But at the same time I am mad as hops about not being a violinist. How I hate that conservatory in Leipzig! But to the matter at hand: this "oddity" that you speak of with respect to the use of G# in D major was the thing that drove me out of my mind in 1871. Naturally I stole it at once for use in my Pictures from Folk Life. This phenomenon is something for the musicologist. The augmented fourth can also* be heard in the peasants' songs. It is a holdover from one old scale or another. But which?

'It is hard to believe that no one among us has taken an interest in the study of our national music when we have such rich sources in our folk music – for those who have ears to hear with, hearts to feel with, and the knowledge to transcribe them. At the moment it seems to me that it would be a sin to arrange the dance tunes for piano. But that sin I probably will commit sooner or later. It is too tempting.'

And commit it he did. In the autumn of 1902 he set to work on the task, and within six months he had completed *Norwegian Peasant Dances*, op. 72. Thanks to his status with Edition Peters in Leipzig he also managed to get them published. The Peters edition included a lengthy preface by Grieg, describing his work and something of his views on the politics of art, as well as the background stories to some of the dance tunes. It is interesting to note that Grieg dedicated *Norwegian Peasant Dances* to the German musicologist Hermann Kretzschmar.

One may ask whether these pieces are Hardanger fiddle dances arranged for piano. And was it right of Grieg to make use of this material? These questions have been debated ever since the publication of *Norwegian Peasant Dances*. A good number of musicians, fiddlers and musicologists are of the opinion that Grieg not only 'committed a sin', but that in doing so he also damaged the attempt to gain recognition for the status of folk music. For a start, some scholars and fiddlers believe that Halvorsen's transcriptions were far from true to Dahle's tradition. This is evidenced in the wax cylinder recordings made by Dahle, and in the performances of his grandsons Johannes and Gunnar, who learned to play from their grandfather. What's more, Grieg took some considerable liberties when adapting the dance tunes to the technical limitations and timbre of the piano. The composer and folk music expert Eivind Groven went so far as to say that when he heard Grieg's *Norwegian Peasant Dances* for the first time, he was left with the feeling that this was a parody of the music he knew from Telemark.

WAS IT EVER GRIEG'S INTENTION TO PRODUCE FOLK MUSIC?

Grieg said and wrote a great deal on the subject of his use of folk music, but in all these quotations he never claimed to have tried *writing* folk music – with the sole exception of *Solveig's Song* in

fact, to obtain a definite form. The few passages in which I considered myself authorised as an artist to add to, or work out, the given motives will easily be found, on comparing my arrangement with the original, written down by Johan Halvorsen, in a manner reliable even for research work, and published by the same firm. In spite of the fact that "Slåttene" will sound a little third higher on the Hardanger fiddle, I have – to get a fuller sound on the piano – kept the key like the original written version.' Edvard Grieg

Grieg's preface to Norwegian Peasant Dances.

'Naturally, many of the little embellishments, characteristic of the peasant's fiddle and of their peculiar manner of bowing, cannot be reproduced on the piano, and were accordingly omitted.' Edvard Grieg in the preface to the Peters edition of Norwegian Peasant Dances. (PHOTO: VIDAR LANDE)

The Australian pianist and composer Percy Grainger (1882–1961) was a source of great encouragement for Edvard Grieg in his later years. (EGM)

'And how Percy Grainger played several of them as arranged for piano! (*Norwegian Peasant Dances*, op. 72) There is no Norwegian pianist at the moment who can match him, and that is significant in more ways than one. It shows that we still do not have a Norwegian pianist who has enough understanding to tackle such challenges. It also shows that this can be found elsewhere – yes, even in Australia, where the marvellous Percy Grainger was born. In general, this harangue about having to be a Norwegian in order to understand Norwegian music, and especially to perform it, is sheer nonsense. Music that has staying power, in any case, be it ever so national, rises high above the merely national level. It is cosmopolitan.' (Edvard Grieg's diary)

'Myllarguten', Torgeir Augundsson (1801–1872). (EGM)

Peer Gynt. For Grieg the important thing was to build on the *authenticity* of folk music in his works. In this way he also hoped to help increase respect for Norwegian folk music at home and in Europe. He did this as a conscious contribution to the building of Norway as an independent nation. Therefore it was important for him to use this material in the medium in which he excelled, namely pieces for solo piano.

When Grieg performed six of his *Norwegian Peasant Dances* at a concert in Oslo in 1906, the response from the audience and the press was lukewarm. It grieved Grieg that *Norwegian Peasant Dances* had not struck home as he had expected. The audience and music critics were more interested in his early works. *'I hope that I can continue to develop as long as I live. That is my fondest wish. The understanding of the general public will come in due course.'* (*Diary entry, 21 March 1906*)

However, Grieg was vindicated just a few days later when he performed the same concert at cut-rate ticket prices in a missionary hall that seated 3000 people. *Norwegian Peasant Dances* was an unmitigated success!

'*In general: the attentiveness and understanding of this audience was much greater and more genuine.*' (*Diary entry, 27 March 1906*) Once again it was the 'man in the street' who showed the greatest enthusiasm for Grieg's music.

If we compare *Norwegian Peasant Dances* with for instance *Lyric Pieces*, we are struck by the radical difference between them. In *Norwegian Peasant Dances* we find an expression only occasionally glimpsed before, and technically *Norwegian Peasant Dances* is extremely demanding with numerous trills, ornamentations and rhythmic intricacies. There is also a dissonant use of harmony more typical of expressionism than romanticism.

Few Norwegian pianists performed this work in Grieg's day. However, the person who lit up Grieg's old age with his absolutely brilliant interpretation of *Norwegian Peasant Dances* was the young Australian pianist Percy Grainger. He represented all that Grieg hoped for and believed in, namely: youth. '*Indeed, if anyone can be said to be right, it is the younger generation. In fact, I would go so far as to say that it is only the younger generation that is right. So, if we wish to have any right to life, we must commit ourselves to feeling as the young do.*'

According to Johan Halvorsen a number of students in Paris 'discovered' *Norwegian Peasant Dances* around 1910, and this work was studied and played with great interest, for it was seen as representing '*le nouveau Grieg*'.

The Hungarian composer and musicologist Béla Bartók was in Paris at this time, and when he came across Grieg's *Norwegian Peasant Dances*, he was so enchanted that he decided there and then that he must travel to Norway to experience the country where this fantastic music came from. On the advice of the composer Frederick Delius (described by Grieg as 'Norway crazy'), Bartók set out on a four-week trip through Norway in 1912, right up to Lofoten in North Norway, where he heard traditional folk songs and dance tunes. He also purchased a Hardanger fiddle on his trip.

In his academic articles on the folk music of Hungary, Bartók also referred to Norwegian folk music, placing it within a wider European tradition. The Norwegian *slaatt* and Rumanian *joc* were mentioned as typical instrumental folk dances with characteristic short motifs that were repeated over and over.

The Anglo-German composer Frederick Delius (1862–1934) was allowed to pursue a career as a composer following Grieg's recommendation to Delius' father who was an industry magnate. Delius, whom Grieg described as 'Norway crazy', wrote a number of pieces associated with Norway and set texts by Bjørnson and Ibsen to music. (EGM)

Béla Bartók
(1881–1945).

Zoltan Kodaly
(1882–1967).

Grieg's use of folk music was a source of inspiration for Bartók in his own compositions. A great many of his works contain motifs and thematic material which he collected in his native country with Zoltan Kodaly. There is also a touching story from the latter part of Béla Bartók's life, after he had emigrated to the USA. One day in 1944 Bartók was visited by a fellow Hungarian, the conductor Antál Doráti. Bartók went into the kitchen to make a pot of tea, and while he was out of the room Doráti had a look at what was lying on Bartók's desk. Among other things he found an open score of Grieg's *Piano Concerto in A minor*. Grieg's romantic concerto is a far cry from Bartók's expressionistic style, and Doráti smiled a little to himself at finding Grieg on the desk, and he made some comment to this effect when Bartók came back in with the tea. Bartók replied earnestly that it was important to study Grieg, for it should always be remembered that '*Grieg was the first to cast off the yoke of Germany.*'

The direct and at times almost brutal style in many of the *Norwegian Peasant Dances* is somewhat reminiscent of the style Bartók 'invented' with his piano piece *Allegro Barbaro* (1911), known as *barbarism*. But in the midst of the uncompromising, coarse dance tunes there are also delicate, exquisite moods that point more in the direction of impressionism. As well as being a treasure trove for pianists, these pieces have been a source of inspiration to other composers throughout the twentieth century within classical music and jazz.

Opus 72 contains many different kinds of dances and several bridal marches. Of course, it is possible to dance to them, but most of them were probably originally intended as so-called *dances for an audience*, i.e. the concert repertoire of rural Norway at that time. The fiddlers were professional musicians, composers and artists.

Of the three bridal marches, *Myllarguten's Bridal March* is the most unusual, but the first bridal march in the opus is *Giboen's Bridal March*, no. 1. We follow the bridal procession as it approaches, passes right by us and continues on its way. This procession is portrayed in a light, playful tone, but there is a heavy undertone suggesting that all might not be as well as it seems.

In *Bridal March from Telemark*, no. 3 the mood is much lighter throughout, in the tones of the now well-known and much-loved bridal march from Seljord.

But when we get to *Myllarguten's Bridal March*, no. 8, we are left in no doubt that this is no ordinary bridal march. It sounds more

Edvard Grieg in his favourite surroundings. (BOB)

like a funeral march and that is really what it is. Myllarguten, a fiddler, had a sweetheart, Kari, who he had hoped to marry some day. However, a professional fiddler was constantly on the road and was therefore not regarded as a good match for a farm girl. So Kari was married off to another suitor. Myllarguten sat behind a rock in the graveyard of the church on the day of Kari's wedding,

Edvard Grieg photographed in 1905 by Nicola Perscheid in Leipzig. (BOB)

and played this pained march as the bridal party passed. It is a sorrowful bridal march in the major. This piece inspired Grieg on many levels and he created a magnificent tone poem out of it.

Two of the *hallings* (folk dances in 2/4 time), *Halling from the Fairy Hill* (no. 4) and *Røtnams-Knut. Halling* (no. 7) are unusual in that Grieg has added a quiet, contrasting middle section. He often used the ABA form in his compositions and here it helps develop the material into well-structured pieces.

Grieg also used *Røtnams-Knut* in his *Album for Male Voices*, op. 30 (no. 12). Røtnams-Knut, who came from Hallingdal, was a dreaded figure throughout his home county of Telemark. He would appear, whether invited or not, at all important occasions, be they weddings or funerals, and wherever he went, he always started fights. He was so strong and arrogant that there was no one capable of throwing him out. But one day a new priest arrived in the parish, and Røtnams-Knut's days as a troublemaker were numbered. The very next time he started a fight, the new incumbent grabbed him and threw him straight through the door – without stopping to open it first! Word has it that the hole in the door is still there to this day.

The work opens with *Gibøen's Bridal March*, followed by *John Vaestafae's Springar*. Grieg sets us spinning in this intense *springar* rhythm (3/4 time), and he sends the theme up and down the keyboard, high and low. The dance gets more and more intense, and we feel the dancers spinning until they drop. The other *springar* dances are not half as wild as this one, but they are incredibly richly ornamented, with complex harmonic bases. This is dance music to challenge and inspire the most quick-footed of dancers.

Myllarguten's Ganger (no. 6) builds up in a huge crescendo. From a thin filigree of trilling ornamentation this silver thread twists and twines until it becomes a thick, rich silver wire.

In *The Goblins' Bridal Procession at Vossevangen* (no. 14) Grieg paints a fairytale landscape before the bridal party approaches with confident strides. Here is an abundance of ceremony and pomposity, and a definite twinkle in the eye.

With *Norwegian Peasant Dances* Grieg took a bold, powerful step into the next century. This music was something quite new. It did not recall times gone by, rather it pointed forwards, both musically and in terms of music politics.

The debate about the 'sin' which Grieg did or did not commit is really a theoretical issue, quite separate from the work itself, for *Norwegian Peasant Dances*, op. 72 is first and foremost a work of art created for the piano for use in the concert hall. It represents the very best of its genre. Grieg was well aware that he would have to sacrifice many details and timbres present in the original material for Hardanger fiddle, but he also knew that he could raise these folk tunes 'to an artistic level' by structuring the material and giving it a fixed form. The whole of his genius and his will to 'elevate the people to art' were gathered in this inspired work.

Grieg and politics

(THG)

'And then, all the political party snobbery! No, the older I grow, I say to myself: not conservative, not liberal – but both. Not subjective, not objective – but both. Not realist, not idealist – but both. The one should mingle with the other and end up in a higher unity… But now farewell and to hell with all philosophy…!'
EDVARD GRIEG

GRIEG WAS A RADICAL and this coloured his political views all his life. During his first stay in Copenhagen in 1863–1864, he was one of the founders of the Euterpe music society (modelled on the society of the same name in Leipzig) in protest against professional music circles in Copenhagen. According to Euterpe's founders the self-important Music Association there, run by the established music scene and the bourgeoisie, never gave progressive young musicians a look in. The idea of Euterpe was to create an arena for new Nordic music, and the two Norwegians on the governing board were, of course, Grieg and Nordraak, alongside the Danes CF Emil Hornemann, Louis Hornbeck and Gottfred Matthison-Hansen. The society got off to a flying start and at its opening concert it was honoured by a prologue written by the ageing yet young-at-heart Hans Christian Andersen.

This brought Grieg to the attention of the Queen of Denmark, who invited the young Norwegian artist to an audience at the Royal Palace. At first Grieg was determined to refuse the invitation, for after all, he was an arch-republican! In the end he was persuaded to accept the invitation, but his attitude to monarchy, the nobility and all institutions of authority remained unchanged throughout his life. His comment that it was Bjørnson who made him a democrat may perhaps be taken to mean that it was through Bjørnson that he really learned to understand the political game and to use his radical powers within the political system in a democratic way. Grieg was particularly active politically in the period leading up to the dissolution of the Swedish–Norwegian Union, when he attempted through speeches and letters to use his position in Norway and abroad to persuade all the involved parties, particularly the major powers, to avoid escalation of the conflict.

'In a time, like ours, when nationality in all aspects is playing such an important role, it is easy to understand our efforts in developing the national element in language, in poetry and art. And even though there are efforts done along other lines, we are all striving for the same goal – the independence and development of our nation. Music is an arena for our struggle, too.'
EDVARD GRIEG

Edvard Grieg (1907). (BOB)

245

Edvard Hagerup Bull
(1855–1938). (BOB)

Edvard Hagerup Bull,
Edvard Grieg's first cousin,
was Minister of Justice in
the government of Chris-
tian Michelsen in 1905.
He was a lawyer, conservative politician and minister
– both as Minister of Justice
and Chancellor of the
Exchequer after 1905.

He even accompanied Fridtjof Nansen to Windsor on a mission to convince King Edward VII of England of the need to intervene and avoid the outbreak of war, and he sent the same message by telegram to Emperor Wilhelm II.

However, this was not the first time Grieg had taken a clear stance on political matters in Norway; he had long campaigned for the position of art and artists in Norwegian society. This led to a deep personal conflict with one of the members of the Norwegian parliament. Grieg and two other composers, Johan Svendsen and Iver Holter, had given their support to an application by the young, extremely talented composer Christian Sinding for a public annual grant for artists. Johannes Helleland, a member of parliament from Hardanger, strongly opposed this application (as he did anything that cost money). In a public debate in parliament he stated:

'We have received a recommendation of a composer, from one of our most highly regarded composers. This recommendation was, however, so hollow that it consisted of nothing but empty phrases, it was totally devoid of meaning.'

Grieg was furious and sent an indignant letter to Johannes Helleland which was published in the Norwegian newspaper *Verdens Gang*. He wrote that he could not go into the details of the case or argue one way or the other, but that he was determined to use the only channel available to him – the newspaper – to protest on behalf of himself and his fellow composers for the slur Helleland had cast on them.

'How are we to understand this? Do you really not realise that by your words you are throwing suspicion on and even deriding those men who have put their names to this application to the Norwegian Parliament? How dare you seriously assume that these men would bear unreliable testimony to their nation's parliament? What justification do you have for such an assumption? One thing is certain: your way of thinking does not belong in the legislative body of Norway. It is quite simply shameful. I, for my part, can take this accusation lightly, as can my fellow composers. Nonetheless it should be stressed publicly that you deserve much harsher words than these for the unacceptable manner in which you have attempted in our national parliament to cast a slur on the name of these men, whose life's work would unfortunately appear to be far beyond your powers of comprehension.' (Verdens Gang, 1 June 1891)

Over the next few years Grieg received frequent invitations from French impresarios, and Colonne tried several times to get him to come to Paris. Grieg would have liked to accept, but he felt uneasy at having no new orchestral works to present, and what's more, he was worried about the kinds of reaction that might come from the audience:

'Mr Henri Rochefort and several anonymous letter-writers have promised me a caning if I dare to set foot in Paris!' (Letter to Colonne, 22 September 1902)

Colonne replied:

'There is no reason for your anxiety. We started playing your beautiful music again ages ago, and I am certain that your return will be welcomed. And I repeat, my dear friend, you can come back without fear. The storm has passed, and France is now in the hands of reasonable people. There is still the odd mad dog running round barking, but they do not bite.' (Letter to Grieg, 25 September 1902)

Grieg allowed himself to be persuaded by these assurances, but when he arrived in Paris on 17 April 1903, he soon realised that the Dreyfus affair was by no means a thing of the past. Just a few weeks previously the socialist leader Jean Jaurés had tried to get Dreyfus's case reopened, in the hope of achieving a full acquittal. The conflict broke out in earnest once more, passions ran high and in the days leading up to Grieg's concert the newspapers were full of letters urging people to demonstrate against *'Grieg, the Dreyfus supporter'.* Colonne, who had promised to protect him, had suddenly disappeared to Spain. Grieg dared not leave his hotel room, and was accompanied to and from the concert hall by a police escort. A number of political demonstrators had gathered there, and Grieg was met with boos and jeers as he entered the podium. Once the most active demonstrators had been removed, Grieg conducted a successful concert that was warmly received by the audience, but the papers were ruthless in their criticism. The only newspaper to print an unbiased and positive critique was *Le Figaro*, whose reviewer was the composer Gabriel Fauré.

The Dreyfus case played a huge role in the development of the Third Republic and modern-day France. It accentuated the lines of demarcation between social and political fronts and led eventually to the separation of Church and state. The bitter oppositions lasted for more than a generation. Had Grieg fully understood how complex and politically inflamed the Dreyfus case

Impresario Édouard Judas Colonne (1838–1910) organised important concerts including at the Chatelét Theatre – the largest concert hall in Paris.
(EGM)

251

THE DREYFUS CASE

In June 1899 Grieg received a letter from the French musicologist Jules Combarieux asking him to respond to a series of questions of principles highly relevant to the Dreyfus case. In his reply of 22 June 1899 Grieg wrote: 'Nothing is easier for sound reason and the modern sense of justice than to answer your questions:

1. The problem, as the Dreyfus case makes evident in our day, is the eternal human one: Which power is stronger, the physical or the intellectual?

2. There is no case in which a man should be convicted without having been informed regarding all the motives on which the accusation is based.

3. Concern for the state can never have greater importance than the recognition of a person's innocence.

4. The honour of a professional group cannot be tarnished as the result of an error committed by one of its members.

5. There is no such thing as the honour of a professional group.

6. A court that condemned a man and later acknowledged his innocence would only gain in authority and respect.

7. A conflict may occur between a nation's intelligentsia and the raw power represented by the army – but such a conflict, fortunately, can be resolved.

8. It is above all science and art that ideally represent the people of one nation to those of another.'

Grieg's attack on the French authorities: 'How shall France survive since Edvard will not conduct there? Edvard Grieg and La France'. Caricature from the comic Vikingen, *1899.* (EGM)

was, he might perhaps have been a little more cautious. As he wrote to his publisher some time later:

'I ought to have remembered that discretion is the better part of valour.' (Letter to Max Abraham, 5 October 1899)

However, Grieg received heartfelt recognition from Georg Brandes, the great Danish critic and scholar, who wrote to Grieg:

'No Norwegian is better known or more greatly admired than you. My tribute to you is not simply for your art, of which there are more expert judges than me. On a purely human level you moved me by your honourable and bold conduct in the Dreyfus affair.' (Letter from Georg Brandes to Grieg, 30 June 1903)

The Dreyfus affair was not the first time Grieg concerned himself with international politics. On the death of Emperor Wilhelm I in 1888, Grieg recognised that there was a real possibility of revolution in Germany and he wrote to his friend Frants Beyer:

'The revolution against the great iron oppression will come in this country [...] but it will happen only when people cry out in despair, for it is unbelievable how servile and well-tamed the populace is.' (Letter to Frants Beyer, 21 March 1888)

Edvard Grieg and Arthur de Greef photographed in Bergen. de Greef was one of the finest pianists of his day, and he performed Grieg's Piano Concerto in A minor *all over Europe. They were close friends, de Greef commissioned the* Concerto no. 2 in B minor *from Grieg. Sadly this never got any further than a few rough sketches of ideas. de Greef was a leading figure in the music life in his native Belgium and taught at the Brussels Conservatory.* (EGM)

When riots and fighting broke out in Russia in the wake of Russia's attack on Japan and the internal turmoil, Grieg was outspoken in his refusal to visit this *'tyranny of the tsars'*. He felt ashamed that artists could talk of culture and civilisation while people were being slaughtered. The closing remark in a letter from Grieg to the impresario Alexander Siloti sums up the founding principle of Grieg's life and art:

'One must first be a human being. All true art grows out of that which is distinctively human.' (Letter to Alexander Siloti, 29 October 1904)

A letter to his Russian friend, the violinist Adolf Brodsky, shows Grieg's compassion for the Russian people:

'We Norwegians never kiss! But I would willingly make an exception for all the poor, persecuted Russian people. I wish I could place a bomb under the Russian government and administration, starting with the tsar! They are the worst criminals of our time!' (Letter to Adolf Brodsky, 26 April 1905)

'Revolution in Norway. The king is asked to abdicate' was the Swedish newspaper Afonbladet's reaction to Norway's secession from the union in 1905. 'Freedom is: the struggle for freedom!' wrote Edvard Grieg. (THG)

His participation in the social debate leading up to the dissolution of the Swedish–Norwegian Union in 1905 shows us his
analytical powers (see his letter to Aulin), his emotional involve-
ment (*'These damned Bernadottes! When the time comes I'll take
part in throwing them out!'*) and the fact that he was more than
capable of putting his views into action (his contact with King
Edward VII and Emperor Wilhelm II).

Grieg summed up his feelings about this struggle in his diary
on New Year's Eve 1905:

*'Now the year 1905 – the great year – goes to rest, and I part
from it with deep gratitude because I experienced it! And yet, without
the youthful dreams that this year has made real, my art would not
have had its proper background. The longings have transformed my
personal experiences into tones. Had the 7th of June come in my
youth, what would have happened? No, it is good that things happened as they did. The lifelong struggle has been the greatest good fortune both for the individual and for the nation. Freedom is: the struggle
for freedom!'*

'ONE MUST FIRST BE A HUMAN BEING'

Throughout his life Grieg demonstrated true brotherly love towards his fellow men, both in the way he treated his friends and in
his ability and willingness to fight against all injustice and tyranny.

There are countless examples of this aspect of Edvard Grieg's
character: he performed at charity concerts, and he frequently gave
financial support to people he knew and people he did not know,
usually in secret if at all possible. He was also quick to react to
cases of injustice towards others. This warm humanity came naturally to Grieg, and he seemed almost embarrassed when people
thanked him for his generosity. After helping his old friends, the
Matthison-Hansens in Copenhagen, with the gift of a fairly large
sum of money in 1904, he wrote a jovial, dismissive letter in which
he flatly denied being a benefactor:

*'Dear friend! I have done absolutely nothing for you. I have now
and then given myself pleasure. That is all. For that matter, I totally
disagree with Georg Brandes, who says that love is "to make another
happy!" Hell, no! Love is to make oneself happy. That is the big secret
that Christianity will not admit: that egoism lurks even within love –
insofar as it produces contentment and a feeling of happiness. For that
reason, however, egoism is also, ideally, a genuine article when it is*

expressed sincerely and not – like margarine!' (Letter to Gottfred Matthison-Hansen, 29 June 1904)

If he thought that people had been treated badly, he always came to their defence, and he was liberal with praise and encouragement of other artists and composers.

However, he also expected generosity and courtesy from others. There is an amusing anecdote dating from Copenhagen in 1903, related in the second volume of the Swedish composer Hugo Alfvén's autobiography, *Tempo Furioso*, where Alfvén paints a fairly sarcastic picture of Nina and Edvard Grieg:

'My next trip abroad was to Spain, and I left home at the end of February. I stopped over for a fortnight in Copenhagen at the home of Peder Severin and Marie Krøyer, where I also made the acquaintance of a number of their friends. A few days before I was due to set off for Spain, I decided to repay their hospitality by inviting them to a smart dinner at the Hotel Phenix. It turned out to be a lively party, but it very nearly cost me my trip to Spain. I had a fair amount of money with me to cover my travel expenses, and this was to be handsomely augmented by the fee I had been promised by the chief editor of Svenska Dagbladet, Helmer Key, for writing travelogues from Spain, at the princely rate of 100 Swedish kroner per letter. Although I knew I was (and still am, unfortunately) an appalling writer, I had been bold enough to agree to this plan. What won't people do for money?! I had funds enough to reach the Spanish border, but from there onwards I would have had to live extremely frugally had it not been for the income I had been promised for my travelogues. My goodness, how many of those I was planning on writing!

'Dinner at the Phenix had just begun, we were enjoying our smorgasbord and discussing what to order afterwards, when the door opened and Edvard Grieg and his wife entered the hotel dining room. They caught sight of us at once, and came over to say hello. I got to my feet and invited them to join us at our table. "With pleasure," Grieg replied, and they sat down.

'I must mention here that shortly before this, Krøyer had painted a portrait of the Griegs, in which Edvard is sitting at the piano accompanying Nina, who is standing by his side singing one of his songs with great gusto. The painting now hangs in the National Museum in Stockholm. Krøyer had made an etching of this picture, and presented me with a copy, complete with a personal inscription. Edvard and Nina had been so kind as to sign my etching when visiting the Krøyers a few days earlier, which of course increased the value of the picture enorm-

Hugo Emil Alfvén (1872–1960) drawn by Krøyer. (BOB)

Hugo Emil Alfvén, Swedish composer and conductor. In 1898 Alfvén was a guest for a fortnight at the home of Norwegian-born painter Peder Severin Krøyer and his wife Marie in Bergensgade in Copenhagen. As a token of his thanks for their hospitality the young Alfvén invited the Krøyers to a fancy dinner at Hotel Phenix. It should be mentioned that at this time Alfvén was having an affair with the much admired Marie Krøyer. In 1903 she left Krøyer to be with Alfvén, and they married in 1912 (Krøyer died in 1908). This marriage too was extremely stormy.

Peder Severin Krøyer
(1851–1909) and Marie
Triepcke Krøyer
(1867–1940).

Peder Severin Krøyer's portrait from 1898: 'Edvard Grieg accompanies his wife'.
(NATIONAL MUSEUM, STOCKHOLM)

ously. Here was the perfect opportunity to show my gratitude, so I asked if I could order them something.

"How very kind," Grieg said, and turned to his wife. "How about oysters and champagne, my dear?"

"That would be lovely," she replied, "but I would love a bit of Russian caviar with it. That's my absolute favourite."

"Same all round, then?" I asked the Krøyers. Søren nodded in agreement, while Maria sent me a troubled glance.

'So I ordered oysters, Russian caviar and champagne for all five of us. Not just once, but repeatedly, since Mr and Mrs Grieg were quite insatiable. Edvard downed oysters like an elephant gobbling up oats, it was really quite a feat for such a tiny man. And when it came to the caviar, Nina was quite his equal. As far as the champagne was concerned, I cannot really speak, for all five of us were equally thirsty. When we got to dessert, the ladies took the lead, while we men soon caught up with them in downing quantities of coffee, liqueur and cognac.

'As the evening progressed, I got more and more worried about the bill. My budget didn't stretch to a meal of this extravagance. The Spanish border was growing fainter by the minute, and when I got

The photographer Anders Beer Wilse took this photo of Nina and Edvard Grieg in the lounge of Westminster Hotel in Kristiania (Oslo). (EGM)

home to my room in Bergensgade and calculated what was left of my travel budget, it disappeared altogether. Once I had got to Spain I would be able to survive on the fees for my travelogues, but what help was that when I no longer had the means to get as far as the promised land? Dear Lord, how I hated that pair of little Norwegian trolls just then, with their oh so bloated stomachs that evening!'

After that fateful evening, Alfvén had no choice but to telegraph Helmer Key in Stockholm, asking to borrow money for his trip. The initial answer he got did nothing to allay his fears: *'I do not lend people money!'* but in the end Key agreed to Alfvén's request. Once Alfvén was assured of this loan, his opinion of the Griegs became a little less critical.

'The first time I met Edvard Grieg was in the autumn of 1906, when he and his wife, Nina, had arrived in Oslo on their way to Copenhagen, and they stayed at Westminster Hotel.

'It was a very wet and cold day, and they had obviously not started to turn the heating on in the hotel rooms. When I arrived on time, Edvard Grieg was walking to and fro in the lounge wearing his winter coat.

'He received me in a very gracious manner. When I had made myself ready in the lounge where the grand piano was placed, I was allowed to place Grieg in whichever positions I liked. He uttered no protestations, even though I understood he was not at his very best that day. I could see that he was freezing. I took some photos of him and his wife Nina sitting at the piano.

'Later I took more pictures of Grieg here at Westminster Hotel – they were like birds coming from Hardanger or Bergen, heading for a milder climate in the south'. (Anders Beer Wilse in his book *Norwegian Landscape*).

Dr. Ed. Grieg
i/s. Heim Troldhougen
am 25. Juli 07.

Hoenisch phot. 1907

One of the last pictures of Edvard Grieg, taken at Troldhaugen on 25 July 1907.
(EGM)

Four Psalms, opus 74

RETURN TO THE RELIGIOUS FASCINATION OF CHILDHOOD

EDVARD GRIEG'S DEEPEST theological discussions were with the Reverend Johann Andreas Budtz Christie (1842–1929), a priest whom Grieg met in his Hardanger period in the mid-1870s. At this time Grieg was facing a multitude of personal and artistic problems, and it is likely that his *'hard spiritual struggle'* also included religious doubt and torment. The dogmas of conservative Christianity felt like a straitjacket to him. He regarded Jesus not so much as the Son of God, but as a prophet who represented an ideal for independent, modern humanity, and he was far from comfortable with the idea of Jesus as saviour of the world or the awaited Christ, as taught by the Church.

In a letter to Christie on 30 January 1888 Grieg wrote: *'I believe in people, and I believe in God, and I still believe that the God who has created human beings has had something good in view for them. Otherwise I would not want to live for another moment …'*

Grieg's final work was *Four Psalms*, op. 74 for mixed chorus a cappella with baritone solo. This masterpiece, based on folk music and traditional Norwegian hymns, has a thoroughly groundbreaking, modern idiom. It was the first time that Grieg made use of religious texts and melodies to any great extent – a number of religious songs and folk tunes can be found in his earlier works, but *Four Psalms* is the first (and only) instance of the composer treating religious material systematically in a cyclical composition.

It would be wrong to say that Grieg was deeply concerned with religious matters, but at various points in his life we catch glimpses

The Revd Johan Andreas Budtz Christie (1842–1929) became Grieg's friend and confidant during his stay in Hardanger. They remained firm friends, and Christie was one of few priests whom Grieg ever trusted.
(EGM)

The plaque in Strandgaten 208.

'I could mention many small triumphs of those years that had a decisive influence on my imagination. For example, as a little boy I was allowed to watch funeral processions, to attend auctions and so on – so that afterwards, mind you, I might report all my impressions to my family. If I had been forbidden to do this, to follow my childish instincts, who knows whether my imagination might not have been shackled or turned in a direction from its true nature.'
(Edvard Grieg in My *First Success*)

'Opposite the school there lived a young lieutenant who was a passionate lover of music and a skilful pianist. I fled to him with my fledgling attempts at composition and he showed such interest in them that I always had to make copies for him. That was a success of which I was not a little proud ... I have often thought with gratitude of my friend, the lieutenant, who later advanced to the rank of general, and of the encouraging recognition that he accorded to my →

Strandgaten 152 (second building from the left) was Edvard Grieg's childhood home in Bergen. Strandgaten was the main street in Bergen, with narrow streets and alleys leading off it down to the sea. The actual building in which Edvard Grieg was born and spent his childhood was destroyed in an explosion in the harbour in April 1944, but it is still possible to find the position of the house, marked by a plaque at the current Strandgaten 208. (EGM)

of his thoughts on questions of faith. Despite being Grieg's last work, *Four Psalms*, op. 74 does not really represent any kind of conclusion of his output; indeed in many ways it points towards a new tonality, a new way of thinking and a new era.

CRITICAL OBSERVATION AND FASCINATION

As a child Edvard Grieg was deeply absorbed by religious matters and ceremonies. The adult world, with its rituals and gatherings, held a great attraction for him and his vivid imagination. For instance, he used to sneak into the auction houses of his hometown of Bergen, fascinated by the peculiar behaviour of the grownups there, the quick-tongued auctioneers, the atmosphere of the auction room and the unwritten rules of the game. Edvard often watched funeral processions making their way slowly along his street. The black mourning garb, black horses and black carriages with coffins draped in black material, complete with hired mourners, had a huge melancholy impact on him. These sombre pro-

first artistic efforts. That, to my boyish temperament, was a pleasant contrast to all the jabs and scoldings that I constantly experienced at school.'
(Edvard Grieg in My *First Success*)

On St Peter's Square Edvard Grieg watched Pope Pius IX being carried round under a canopy. (THG)

cessions held such a total fascination for him that he actively sought out funeral processions in other parts of the town too.

All these impressions on his sensitive nature found their outlet in the 'sermons' he preached to his parents as they dozed after dinner. Perhaps his long-suffering parents endured Edvard's earnest homilies in the secret hope that he might one day follow in the footsteps of many of his mother's family and enter the priesthood – a great many of Gesine Hagerup's relatives had been priests, including several who became bishops.

His fascination for such morbid things as funeral processions lasted beyond his childhood years. He wrote the following in his diary shortly before Christmas 1865 after witnessing a funeral procession in Rome: '*Powerful, gripping impression. The monks bellowed on two notes (interval of a sixth) with a strange effect.*'

Pope Pius IX.

An example of Grieg's thoughts on the Church, its practices and its spiritual leaders can be read in the diary of his stay in Rome in 1865–1866. On Christmas Day 1865 he attended mass at St Peter's Basilica and watched as Pope Pius IX was carried around under a canopy to bless the kneeling masses outside on St Peter's Square.

'*Strange impression to see the assembled crowd kneel as soon as the old, grey-haired and apparently world-weary man passed them. He looked pale and scarcely opened his eyes except when he shakily stretched out his arm, once to each side; then he also allowed his wan glance to scan the kneeling multitude. His facial expression was gentle and intelligent – indescribably attractive, actually, and of a sort to elicit a positive reaction. I can understand how one could learn to like him if one got*

'We have come to the end of the road with crescendo and fortissimo. Now we are playing our diminuendo; and a diminuendo can in fact be beautiful.'
EDVARD GRIEG

The last photographic portrait of Edvard Grieg was taken in Kiel in the spring of 1907. He had just finished a hectic series of concerts in Munich, Berlin and Kiel, and was about to return home to Troldhaugen for the summer. (EGM)

to know him – even if one did not applaud his biases.' (Diary entry, 25 December 1865)

Grieg regularly visited a number of churches during his stay in Italy, but mostly as a concertgoer or to study ecclesiastical art and architecture. He was overwhelmed by the opulence and sheer quantity of art, particularly in St Peter's Basilica and the Vatican. The following reflection is typical of Grieg:

'When one hears that this enormous church exists only for show, one cannot help asking the question: where in the world does all the money come from? For as everyone knows, the country is anything but rich! Ah yes, the people are coerced into paying this enormous church tax because that is pleasing to God! The terrible illusion that the worship of God consists of building majestic temples that can, indeed, be admired – but for the sake of which the people sigh in bondage and misery.' (Diary entry, 18 February 1866)

Grieg's relationship to the Church became increasingly strained as he grew older. He was extremely distrustful of, and rebellious towards, the power structure of the Church and its leaders. Grieg himself was an extremely anti-authoritarian person, and the dogmas and power seeking of the Church, together with the clergy's lack of knowledge and integrity, were like a red rag to a bull. As he wrote:

'It is my opinion that Carthage ought to be destroyed. And my Carthage is in fact the clergymen. I can't swallow them. I spew them up again and can never get rid of their repulsive, greasy and nauseating taste. They sprawl all over everything.' (Letter to Frants Beyer, 27 March 1902)

He wrote the following to Jonas Lie in 1897 about the Church's teaching, which at that time contained a hefty dose of pietism:

'I am now beginning to understand that we have only one enemy, but it is an implacable one which, as things unfortunately are, it is our inescapable duty to arm ourselves against. It is sad that all the money can't rather be used to enlighten the country so as to clear the air of that damned pietism that paralyses the common sense of the people. Pietism and the Swedes – let us take up arms and be on guard against both.' (Letter to Jonas Lie, 3 August 1897)

In a letter to Bjørnson he made this attack on the Church: 'All these clergymen who stifle every good aspiration among us! There is just one thing that we all should do: get out of the state Church, this lizard that in addition to its complete impotence has nothing but a poisonous stinger to sting with.' (Letter to Bjørnstjerne Bjørnson, 10 July 1897)

However, while Grieg was deeply unhappy with the practices of the Church, he was nevertheless concerned with theological and spiritual questions.

FAITH AND DOUBT

Both of Edvard Grieg's parents were devout Christians. Alexander Grieg's many letters to his son bear witness to his religious beliefs, through his exhortations and reflections. In 1869, for instance, after hearing about Nina and Edvard's well-received concert in Copenhagen, his letter of congratulations included the following reminder: *'I hope that you won't let yourselves be ensnared by all the praise that you have been receiving of late, but that you will both humbly give God the glory. For whatever we are able to accomplish comes from Him.'*

In later years, when Alexander Grieg's business hit hard times, he said that his faith comforted and sustained him and that he put his trust in the Lord.

At times Grieg's thoughts on religious matters crop up in his extensive correspondence. This was, of course, most notable at times of spiritual turmoil, for instance after the deaths of his parents, and a few years later when he found himself in an emotional tug-of-war between his burning desire for freedom as an artist on the one hand and the demands of love and fidelity on the other.

When Edvard and Nina Grieg's marriage nearly collapsed, Frants Beyer did his best to get his friend to reconsider. In July 1883 Grieg wrote to Beyer:

'In which cases shall individuality be opposed and in which shall it not? For we are hopefully in agreement that it neither can nor should always be opposed. Fighting against individuality is one of Christianity's basic principles that in our time has become a stock phrase of the clergy – and it leads straight to the devil, away from all truth and spiritual freedom [...] if I demand that each individual shall act according to what I consider right, and if I judge people's actions in accordance with this principle, then I am committing an injustice [...] that is medieval in origin and based on ignorance and narrow-mindedness.' (Letter to Frants Beyer, 29 July 1883)

It was Grieg's belief that no one had a universal right to define right and wrong as the Church had done for generations, imposing guilty consciences on people through its judgement. Everyone had the right to believe that something was wrong and to fight for that conviction, but no earthly being had the right to condemn a person to eternal damnation.

As usual he spoke most freely in his letters to Bjørnson:

'Whether one believes in God, Satan, Christ along with the Holy

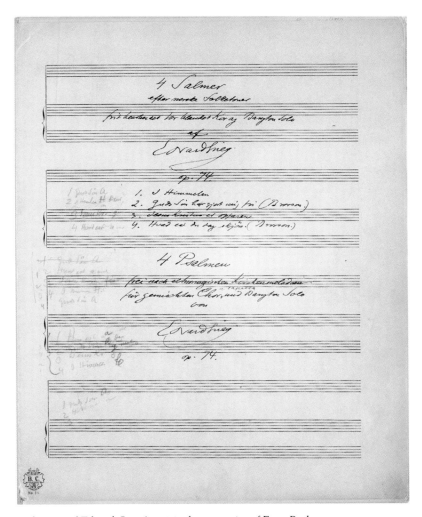

Title page of Edvard Grieg's original manuscript of Four Psalms. (BOB)

Ghost and the Virgin Mary, in Mohammed or in nothing, it is still the case [...] that the mystery of death cannot be explained away. It is this mystery which I have thought of finding a way of expressing. The Old Testament has, in both content and style, passages of absolutely dazzling fervour and power – the Psalms of David, for example – especially where they deal with the transitoriness of life. I am able to find less of what I am seeking regarding the complete abandonment to thoughts of death combined with a belief in universal love, whether or not there is a life after death. For the idea of "security at any price" does not interest me in the least. Atheists and dogmatic Christians are equally abhorrent to me.' (Letter to Bjørnstjerne Bjørnson, Christmas Day 1890)

Edvard Grieg's original manuscript of God's Son Hath Made Me Free. (BOB)

There was one occasion on which Grieg showed a particular interest in a religious movement. During a visit to Birmingham in 1888 he came across the Unitarian movement, and for the first time discovered an approach to Christianity which was very much in keeping with his own religious feelings, and which satisfied the demands of his keen intellect. The non-dogmatic Unitarian faith with its strong humanistic ideals was precisely in keeping with Grieg's own outlook. Another Norwegian, the author Kristofer Janson, whose poems Grieg set to music, taught for many years at Vonheim Folk High School in Gausdal, before emigrating to Minnesota where he became a Unitarian minister.

Grieg wrote an enthusiastic letter to Beyer after meeting Stop-ford Brooke, a former Anglican priest and leader of this movement.

'*A large, wonderful, radiant person, full of fire and strength. We talked about this and that: about the Unitarian faith and socialism, about Ibsen and Bjørnson, also a bit about politics [...] and I dare say that he felt exactly as I do about these things.*' (*Letter to Frants Beyer, 16 March 1888*)

Grieg remained a Unitarian for the rest of his life, as did his wife Nina and his closest friend Frants Beyer.

THE WORK

In the light of Grieg's religious stance and his attitude to dog-matic orthodox Christianity, his choice of texts and melodies for *Four Psalms* seems almost a little strange. The theology in *God's Son Hath Set Me Free* and *Jesus Christ Our Lord Is Risen* is a far cry from Grieg's personal ideas on divinity. Nevertheless, he – like many others – must have been spellbound by the beauty and richness of the Baroque poetry of Hans Adolf Brorson (nos. 1 and 2), Hans Thomissøn (no. 3) and Laurentius Laurentii Laurinus (no. 4) and the religious folk tunes that twist and coil around these texts like gorgeous garlands and decorations.

This combination triggered an impressive spate of creativity, particularly given Grieg's advanced age and poor health. Admit-tedly, he had experienced a huge surge of creative output when he received the folk tunes from Johan Halvorsen on which he based his *Norwegian Peasant Dances*, op. 72, but due to his ever-declining health, neither he himself nor anyone else really expected him to produce any more works on a larger scale.

However, in the summer of 1906 he turned once again to good old Lindeman. He completely fell for Lindeman's hymn tunes. To start with he played with the idea of adding to the *Album for Male Voices*, op. 30, but this time he wanted to compose for mixed choir and baritone soloist.

He composed three of the psalms at Troldhaugen that summer, and the fourth, *How Fair is Thy Face*, was completed at the Hotel Westminster in Oslo that autumn. He placed this indescribably beautiful piece – his very last composition ever – at the opening of the set of four.

Four Psalms bears witness once more to Grieg's genius in his treatment of folk tunes; his ability to extend the melodic, harmo-

Berlin, April 1907: Edvard Grieg visits Pianola-Haus Berlin, Leipziger Strasse 110, and listens to the pianola recordings he made in Leipzig on 11 April 1906.
(EGM)

nic and rhythmic arches produced a power and sincerity of expression to be found only in true masterpieces.

As in *Norwegian Peasant Dances*, op. 72, Grieg's rhythmic, harmonic and dynamic treatment are extremely radical in this work. For instance in *God's Son Hath Set Me Free* he employs bitonality between the soloist and the choir. In the middle section the soloist sings in B flat major while the choir sings in B flat minor, and we feel the struggle of the forces of light against the forces of darkness

– '*Dazu ward ich erkauft zu schwer, der Sünde Glückspiel lockt nicht mehr*'.

This of course creates the desired harmonic tension. The piece concludes in victorious unanimity in B flat – '*Mein Herze in mir lacht, schau ich des Grabes Nacht*'. The harmonic and dynamic variations in this piece make it one of Grieg's most modern works, combining Brorson's colourful Baroque text with his own incredibly expressive music.

The first piece, *How Fair is Thy Face*, is a fine example of the constant shifting from major to minor of which Grieg was so fond. The choir and soloist sing antiphonally (verse and response form) and the soloist's short phrases are accompanied by a colourful harmonic base in the choir. After three verses, the first verse returns and is expanded on dynamically and harmonically. The choir reaches a dramatic peak at the words '*Du allerlieblichster Gottessohn*' before gliding back to support the soloist once more. The accompanying chord at this point is in the major, but this time the soloist's phrase is in a melancholy minor. The piece finishes with yet another harmonic and dynamic swell, and we are led to the conclusion at '*All mein Eigen das ist auf ewig dein*' on an ambiguous harmonic base, scarcely knowing whether to expect a major or minor chord at the end.

The third piece, *Jesus Christ Our Lord Is Risen*, is also antiphonal. It has a very liturgical air, not least due to the repeated response-like *Kyrie eleison* (Lord, have mercy). As David Monrad Johansen, a fellow Grieg specialist, put it, it is as though Grieg '*… took this beautiful folk tune from rural Norway and placed it in a magnificent Gothic cathedral*'.

In the fourth piece, *In Heav'n Above*, Grieg's luxuriant harmonies blend with the text's praise of the glory of heaven to create an exquisite hymn.

In each of the *Four Psalms* Grieg allows the text to shape the musical form, giving the work a feeling of naturalness (it is very idiomatically written), despite the archaic language. The same is true of the challenges of dynamic and vocal range, independence between the different voices and musical expression. It is steeped in naturalness – just as it should be!

Grieg's style in *Four Psalms* is modern and challenging, but nevertheless typically Grieg. This work is a fantastic example of his creativity and his ability never to look backwards, but always forwards.

His last summer: Edvard and Nina Grieg at Troldhaugen in 1907. (BOB)

The legacy of Grieg's music and personality is greatly to be respected. If we look and listen carefully, they may help us map out our way forward, whether we follow in the same direction as him, or whether we choose to break out in a new direction. The important thing is that we make conscious choices. In writing this book I have had to make many choices as to what to include when it comes to Grieg's music, his personality and the times in which he lived, so in many ways this book says a lot about me too. That is as it may be. I have set out to present *my* Grieg, and my hope is that this book may inspire its readers to discover *their* Grieg.

Edvard Grieg seen from a French point of view. The French music journal Musica *printed this caricature in September 1904 – Edvard Grieg with his characteristic hair and melancholic eyes.* (EGM)

Notes

1   Grieg Complete Songs, Edition Peters, translated by WH Halverson.
2   Translation by Diane Oatley, published at www.ibsen.net
3   Quotations from Ibsen's Peer Gynt are from the Oxford World's Classics edition, translated by C Fry and J Fillinger.
4   Grieg Complete Songs, Edition Peters, translated by WH Halverson.
5   Grieg Complete Songs, Edition Peters, translated by WH Halverson.
6   Source: Festschrift for birthday in 1907.
7   Translation by Beryl Foster, published in Bergljot: A forgotten masterpiece.
8   Grieg Complete Songs, Edition Peters, translated by WH Halverson.
9   Grieg Complete Songs, Edition Peters, translated by WH Halverson.
10 Grieg Complete Songs, Edition Peters, translated by WH Halverson.
11 Grieg Complete Songs, Edition Peters, translated by RK Stang.
12 Grieg Complete Songs, Edition Peters, translated by RK Stang.
13 Grieg Complete Songs, Edition Peters, translated by RK Stang.
14 Grieg Complete Songs, Edition Peters, translated by RK Stang.

Index of names

Index of compositions and works

Bibliography

Andersen, Rune J. Edvard Grieg. Oslo: Cappelen. 1993

Asafjev, Boris. Grieg. Oslo: Solum, 1992

Bakke, Reidar. Grieg og Sibelius. Trondheim: Tapir, 2006

Bartók, Béla. The Folklore of Instrumental Music in Hungary. Budapest: Zene-közlöny, 1911

Benestad, Finn. Edvard Grieg. Oslo: Uten-riksdepartementet, 1991

Benestad, Finn and Bjarne Kortsen (ed). Brev til Frants Beyer 1872–1907. Oslo Universitetsforlaget, 1993

Benestad, Finn and Dag Schelderup-Ebbe. Edvard Grieg: Chamber music. Oslo Scandinavian University Press, 1993

Benestad, Finn and Dag Schelderup-Ebbe. Edvard Grieg: Mennesket og kunst-neren. Oslo: Aschehoug, 1980.

Benestad, Finn and Dag Schelderup-Ebbe. Johan Svendsen: Mennesket og kunst-neren. Oslo: Aschehoug,1990

Benestad, Finn. Brev i utvalg 1862–1907. Oslo: Aschehoug, 1998

Benestad, Finn and Halverson, William H. Edvard Grieg. Letters to Colleagues and Friends. Colombus, Ohio: Peer Gynt Press, 2000

Bengtson, Ingmar. Musikvetenskap. Oslo: Universitetforlaget, 1973

Bergen Public Library, Edvard Grieg Archives. Manuscripts, letters, photos, Griegiana, etc. http://www.bergen.folkebibl.no/grieg-samlingen/engelsk/grieg_intro_eng.html

Bergen Public Library: Newspaper cuttings: Edvard Grieg's 60th birthday, 15 June 1903. Edvard Grieg's death, 4 September 1907. Unveiling of Grieg statue in centre of Bergen,1917. Centenary of Edvard Grieg's birth, 1943.

Beyer, Marie (ed). Brev fra Edvard Grieg til Frants Beyer 1872–1907. Kristiania Steenske forlag, 1923

Bjørndal, Arne. Edvard Grieg og folke-musikken. Bergen 1951

Bredal, Dag. Edvard Grieg. Oslo: Aventura, 1992

Brock, Hella. Edvard Grieg. Eine Biographie. Zürich: Atlantis Musikbuchver-lag, 1998

Brodsky, Anna. Recollections of a Russian Home. London,1904

Bøe, Finn. Trekk av Edvard Griegs person-lighet. Oslo: Grundt Tanum, 1949

Carley, Lionel. Edvard Grieg in England. London: Boydell&Brewer Ltd, 2006

Carley, Lionel. Grieg and Delius. London, 1993

Caron, Jean-Luc. Edvard Grieg et Paris. Brou-sur-Chantereine: AFCN, 1994

Cederblad, Johanne Grieg. Edvard Grieg. Stockholm: Lindfors bokförlag, 1946

Cederblad, Johanne Grieg. Sangen om Norge. Oslo: Gyldendal, 1948

Cherbuliez, Antoine Elisée. Edvard Grieg. Zürich: Albert Müller Verlag, cop. 1947

Closson, Ernest. Edvard Grieg et la musique Scandinave. Paris: Fischbacher, 1892

Cooke, James Francis. Edvard Hagerup Grieg. Philadelphia: Presser, cop. 1928

Cuypers, Jules. Edvard Grieg. Haarlem: Gottmer, cop. 1948

Dahl, Erling jr. Troldhaugen. En veiviser til Edvard Griegs hjem. Bergen: EGM, Troldhaugen, 1996

Dahl, Erling jr. Edvard Grieg. Kort biografi. Bergen: EGM Troldhaugen, 2001

Dahl, Erling jr. and Tønnes H. Gundersen. Edvard Grieg. Portrettene. Bergen: EGM, Troldhaugen, 1996

Dahl, Erling jr. and Monica Jangaard (ed). Edvard Grieg art and identity (Norwegian/German/French/English) Bergen: EGM, Troldhaugen, 2000

Dahl, Per. Jeg elsker deg på 252 måter. Oslo: Solum forlag, 1993

Dahl, Per. Jeg elsker deg. Lytterens alternativ. Stavanger: PhD dissertation University of Stavanger, 2006

Deucher, Sybil. Edvard Grieg. London: Faber and Faber, 1950

Edvard Grieg Museum, Troldhaugen. www.troldhaugen.no

Eikenes, Eivind AC. Edvard Grieg fra dag til dag. Stavanger: Eikenes, 2007

Fett, Tryggve. Edvard Grieg mellom Bjørnstjerne Bjørnson og Henrik Ibsen.

Gamle Bergen, 1993

Finck, Henry Theophilus. Edvard Grieg. New York; London: John Lane Company; John Lane, The Bodley Head, 1906

Finck, Henry Theophilus. Grieg and his music. New York, 1929

Flaten, Trine Kolderup (ed). Grieg, Edvard Dagbøker. Bergen: Bergen Public Library, cop 1993

Fosheim, Minken. Eventyret om Grieg. Oslo: Cappelen, 1998

Foster, Beryl. The songs of Edvard Grieg. Aldershot: Scolar Press, 2007

Gaukstad, Øystein (ed). Edvard Grieg. Artikler og taler. Oslo, 1957

Grieg, Edvard. Artikler og taler. Oslo: Gyldendal, 1957

Grieg, Edvard. Brev i utvalg Bind I og II. Til norske mottagere. Oslo: Aschehoug, 1998

Grieg, Edvard. Grieg and Delius. London: Marion Boyars, 1993

Grieg Anniversary 1993 Catalogue. Bergen: Grieg Anniversary 1993

Grieg Anniversary 1993 (ed). «Lillegrieg». Bergen: Grieg Anniversary 1993

Grinde, Niels. Norsk musikkhistorie. Oslo, 1971

Gundersen, Tønnes H. Edvard Grieg – Art and Identity. Katalog til utstilling. EGM, Troldhaugen, 2002

Herresthal, Harald. Edvard Grieg med venner og uvenner. Bergen: EGM, Troldhaugen, cop. 1997

Herresthal, Harald. Grieg et Paris. Caen: Presses Universitaires de Caen, cop. 1996

Herresthal, Harald. Med spark i gulvet og quinter i bassen. Oslo Universitetsforlaget, 1923

Horton, John. Edvard Grieg. Oslo: Dreyer, 1978

Hurum, Hans Jørgen. Edvard Grieg. Schools edition. Bergen: J W Eides boktrykkeri, 1953

Hurum, Hans Jørgen. I Edvard Griegs verden. Oslo: Gyldendal, 1959

Hurum, Hans Jørgen. Vennskap. Oslo: Grøndahl, cop. 1989

Haavet, Elisabeth. Nina Grieg. Oslo: Aschehoug, 1998

Jangaard, Monica (ed). Bergen og Troldhaugen. Møteplasser og impulser. Bergen: EGM, Troldhaugen, 2003

Jangaard, Monica (ed). Edvard Grieg i kulturbyen. Bergen: EGM, Troldhaugen, 2000

Johannessen, Karen Falch. Edvard Grieg. Oslo: Biblioteksentralen, 1993

Johansen, David Monrad. Edvard Grieg. Oslo: Gyldendal, 1934

Jordan, Sverre. Edvard Grieg. Bergen: Eide, 1954

Kayser, Audun. Edvard Grieg. Bergen: John Grieg, cop. 1992

Kayser, Audun. Troldhaugen. Bergen: John Grieg, 1980

Kayser, Audun. Edvard Grieg. I ord og toner. Bergen: Eide forlag, 1992

Kortsen, Bjarne (ed). Grieg, Edvard Grieg the writer Volume I. Essays and articles. Bergen, 1972

Kortsen, Bjarne (ed). Grieg, Edvard Grieg the writer Volume II. Letters to Frants Beyer. Bergen, 1972

Lawford, Irene. Edvard Grieg and his publishers, Max Abraham and Henri Hinrichsen. London: Peters, cop. 1997

Layton, Robert Grieg. London: Omnibus, 1998

Løtveit, Eilif B (ed). Edvard Grieg og 1905. Bergen: EGM, Troldhaugen, 2005

Møller, Arvis. Gjendine. Oslo: Cappelens forlag, 1976

Nagelhus, Lorents Aage. Edvard Grieg og folkemusikken. Oslo: Norsk musikforlag, 2004

Norsk musikksamling (ed). Det var dog en herlig tid, trods alt. Oslo: Norsk musikksamling, Universitetsbiblioteket, 1993

Odéen, Kristi Østtveit. Følg frosken! Bergen: Bergen kommune, Edvard Grieg Museum Troldhaugen together with Barnas Hus, 1998.

Oelmann, Klaus Henning. Edvard Grieg. Engelsbach; Cologne; New York: Hänsel-Hohenhausen, 1993.

Paulsen, John. Min første sommer i København o.a. erindringer. Oslo: Gyldendal, 1908

Reznicek, Ladislav. Edvard Grieg og tsjekkisk kultur. Oslo: Biblioscandia, 1975.

Röntgen, Julius. Julius Röntgen og Edvard Grieg. Bergen: Alma Mater, cop. 1994.

Schjelderup, Gerhard. Edvard Grieg. Leipzig: CF Peters, 1908.

Skyllstad, Kjell. Grieg's forbidden symphony. Studia Musicologica Norvegica no.19, 1993

Solås, Eyvind. Ensom vandrer. Oslo: Aschehoug, 1993.

Staveland, Hanna de Vries. Julius Röntgen og Edvard Grieg: Et musikalsk vennskap. Bergen, 1994

Storaas, Reidar. Edvard Grieg. Bergen: Bergens Tidende, 1993.

Storaas, Reidar. Edvard Grieg i Hardanger. Ullensvang herad, 1993.

Storaas, Reidar. Fest og spill i 35 år. Bergen: Eides forlag, 1987

Thompson, Wendy. Edvard Grieg. Watford: Exley, 1995.

Torsteinson, Sigmund. Femti år med Troldhaugen. Oslo, 1971

Torsteinson, Sigmund. Troldhaugen. Nina og Edvard Griegs hjem. Oslo: Gyldendal, 1959/1962

Volden, Torstein. Studier i Edvard Griegs Haugtussanger. Oslo: University of Oslo, dissertation, 1967

Wenzel Andreasen, Mogens. Grieg og Danmark. Copenhagen: Engstrøm & Sødring, 1993

Olaf Gulbransson's drawing of Edvard Grieg made for the German satirical journal Simplicissimus *(no. 2, 1905/06).*

(EGM)

Opus list

FOUR PIANO PIECES, OP. 1 (1861–1863)
1. Allegro con leggerezza
2. Non Allegro e molto espressivo
3. Mazurka
4. Allegretto con moto

FOUR SONGS OP. 2 FOR ALTO VOICE
PIANO. (1861)
1. Die Müllerin (Chamisso)
2. Eingehüllt in graue Wolken (Heine)
3. Ich stand in dunkeln Träumen (Heine)
4. Was soll ich sagen (Chamisso)

POETIC TONE PICTURES, OP. 3
FOR PIANO. (1863)
1. Allegro ma non troppo
2. Allegro cantabile
3. Con moto
4. Andante con sentimento
5. Allegro moderato
6. Allegro scherzando

SIX SONGS, OP. 4 FOR ALTO VOICE
AND PIANO. (1863–64)
1. Die Waise (Chamisso)
2. Morgenthau (Chamisso)
3. Abschied (Heine)
4. Jägerlied (Uhland)

5. Das alte Lied (Heine)
6. Wo sind sie hin? (Heine)

MELODIES OF THE HEART, OP. 5
FOR VOICE AND PIANO. (1864–65)
(H. C. ANDERSEN)
1. Two Brown eyes
2. The Poet's Heart
3. I Love But Thee
4. My Mind Is Like a Mountain Steep

HUMORESQUES, OP. 6 FOR PIANO.
(1865)
1. Tempo di Valse
2. Tempo di Menuetto ed energico
3. Allegretto con grazia
4. Allegro alla burla

PIANO SONATA IN E-MINOR, OP. 7
(1865)
1. Movement: Allegro moderato
2. Movement: Andante molto
3. Movement: Alla Menuetto, ma poco
   più lento
4. Movement: Finale. Molto allegro

VIOLIN SONATA NR. 1 IN F-MAJOR,
OP. 8. (1865)
1. Movement: Allegro con brio
2. Movement: Allegretto quasi andantino
3. Movement: Allegro molto vivace

SONGS AND BALLADS OP. 9.
FOR VOICE AND PIANO (1863–66)
(ANDREAS MUNCH)
1. The Harp
2. Cradle Song
3. Sunset
4. Outward Bound

FOUR SONGS, OP. 10 FOR VOICE AND
PIANO. (1864–66) (CHR. WINTHER)
1. Thanks
2. Woodland Song
3. Song of the Flowers
4. Song on the Mountain

IN AUTUMN, OP. 11.
A Fantasy for piano four hands. (1866).
Orchestrated in 1887.

LYRIC PIECES I, OP. 12. (1865–67)
1. Arietta
2. Waltz
3. Watchman's Song
4. Fairy Dance
5. Folk Song
6. Norwegian
7. Album Leaf
8. National Song

VIOLIN SONATA NR. 2 IN G-MAJOR, OP. 13
(1867)
1. Movement: Lento doloroso – Allegro
   Vivace
2. Movement: Allegretto tranquillo
3. Movement: Allegro animato

TWO SYMPHONIC PIECES, OP. 14.
ARRANGEMENT FOR PIANO FOUR HANDS.
(1864) (2. OG 3. MOVEMENT FROM
SYMPHONY IN C MINOR.)
1. Adagio cantabile
2. Allegro energico

FOUR SONGS, OP. 15 FOR VOICE
AND PIANO. (1864–68)
1. Margaret's Cradle Song. (Ibsen)
2. Love (H.C. Andersen)
3. Folk song from Langeland
   (H.C. Andersen)
4. A Mother s Grief (Chr. Richardt)

PIANO CONCERTO IN A-MINOR, OP. 16.
(1868)
1. Movement: Allegro molto moderato
2. Movement: Adagio
3. Movement: Allegro moderato molto e
   marcato

25 NORWEGIAN FOLK SONGS AND
DANCES.(«ARRANGED FOR PIANO»),
OP. 17. (1869) FR L.M. LINDEMAN'S
COLLECTION
1. Springar
2. The Swain
3. Springar
4. Nils Tallefjorden
5. Dance from Jølster
6. Wedding Tune
7. Halling
8. The Pig
9. Religious Song
10. The Wooer's Song
11. Heroic Ballad
12. Solfager and the Snake King
13. Wedding March

14. I Sing with a Sorrowful Heart
15. Last Saturday Evening
16. I Know a Little Maiden
17. The Gadfly and the Fly
18. Peasant Dance
19. Hølje Dale
20. Halling
21. The Woman from Setesdal
22. Cow Call
23. Peasant Song
24. Wedding Tune
25. The Raven's Wedding

NINE SONGS, OP. 18 FOR MEZZO-
SOPRANO AND PIANO (1865–69)
1. Moonlit Forest (H.C. Andersen)
2. My Darling is as White as Snow
   (H.C. Andersen)
3. The Poet s Farewell (H.C. Andersen)
4. Autumn Storms (Chr. Richardt)
5. Poesy (H.C. Andersen)
6. The Young Birch-Tree (Jørgen Moe)
7. The Cottage (H.C. Andersen)
8. The Rosebud (H.C. Andersen)
9. Serenade for Welhaven (Bjørnson)

PICTURES FROM FOLK LIFE, OP. 19
FOR PIANO. (1869–71)
1. In the Mountain
2. Bridal Procession
3. From the Carnival

BEFORE A SOUTHERN CONVENT, OP. 20.
(1871) TO PIECES FROM BJØRNSON'S
«ARNLJOT GELLINE»
1. Who Knocks So Late at the Cloister
   Door? (For soprano- and alto voices and
   orchestra)
2. From Guilt, from Sin, to God Come In.
   (For 4 part female voices and orchestra)

FOUR SONGS FROM «FISKERJENTEN» BY
BJØRNSON, OP. 21 FOR VOICE AND PIANO
1. The First Meeting
2. Good Morning!
3. To Springtime my Song I'm singing
4. Say What You Will

SIGURD JORSALFAR, OP. 22. INCIDENTAL
MUSIC TO BJØRNSON'S DRAMA. (1872)
1. Introduction.
2. Borghild's Dream
3. At the Matching Game
4. Northland Folk
5. Homage March
6. Interlude I
7. Interlude II.
8. The King's Song

PEER GYNT, OP. 23. INCIDENTAL MUSIC
TO IBSEN'S DRAMA. (1874–75)
1. Introduction and At the Wedding
2. Bridal Procession
3. Halling and springar
4. The Abduction of the Bride.
   Ingrid's Lament.
5. Peer Gynt and the Herd Girls
6. Peer Gynt and the Woman in Green
7. In the Hall of the Mountain King
8. Dance of the Mountain King's
   Daughter
9. Peer Gynt Hunted by the Trolls
   Peer Gynt and the Bøyg
10. Deep in the Forest
11. Solveig's Song
12. The Death of Mother Aase
13. Interlude. Morning Mood
14. The Thief and the Receiver
15. Arabic Dance
16. Anitra's Dance
17. Peer Gynt's serenade

18. Solveig's Song
19. Interlude. Peer Gynt's Homecoming
20. Solveig Singing.
21. Night Scene.
22. Whitsun Hymn
23. Solveig's Cradle Song

BALLADE I G-MINOR, OP. 24. (1875–76)
(BALLADE IN THE FORM OF VARIATIONS
ON A NORWEGIAN MELODY FROM
L.M. LINDEMAN'S COLLECTION)

SIX SONGS, OP. 25 FOR VOICE AND
PIANO. (1876) (HENRIK IBSEN)
1. Fiddlers
2. A Swan
3. Album Lines
4. With a Water Lily
5. Departed!
6. A Bird-Song

FIVE SONGS OP. 26 FOR VOICE AND
PIANO. (1876) (JOHN PAULSEN)
1. Hope
2. I Walked One Balmy Summer Eve
3. You Whispered That You Loved Me
4. The First Primrose
5. Autumn Thoughts

STRING QUARTET NR. 1 IN G-MINOR,
OP. 27. (1877–78)
1. Movement: Un poco Andante – Allegro
   molto ed agitato
2. Movement: Romanze: Andantino
3. Movement: Intermezzo: Allegro molto
   marcato
4. Movement: Finale. Lento – Presto al
   Saltarello

ALBUM LEAVES , OP. 28 FOR PIANO.
(1864– 78)
1. Allegro con moto
2. Allegretto espressivo
3. Vivace
4. Andantino serioso

IMPROVISATIONS ON TWO NORWEGIAN
FOLK SONGS, OP. 29 FOR KLAVER. (1878)
1. Andante
2. Allegretto con moto

ALBUM FOR MALE VOICES, OP. 30.
(1877–78) ARRANGEMENTS FOR SOLI
OG MALE CHORUS. FROM L.M.
LINDEMAN'S COLLECTION.
1. I Lay Down So Late
2. Children's Song
3. LittleTorö
4. Halling
5. It is the Greatest Foolishness
6. Springar
7. Young Ole
8. Halling
9. Fairest Amng Women
10. The Great White Host
11. The Gypsy Lad
12. Røtnams-Knut

LAND SIGHTING, OP. 31 FOR BARYTONE,
MALE CHORUS AND ORCHESTRA. (1872)
(BJØRNSTJERNE BJØRNSON)

THE MOUNTAIN THRALL, OP. 32 FOR
BARYTONE, STRING ORCHESTRA AND
TWO HORNS. (1877–78)

TWELVE SONGS TO POEMS BY
A.O.VINJE,
OP. 33 FOR VOICE AND PIANO (1873–80)
1. The Youth

2. Last Spring
3. The Wounded Heart
4. The Berry
5. Beside the Stream
6. A Vision
7. The Old Mother
8. The First Thing
9. At Rondane
10. A Piece on Friendship
11. Faith
12. The Goal

TWO ELEGIAC MELODIES, OP. 34.
TWO VINJE-SONGS INSTRUMENTATED
FOR STRING ORCHESTRA. (1880)
1. The Wounded Heart
2. Last Spring

NORWEGIAN DANCES, OP. 35
FOR PIANO FOUR HANDS (1880)
1. Allegro marcato
2. Allegretto tranquillo e grazioso
3. Allegro moderato alla marcia
4. Allegro molto- presto e con brio

CELLO SONATA IN A-MINOR, OP. 36.
(1882–83)
1. Allegro agitato
2. Andante molto tranquillo
3. Allegro. Allegro molto e marcato

WALTZ CAPRICES, OP. 37
FOR PIANO FOUR HANDS (1883)
1. Tempo di Valse moderato
2. Tempo di Valse

LYRIC PIECES II, OP. 38
FOR PIANO. (1883)
1. Berceuse
2. Folk Song
3. Melody

4. Halling
5. Springar
6. Elegy
7. Waltz
8. Canon

SIX SONGS (OLDER AND NEWER), OP. 39
FOR VOICE AND PIANO (1869–84)
1. From Monte Pincio (Bjørnson)
2. Hidden Love (Bjørnson)
3. Upon a Grassy Hillside (Jonas Lie)
4. Among Roses (Kristofer Janson)
5. At the Grave of a Young Wife
   (O.P. Monrad)
6. Hearing a Song (N. Rolfsen)

HOLBERG SUITE, OP. 40 FOR PIANO.
(1884) FOR STRING ORCHESTRA (1885)
1. Preludium
2. Sarabande
3. Gavotte
4. Air
5. Rigaudon

TRANSCRIPTIONS OF ORIGINAL SONGS I,
OP. 41. (1884)
1. Cradle Song (op. 9, nr. 2.)
2. Little Haakon (op. 15, nr. 1)
3. I Love Thee (op. 5, nr. 3)
4. She is so White (op. 18, nr. 2)
5. The Princess (no opus number. EG 133)
6. To Spring (op. 21, nr. 3)

BERGLIOT, OP. 42. MELODRAMA
(1871/1885) (BJØRNSON)

LYRIC PIECES III, OP. 43 FOR KLAVER.
(1886)
1. Butterfly
2. Solitary Traveller
3. In my Native Country

4. Little Bird
5. Eroticon
6. To Spring

REMENISENCES FROM MOUNTAIN AND FJORD OP. 44. (1886) (HOLGER DRACHMANN)
1. Prologue
2. Johanne
3. Ragnhild
4. Ingebjørg
5. Ragna
6. Epilogue

VIOLIN SONATA NR. 3 IN C-MINOR, OP. 45. (1886–87)
1. Movement: Allegro molto ed appassionato
2. Movement: Allegretto espressivo alla romanza
3. Movement: Allegro animato

PEER GYNT-SUITE NR. 1, OP. 46. SUITE FOR SYMPHONY ORCHESTRA. (1887–88)
1. Morning Mood (op. 23, nr. 13)
2. The Death of Aase (op. 23, nr. 12)
3. Anitra's Dance (op. 23, nr. 16)
4. In the Hall of the Mountain King (op. 23, nr. 8)

LYRIC PIECES IV, OP. 47 FOR PIANO. (1886– 88)
1. Waltz-Impromptu
2. Album Leaf
3. Melody
4. Halling
5. Melancholy
6. Springar
7. Elegy

SECHS LIEDER, OP. 48 / SIX SONGS, OP. 48. (1884–89)
1. Gruss / Hilsen / Greeting (Heine)
2. Dereinst, Gedanke mein / Jeg vet, min tanke / One Day, O Heart of Mine (Geibel)
3. Lauf der Welt / Verdens gang / The Way of the World (Uhland)
4. Die verschwiegene Nachtigal / Nattergalen / The Nightingale's Secret (Vogelweide)
5. Zur Rosenzeit / I rosentiden / The Time of Roses (Goethe)
6. Ein Traum / En drøm / A Dream (Bodenstedt)

SIX SONGS, OP. 49 FOR VOICE AND PIANO. (1886–89) (HOLGER DRACHMANN)
1. Tell Me Now, Did You See the Lad
2. Rocking, Rocking on Gentle Waves
3. Kind Greetings, Fair Ladies
4. Now is Evening Light and Long
5. Christmas Snow
6. Spring Showers

SCENES FROM «OLAV TRYGVASON», OP. 50. (1873. REV. 1888) (OPERA FRAGMENT. TEXT BY BJØRNSON)
1. Concealed in the Many Enticing
2. You, Coming out of Urd's Well
3. Evil Man's Evil Genius
4. Thank you for Speaking
5. Give All Gods a Toast of Joy
6. All Goddesses
7. The Eternal Religion of the Ases

OLD NORWEGIAN MELODY WITH VARIATIONS, OP. 51 FOR TWO PIANOS. (1890)

TRANSCRIPTIONS OF ORIGINAL SONGS II,
OP. 52. (1890)
1. A Mother's Grief (op. 15, nr. 4)
2. The First Meeting (op. 21, nr. 1)
3. The Poet's Heart (op. 5, nr. 2)
4. Solveig's Song (op. 23, nr. 19)
5. Love (op. 15, nr. 2)
6. The Old Mother (op. 33, nr. 7)

TWO MELODIES FOR STRING ORCHESTRA
OP. 53 (1890)
1. Norwegian (op. 33, nr. 12)
2. The First Meeting (op. 21, nr. 1)

LYRIC PIECES V, OP. 54 FOR PIANO.
(1891)
1. Shepherd's Boy
2. Gangar
3. March of Trolls
4. Notturno
5. Scherzo
6. Bell Ringing

PEER GYNT-SUITE NR. 2, OP. 55. SUITE
FOR SYMFONY ORCHESTRA (1891)
1. The Abduction of the Bride.
   Ingrid's Lament (op. 23, nr. 4)
2. Arabian Dance (op. 23, No 15)
3. Peer Gynt's Homecoming. Stormy
   Evening on the Sea (op. 23, nr. 19)
4. Solveig's Song (op. 23, nr. 11)

THREE ORCHESTRAL PIECES FROM
«SIGURD JORSALFAR», OP. 56 (1892)
1. Prelude. In the King's Hall (op. 22,
   nr. 2)
2. Intermezzo («Borghild's Dream»)
   (op. 22, nr. 1)
3. Homage March (op. 22, nr. 4)

LYRIC PIECES VI, OP. 57 FOR KLAVER.
(1893)
1. Vanished Days
2. Gade
3. Illusion
4. Secret
5. She Dances
6. Homesickness

FIVE SONGS, OP. 58. (JOHN PAULSEN)
FOR VOICE AND PIANO. (1893–94)
1. Homeward
2. To the Motherland
3. Henrik Wergeland
4. The Shepherdes
5. The Emigrant

SIX ELEGIAC SONGS OP. 59 FOR VOICE
AND PIANO. (1893–94) (JOHN PAULSEN)
1. Autumn Farewell
2. The Pine Tree
3. To Her I
4. To Her II
5. Good-bye
6. Your Eyes Are Closed Forever

FIVE SONGS (VILHELM KRAG), OP. 60
FOR VOICE AND PIANO (1893–94)
1. Little Kirsten
2. The Mother's Lament
3. On The Water
4. A Bird Cried Out
5. Midsummer Eve

SEVEN CHILDREN'S SONGS, OP. 61
FOR VOICE AND PIANO (1894)
1. The Ocean (Rolfsen)
2. The Christmas Tree (J. Krohn)
3. Farmyard Song (Bjørnson)
4. Fisheman's Song (Petter Dass)
5. Good-night Song for Dobbin(Rolfsen)

6. The Norwegian Mountains (Rolfsen)
7. Fatherland Hymn (Runeberg / Rolfsen)

LYRIC PIECES VII, OP. 62 FOR PIANO.
(1893–95)
1. Sylph
2. Gratitude
3. French Serenade
4. Brooklet
5. Phantom
6. Homeward

TWO NORDIC MELODIES, OP. 63
FOR STRING ORCHESTRA. (1895)
1. In Folk Style Cow
2. Cow Call and Peasant Dance

SYMPHONIC DANCES, OP. 64
FOR ORCHESTRA. (1896–98)
1. Movement: Allegro moderato e marcato
2. Movement: Allegretto grazioso
3. Movement: Allegro giocoso
4. Movement: Andante. Allegro risoluto

LYRIC PIECES VIII OP. 65 FOR PIANO.
(1896)
1. From Early Days
2. Peasant's Song
3. Melancholy
4. Salon
5. Ballad
6. Wedding Day at Troldhaugen

NINETEEN NORWEGIAN FOLK SONGS,
OP. 66 FOR PIANO. (1896) COLLECTED
BY FRANTS BEYER.
1. Cow Call (Lom)
2. It is the Greatest Foolishness (Sunn-møre)
3. A King Ruled in the East (Sogn)
4. The Siri Dale Song (Årdal in Sogn)

5. It Was in My Youth (Luster in Sogn)
6. Cow Call and Lullaby (Luster in Sogn)
7. Lullaby (Ryfylke)
8. Cow Call (Lom)
9. Small Was the Lad (Østre Slidre)
10. Tomorrow You Shall Marry Her (Lom)
11. There Stood Two Girls (Lom)
12. Ranveig (Lom)
13. A Little Grey Man (Lom)
14. In Ola Valley, in Ola Lake (Østre Slidre)
15. Lulleby (Lom)
16. Little Astrid (Lom)
17. Lullaby (Turtagrø in Sogn)
18. I Wander Deep in Thought (Turtagrø in Sogn)
19. Gjendine's Lullaby (Lom)

THE MOUNTAIN MAID, OP. 67
FOR VOICE AND PIANO. (1895–98)
(ARNE GARBORG)
1. The Enticement
2. Veslemøy – The Young Maiden
3. Blueberry Slope
4. The Tryst
5. Love
6. Kidlings' Dance
7. Hurtful Day
8. At the Brook

LYRIC PIECES IX, OP. 68 FOR PIANO
(1898–99)
1. Sailors' Song
2. Grandmother's Minuet
3. At Your Feet
4. Evening in the Mountains
5. At The Cradle
6. Valse Mélancolique

FIVE SONGS, OP. 69 FOR VOICE AND
PIANO. (1900) (OTTO BENZON)
1. A Boat on the Waves Is Rocking
2. To My Son
3. At Mother's Grave
4. Snail, Snail
5. Dreams

FIVE SONGS, OP. 70 FOR VOICE AND
PIANO. (1900) (OTTO BENZON)
1. Eros
2. A Life of Longing
3. Summer Night
4. Walk With Care
5. A Poet's Song

LYRIC PIECES X, OP. 71 FOR PIANO.
(1901)
1. Once Upon a Time
2. Summer's Eve
3. Puck
4. Peace of the Woods
5. Halling
6. Gone (In Memoriam)
7. Remembrances

NORWEGIAN PEASANT DANCES
(SLAATTER), OP. 72 FOR PIANO.
ARRANGEMENTS FOR PIANO OF
HARDANGER FIDDLE DANCE TUNES,
BASED ON JOHAN HALVORSEN'S TRANS-
CRIPTIONS OF DANCE TUNES PLAYED BY
KNUT DAHLE. (1902–03
1. Gibøen's Bridal March.
2. Jon Væstafæ's Springar
3. Bridal March from Telemark
4. Halling from the Fairy Hill

5. The Prillar from Os Parish (Springar)
6. Gangar after Myllarguten
7. Røtnams-Knut. Halling
8. Bridal March after Myllarguten
9. Nils Rekve's halling
10. Knut Luråsen's halling I
11. Knut Luråsen's halling II
12. Springar after Myllarguten
13. Håvar Gibøen's Dream at the Oterholt
    Bridge (Springar)
14. The Goblins' Bridal Procession at
    Vossevangen (Gangar)
15. The Skuldal Bride (Gangar)
16. The Maidens from Kivledal (Springar
    from Seljord)
17. The Maidens from Kivledal (Gangar)

MOODS, OP. 73 FOR PIANO. (1898–1905)
1. Resignation
2. Scherzo-Impromptu
3. Night Ride
4. Folk Tune from Valdres
5. Homage to Chopin
6. The Students' Serenade
7. Mountain Tune

FOUR PSALMS, OP. 74 FOR MIXED
CHORUS A CAPELLA AND BARITONE
SOLO. (1906) ARRANGEMENTS OF FOUR
OLD NORWEGIAN HYMN TUNES FROM
THE L.M. LINDEMAN'S COLLECTION
1. How Fair is Thy Face (Brorson)
2. God's Son Hath Set Me Free (Brorson).
3. Jesus Christ Our Lord Is Risen
   (Thomisson)
4. In Heav'n Above (Laurentii)

Works without opus number

EG 101 LARVIK S POLKA. FOR PIANO
(1858)

EG 102 TREE PIECES FOR PIANO.
(1858–59)
1. Longing
2. Allegro con moto
3. Allegro assai

EG 103 NINE CHILDREN'S PIECES. FOR
PIANO. (1858–59)
1. Allegro Agitato
2. Pearls
3. Bu Gellert s Grave
4. Prayer
5. Loss
6. Fifth Birthday
7. Allegro con moto
8. Scherzo
9. A Dream

EG 104 SMALL PIECES FOR PIANO.
(1858–59)
1. Allegro agitato
2. Allegro desiderio
3. Molto allegro vivace
4. Andante quasi allegretto
5. Allegro assai

6. Allegro con moto.
7. A Dream. Andante quasi allegretto
8. Allegro assai
9. Pearls. Andante moderato
10. By Gellert's grave. Andante con gravitá
11. Vivace
12. Preludium. Largo con estro poetica
13. Allegretto con moto
14. Allegretto con moto
15. Preludium. Com passione
16. Scherzo. Allegro assai, quasi presto
17. Molto adagio religioso
18. Allegro molto
19. Andante moderato
20. Allegro vivace
21. Loss. Andante moderato
22. Gently, not too fast.
23. Assai, allegro furiose

EG 105 3 PIANO PIECES (1860)
1. Allegro agitato
2. Allegretto
3. Allegro molto e vivace, quasi Presto

EG 106 AGITATO. FOR PIANO (1865)

EG 107 FUNERAL MARCH FOR RIKARD
NORDRAAK. For piano (1866). Arr for
Wind orchestra 1867.

EG 108 THE MELODIES OF NORWAY
«NORGES MELODIER, ARRANGED FOR
PIANO WITH TEXT». ALL TOGETHER 152
PIECES. GRIEG'S OWN ARRANGEMENTS

EG 109 ALBUM LEAF. FOR PIANO. (1878)

EG 110 WHITE CLOUDS. FOR PIANO.
(1898) (UTG. AV JULIUS RÖNTGEN)

EG 111 TUSSELÅT. FOR PIANO. (1898)
(UTG. AV JULIUS RÖNTGEN)

EG 112 DANCING. FOR PIANO. (1898)
(UTG. AV JULIUS RÖNTGEN)

EG 113 PIANO II TO FOUR SONATAS BY
W.A. MOZART (1877)

EG 114 FUGE IN F-MINOR. FOR STRING
QUARTET. (1861)

EG 115 INTERMEZZO. FOR CELLO AND
PIANO. (1866)

EG 116 ANDANTE CON MOTO. TRIO
MOVEMENT FOR PIANO, VIOLIN AND
CELLO IN C-MINOR. (1878)

EG 117 STRING QUARTET NR. 2 IN
F-MAJOR (1891). NOT FINISHED. TWO
MOVEMENTS EDITED BY J. RÖNTGEN 1908.
ALL MATERIAL EDITED BY L. CHILINGIRIAN
1998.

EG 118 PIANO QUINTETT I B-MAJOR
FRAGMENT.

EG 119 SYMPHONY IN C-MINOR
(1863–64)

EG 120 PIANO CONCERTO IN B-MINOR.
FRAGMENT. (1883)

EG 121 SIEHST DU DAS MEER. (GEIBEL)
VOICE AND PIANO. (1859)

EG 122 THE SINGING CONGREGATION
(GRUNDTVIG). VOICE AND PIANO.
(1860)

EG 123 DEVOUTEST OF MAIDENS
(B. FEDDERSEN ETTER C. GROTH).
VOICE AND PIANO (1864)

EG 124 CLARA S SONG. (B. FEDDER-
SEN). VOICE AND PIANO. (1864)

EG 125 THE SOLDIER (H.C. ANDERSEN)
VOICE AND PIANO. (1865)

EG 126 MY LITTLE BIRD (H.C. ANDER-
SEN). VOICE AND PIANO. (1865)

EG 127 I LOVE YOY, DEAR! (CASPARA
PREETZMANN). VOICE AND PIANO (1865)

EG 128 TEARS (H.C. ANDERSEN).
VOICE AND PIANO. (1865)

EG 129 LITTLE LAD (KRISTOFFER JAN-
SON). VOICE AND PIANO. (1866)

EG 130 THE FAIRY GIRL (I) (BJØRNSON).
VOICE AND PIANO. (1867)

EG 131 THE ODALISQUE (CARL BRUN).
VOICE AND PIANO. (1870)

EG 132 THE MINER (IBSEN). VOICE AND
PIANO (1870)

EG 133 The Princess (Bjørnson). Voice and piano. (1871)

EG 134 Sigh (Bjørnson). Voice and piano. (1873)

EG 135 To L.M. Lindeman's Silver Wedding. (1873)

EG 136 To General consul Chr. Tønsberg (J. Bøgh). Voice and piano. (1873)

EG 137 The White, Red Rose (Bjørnson). Voice and piano (1873)

EG 138 The Fairy Girl (II) (Bjørnson). Voice and piano. (1874)

EG 139 Morning Prayer (Fredrik Gjertsen). Voice and piano (1875)

EG 140 On the Ruins of Hamar Cathedral (A.O. Vinje) Voice and piano (1880)

EG 141 The Young Woman (A.O. Vinje). Voice and piano. (1880)

EG 142 The Forgotten Maid (A.O. Vinje). Voice and piano. (1880)

EG 143 Dyre Vaa (Welhaven) Voice and piano (1880)

EG 144 Beneath the Christmas Tree (Nordahl Rolfsen). Voice and piano (1885)

EG 145 The Blueberry (D. Grønvold) Voice and piano (1886)

EG 146 Easter Song (A. Böttger). Voice and piano. (1889)

EG 147 A Simple Song (H. Drachmann). Voice and piano. (1889)

EG 148 You Often Fix Your Gaze (H. Drachmann). Voice and piano (1889)

EG 149 Election Song (Bjørnson). For Male chorus a cappella. (1893)

EG 150 Ave maris stella (Thor Lange) Voice and piano/ Mixed chorus (1893)

EG 151 National Anthem (Johan Paulsen). Voice and piano (1899)

EG 152 Mountain Maid-Songs (A. Garborg) Voice and piano (not in op. 67)
1. The Sparrow
2. Cow Call
3. Doomed
4. In the Hayfield
5. Veslemøy Longing

EG 153 I Loved Him. From the oratory «Peace» (Bjørnson). Voice and piano (1891?)

EG 154 To a Devil (Otto Benzon). Voice and piano. (1900)

EG 155 Christmas Lulleby (Langsted). Voice and piano. (1900)

EG 156 Gentleman-Rankers (Kipling/ Rosenkranz) Voice and piano (1900)

EG 157 DER JÄGER (W. SCHULTZ). VOICE AND PIANO. (1905)

EG 158 CANTATA FOR THE UNVEILING OF THE W.F.K CHRISTIE'S MONUMENT MAY 17. 1868 (P.A. MUNCH). FOR MALE CHORUS AND WIND BAND (1868)

EG 159 DONA NOBIS PACEM. FUGE FOR MIXED CHORUS A CAPPELLA. (1862)

EG 160 FOUR SONGS FOR MALE VOICES. A CAPPELLA (1863)

EG 161 DANMARK (H.C. ANDERSEN). BLANDET KOR MED KLAVER. (1864)

EG162 TWO SONGS FOR MALE CHORUS A CAPPELLA.(JØRGEN MOE) (1867)
1. Evening Mood
2. The Bear Hunter

EG 163 NORWEGIAN SAILORS SONG (BJØRNSON). FOR MALE CHORUS A CAPPELLA. (1869–70)

EG 164 CANTATA TO KARL HALS (BJØRNSON). FOR TENOR, CHORUS AND PIANO (1873)

EG 165 AT J.S. WELHAVEN'S GRAVE (JØRGEN MOE). FOR MALE CHORUS A CAPPELLA. (1873)

EG 166 CHORUS FOR THE SUPPORTERS OF FREEDOM IN SCANDINAVIA (BJØRNSON). FOR MALE CHORUS A CAPPELLA. (1874)

EG 167 AT HALFDAN KJERULF'S STATUE (P.A. MUNCH). FOR TENOR SOLO AND MALE CHORUS. (1874)

EG 168 INGA LITIMOR. FOR BARYTONE AND MALE CHORUS A CAPPELLA. (1877–78)

EG 169 TWO MALE CHORUS SONGS (OLAV LOFTHUS). (1881)
1. My Finest Thought
2. Our Watchword

EG 170 A GREETING TO THE SINGERS (S. SKAVLAN). FOR MALE CHORUS A CAPPELLA. (1883)

EG 171 HOLBERG CANTATA (NORDAHL ROLFSEN). FOR BARYTONE AND MALE CHORUS A CAPPELLA. (1884)

EG 172 FLAG SONG (JOHAN BRUN). FOR MALE CHORUS A CAPPELLA. (1893)

EG 173 GREETINGS FROM KRISTIANIA (JONAS LIE). FOR BARYTONE AND MALE CHORUS A CAPPELLA. (1896)

EG 174 SONG FROM JÆREN (JONAS DAHL). FOR MALE CHORUS A CAPPELLA. (1896)

EG 175 IMPROMPTU TO «GRIEG'S MALE CHORUS IN FORT DODGE, IOWA».(1896)

EG 176 TO OLE BULL (WELHAVEN). FOR MALE CHORUS A CAPPELLA. (1901)

51. Sonaten für Violine und Klavier. Edvard Grieg. Ole Bøhn, violin. Einar Steen-Nøkleberg, piano. Sound-star-ton ; SST 30181.

52. Sonatas for violin and piano. Edvard Grieg. DG 37 525-2. Augustin Dumay, violin. Maria Joao Pires, piano.

53. Cello & piano works. Grieg & Sibelius. Virgin Classics ; VC 5 45034 2. Truls Mørk, cello. Jean-Yves Thibaudet, piano.

54. String quartets. Grieg, Johansen. Naxos 8.550879. Oslo String Quartet.

55. Violinsonater nr. 1-3. Grieg. Naxos: 8 553904N. Henning Kraggerud, violin. Helge Kjekshus, piano.

56. Complete music for cello and piano. Grieg, Delius. Philips ; 454 458-2,. Andrew Lloyd Webber, cello. Bengt Forsberg, piano.

57. String quartets. Edvard Grieg. Hyperion: CDA67117. Chillingirian Quartet. Also published by Troldhaugen – TROLD 11.

58. Complete violin sonatas. Edvard Grieg. Sony Classical ; SK 8909. Arve Tellefesen, violin. Håvard Gimse, piano. Recorded in The Villa at Troldhaugen with Grieg's Steinway piano (1892).

59. Cello sonata ; String quartet. Grieg. Virgin Classics ; 545 505-2, Also on TROLD 17. Håverd Gimse, piano. Sølve Sigerland, violin. Atle Sponberg, violin. Lars Anders Tomter, viola. Truls Mørk, cello. The cello sonata recorded in Grieg s Villa, Troldhaugen with his Steinway (1892).

60. Lyrische Stücke. Edvard Grieg. Deutsche Grammophon ; 419 749-2. Emil Gilels, piano.

61. BIS,The complete piano music , Edvard Grieg; vol. 1 - 9. Eva Knardahl, piano. BIS CD 104 – 112.

62. Slåtter, op. 72 together with the original fiddle tunes. Norwegian dances / Edvard Grieg. Simax ; PSC 1040. Knut Buen, Hardanger fiddle. Einar Steen-Nøkleberg, piano.

63. Holberg suite - Lyriske stykker - Ballade [lydopptak] / Edvard Grieg. - Bergen: Edvard Grieg Museum Troldhaugen ; TROLD 04. Jan Henrik Kayser, piano.

64. The piano music in historic interpretations. Edvard Grieg. Historical recordings. Simax ; PSC 1809. Various artists.

65. Piano music Vol. 1-14. Grieg. Naxos ; 8.550884. Einar Steen-Nøkleberg.

66. Ballade in g minor, op. 24 ; Piano sonata in a minor, op. 7 ; Norwegian peasant dances, "Slåtter", op. 72 . Edvard Grieg. Norsk kulturråd - Polygram ; NKFCD 50029-2 - 439 330-2. Robert Riefling, piano.

67. Grieg playing Grieg Edvard Grieg. Edvard Grieg Museum Troldhaugen ; TROLD 07.

68. Piano sonata ; 7 fugues ; Lyric pieces ; Carnival scene. Edvard Grieg. -DG ; 459 671-2. Mikhail Pletnev, piano.

69. Lyric pieces. Selection of 27 . Edvard Grieg. Håkon Austbø, piano. Regis: RRC 1071.

70. Lyric pieces. Grieg. Leif Ove Andsnes, pinao. Recordes on Grieg s piano, Villa Troldhaugen. EMI Classics: 557296 2/ TROLD 16.

71. Folk dances. Songs: original piano transcriptions. Edvard Grieg. Håvard Gimse, piano. naim ; naimcd059

72. Piano works / Edvard Grieg. Membran Music ; 231555, c2006. Isabel Mourao, piano.

73. Lyrische Stücke. Complete / Grieg. Brilliant Classics ; 99748, 2001. Håkon Austbø, piano.

74. Klavierkonzerte. Schumann / Grieg. - Hamburg: DG ; 410021-2, Krystian Zimmerman, Piano. Berliner Philharmoniker, Herbert von Karajan, conductor.

75. Piano concertos. Grieg & Schumann. Angel ; CDC 7 47164 2. Svatoslav Richter, piano. Monte Carlo Nathional POrchestra, Lovro von Matacic, conductor.

76. Klavierkonzerte. Schumann/Grieg. DG ; 415 850-2. Geze Anda, piano. Berliner Philharmoniker, Rafael Kubelik, conductor.

77. Piano concertos. Tchaikovsky & Grieg. BIS: CD-375, 1987. Roland Pöntinen, piano. Bamberger Symphoniker, Leif Segerstam, conductor.

78. Piano concertos. Grieg & Schumann. Decca ; 417728-2. Radu Lupu, piano. London Symphony Orchestra, André Previn, conductor.

79. Piano concertos. Schumann/Grieg. CBS Records: MPK 44849, 1988 (Masterworks portrait). Leon Fischer, Piano. Cleveland Orchestra, George Szell, conductor.

80. Piano concerto in a-minor and other Scandinavian favourites. EMI; 777N7697692. John Ogdon, piano. Bournmouth Symphony Orchestra and New Philharmonia Orchestra, Paavo Berglund, conductor.

81. Concertos. Grieg & Liszt. BMG ; GD87834. Van Cliburn, piano. The Philadelphia Orchestra, Eugene Ormandy, conductor.

82. Concertos per pianoforte. Franz Liszt, Robert Schumann, Edvard Grieg. (Compact Discoteca). Arturo Benedetti Michelangeli, piano. Ochestre Sinfonica di Roma, Mario Rossi (Grieg).

83. Klavierkonzerte. Schumann, Grieg. EMI ; CDC 754746 2. Lars Vogt, piano. City of Birmingham Symphoni Orchestra, Simon Rattle, conductor.

84. Piano concertos. Mozart & Grieg. Intaglio: INCD 7101. Artur Rubinstein, piano. Philharmonia Orchestra, Carlo Maria Giulini, conductor.

85. Piano concertos. Schumann, Grieg. Sony Classical SK 44 899. Murray Perahia, pinao. Symphonie-Orchester des Bayerischen Rundfunks, Sir Colin Davis, conductor.

86. Piano concertos. Schumann. Grieg. Teldec: 9031-76439-2, (Historic). Arturo Beneditti Michelangeli, piano. Orchestra del Teatro Scala di Milano, Alceo Galliera, conductor (Grieg)

87. Piano concertos. Grieg & Schumann. SONY Records: SRCR 2129. Hiroko Nakamura, piano. Bergen Philmonic Orchestra, Dmitri Kitajenko, conductor.

88. Piano concertos. Grieg and Chopin. Decca ; 467093-2. Jean-Yves Thibaudet, piano. Rotterdam Philharmonic Orchestra, Valery Gergiev, conductor.

89. Piano concerto. Grieg, Debussy. BBCL 4043-2, 2000. (BBC Legends).Arturo Benedetti Michelangeli, piano. New Philharmonia Orchestra, Rafael Frübeck de Burgos, conductor.

90. Solomon plays Grieg & Schumann. Testament ; SBT 1231, 2001. Solomon, piano. Philharmonia Orchestra, Herbert Menges, conductor.

91. Claudio Arrau plays Grieg & Schumann .Bromley: Testament SBT 1233. Claudio Arrau, piano. Philharmonia Orchestra, Alceo Galliera, conductor.

92. Piano concertos. Grieg, Schumann. EMI Classics: 557486 2. Leif Ove Andsnes, piano. Berliner Philharmoniker, Mariss Jansons, conductor.

93. Piano concerto ; In autumn ; Symphonic dances. Grieg. Naxos: 8.557279. Håvard Gimse, piano. Royal Schottish Nathional Orcherstra, Bjarte Engeset, conductor.

94. Piano concerto. Edvard Grieg. 2L, 2009,1 CD + 1 Blu-ray. Super Audio CD. Percy Grainger, pianola. Kristiansand Symfoniorkester, Rolf Gupta, conductor.

95. Piano concertos. Grieg, Schumann. Newton Classics: 8802019. Stephen Kovacecich, piano. BBC Symphony Orchestra, Colin Davis, conductor.

96. Four hymns, op. 74 ; Two religious choirs, EG 15 ; Album for male voices, op. 30. Edvard Grieg. Simax ; PSC 1027. Malmø Chamber Choir,Dan-Olof Stenlund, conductor. Harald Bjørkøy, baritone.

97. Choral works by Edvard Grieg. TROLD 13. Bergen Domkantori, Magnar Mangersnes, conductor. Trond Halstein Moe, baritone, Audun Kayser, pinao.

98. Grieg, op. 61. Nystedt - songs. Bergen Digital: BD 7943CD. Voci Nobili, Maria Gamborg Hellbekkmo, conductor.

99. Choral music. Grieg. The Norwegian Soloist Choir, Grete Pedersen, conductor. BIS: SACD-1661.

100. Choral music. Edvard Grieg. 2L ; 45. Grex Vocalis, Carl Høgset, conductor.

101. String quartets. Grieg & Debussy. Simax Classic: PSC 1201. Vertavo String Quartet.

102. Intimate voices. Grieg, Sibelius, Nielsen. DG 477 5960, 2006. Emmerson String Quartet.

103. String quartet, op. 27 . Grieg. Clarinet quintet, op. 115. Brahms. Myrios Classics: MYR 007. Hagen Quartett.

104. Norwegian dances ; Ballade ; Slåtter: suite for orchestra. Grieg. Naxos. Royal Scottish National Orchestra, Bjarte Engeset, conductor.

105. Olav Trygvason ; Orchestral songs. Edvard Grieg. Åkersberga: BIS ; SACD-1531. Bergen Philharmonic Orchestra, conductor Ole Kristian Ruud, conductor.

106. Piano concerto & Lyric suite. Edvard Grieg. Unicorn Kanchana UKCD2005, 1988. Einar Steen-Nøkleberg, piano. London Symphony Orchestra, Per Dreier, conductor.

107. Piano concerto in a minor / Grieg. Piano concerto no. 2 in A major Liszt; Six lyric pieces, op. 65 / Grieg. Virgin Classics ; VC 7 91198-2 Leif Ove Andsnes, piano. Bergen Philharmonic Orchestra, Dmitri Kitajenko, conductor.

108. Symphonic dances and orchestra songs. Edvard Grieg. Chandos: CHAN 9113. Royal Stockholm Philharmonic Orchestra, Gennady Rozhdestvensky, conductor. Solveig Kringlebotn, soprano.

109. Music for strings. Victoria: VCD 19066. The Trondheim Soloists, Bjarne Fiskum, conductor.

110. Grieg, Edvard. Orkestermusikk. Utvalg. Symphony ; Symphonic dance Classics; VC 7 59301 2. Bergen Philharmonic Orchestra, Dmitri Kitajenko, conductor.

111. Peer Gynt. Edvard Grieg. Hänssler Classics ; CD 98.995. The Academy of St. Martin in the Fields, Neville Marriner, conductor.

112. Music for string orchestra. Grieg. Naxos: 8.557890, 2006. Oslo Camerata, Stephan Barratt-Due, conductor.

113. The complete orchestral music. Edvard Grieg. BIS ; BIS-CD-1740/42, 2008. 8 CDer. Bergen Philharmonic Orchestra, Ole Kristian Ruud, conductor. Various artists.

114. Peer Gynt, op. 23. Complete. Edvard Grieg [a play by Henrik Ibsen]. BIS; SACD-1441/42. - 2 CDer. Bergen Philharmonic Orchestra, Ole Kristian Ruud, conductor. Various artists.

115. Peer Gynt , op. 23. Complete. Grieg. Naxos ; 8.570872. 2 CDer. Malmø Symphony Orchestra, Bjarte Engeset, conductor. Various artists.

116. Piano recital 1994. Grieg, Franck, Ravel. - Holzgerlingen, Germany: Hänssler Classic, 2011: CD 93.712. Svatoslav Richter, piano.

117. Six poems by Ibsen, op. 25. Edvard Grieg. Simax ; PSC 1011. Ellen Westberg Andersen, soprano. Jens Harald Brattlie, piano.

118. Seks sange, op. 48 ; Fire sange, op. 21 ; "Haugtussa", op. 67. Edvard Grieg. Aurora; ARCD 1930. Marianne Hirsti, soprano. Rudolf Jansen, piano.

119. Haugtussa. Edvard Grieg. BMG Ariola ; 74321 117 082. Solveig Kringlebotn, soprano. Kjell Bækkelund, piano.

120. Sanger av Edvard Grieg. Norsk Plateproduksjon, DCD 29. Elisabeth Norberg-Schulz, soprano. Håvard Gimse, piano.

121. Grieg & Schubert songs. Quattro: QCD 9301. Njål Sparboe, bass-baryton, Einar Steen-Nøkleberg, piano.

122. The vocal music in historic interpretations. Edvard Grieg. 1888- 1924. Simax; PSC 1810. 3 CDer. Various artists.

123. Norwegian folk songs and peasant dances from op. 66 & 72. Simax: PSC 1102. Geir Botnen, piano. Reidun Horvei, soprano. Knut Hamre, Hardanger fiddle.

124. Lieder. Edvard Grieg. Deutsche Grammophon ; 437521-2. Ann Sofie von Otter, mezzo. Bengt Forsberg, piano.

125. Songs. Edvard Grieg. Simax, PSC 1089. Per Vollestad, baryton. Sigmund Hjelset, piano.

126. Historic vocal recordings. Edvard Grieg. RCA Victor ; 09026 61827 2. 191 – 1961. Various artists.

127. Complete songs vol. I- VII / Edvard Grieg. Victoria ; VCD 19037 -46. (The Grieg Edition). Various artists.

128. Grieg, Edvard, n., 1843-1907 Sanger. Utvalg Haugtussa ; 14 songs Decca; 440 493-2, Kirsten Flagstad, soprano. Edwin McArthur, piano.

129. Grieg songs. Edvard Grieg Museum, Troldhaugen ; TROLD 12. Ragnhild Heiland Sørensen, soprano. Einar Steen-Nøkleberg, piano.

130. Song recital. Grieg & Dørumsgaard. Testament SBT 1268. Kirsten Flagstad, soprano. Gerald Moore, piano. Philharmonia Orchestra.

131. Haugtussa. Edvard Grieg. NMA 3. Solveig Kringlebotn, soprano. Malcolm Martineau, piano.

132. Grieg songs. Hyerion ; CDA67670. Katarina Karneus, mezzo. Julius Drake, piano.

133. Olav Trygvasson etc. Grieg. DG ; 437 523-2. Gothenburg Symphony Orchestra, Neme Jervi, conductor. Various artists.

134. Olav Trygvasson , Bergljot etc. Grieg. DG ; 437 523-2. Lise Fjeldstad, narrator. Trondheim Symphony Orchestra and Choir, Ole Kristian Ruud, conductor. Various artists.

135. Peer Gynt. op. 23 / Edvard Grieg. TROLD 06. Bergen Philharmonic Orchestra, Dmitri Kitajenko, conductor. Linda Øvrebø, soprano.

136. Slåtter, op. 72 & the Knut Dale slåtter. Edvard Grieg. Simax: PSC 1287. Ingfrid Breie Nyhus, piano. Åshild Breie Nyhus, Hardanger fiddle. Recorded in Grieg s Villa, Troldhaugen on his Steinway(1892).

137. Songs. Grieg. Naxos ; 8.553781. Bodil Arnesen, soprano. Erling Ragnar Eriksen, piano.

138. Toner fra Troldhaugen. Edvard Grieg. Edvard Grieg Museum Troldhaugen; TROLD 02. Olav Eriksen, baryton. Audun Kayser, piano.

139. Grieg and his circle play Grieg. Pearl ; GEMM CD 9933, 1991. Historic recordings rom 190 –1939. Various artists.

140. Piano concerto; Ballade; Lyric pieces. Grieg. BMG Classics GD60897. Arthur Rubinstein, piano. The Philadelphia Orchester, Eugene Ormandy, conductor.

141. Chamber music. Historic recordings. Grieg. BMG Classics ; 09026 61826 2. Fritz Kreisler, violin. Sergei Rachmaninoff, piano. Mischa Elman, violin. Budapest String Quartet. Boston Symphony Orchestra, Serge Koussovitzky, conductor.

142. Piano sonata, op. 7 ; Intermezzo in a minor for cello and piano ; Cellosonata, op. 36 Edvard Grieg. Naxos: 8.550878. Øystein Birkeland, cello. Håvard Gimse, piano.

143. Gieseking plays Grieg. Palladio ; PD 4178. Walter Gieseking, piano. Philharmonia Orchestra, Herbert von Karajan, conductor.

144. Sigurd Jorsalfar, Bergljot mm. Edvard Grieg. BIS: SACD-1391. Bergten Philharmonic Orchestra, Ole Kristian Rud, conductor. Håkan Hagegård, baryton. Gørild Mauseth, narrator.

145. Grieg in a nutshell. BIS 2007. Bergen Philharmonic Orchestra, Ole Kristian Ruud, conductor. Håkan Hagegård, baryton. Marita Sølvberg, soprano. Noriko Ogawa, piano.

146. Visiting Grieg. Simax Classics: PSC 1310. Johannes Weisser, baryton. Søren Rastogi, piano.

147. String quartets. Haydn, Solberg, Grieg. 2L ; 2L53SACD, Engegård String Quartet.

148. Nordic Songs. Grieg among others: EMI Classics ; 5 568842. Barbara Hendricks, soprano. Roland Pöntinen, piano.

149. Forgotten romance. Grieg, Liszt, Rubinstein. RCA Victor: 09026 68290 2. Steven Isserlis, cello. Stephen Hough, piano.
150. Edvard Grieg in jazz mood. Kjell Karlsen Big Band. Universal: 06025 1789907 0
151. Piano sonata with a freely added accompaniment for asecond piano by Grieg. Teldec; 4509-90825-2. Elisabeth Leonskaja and Svatoslav Richter, piano.
152. Mozart – Grieg. 2L ; 40. Tina Margareta Nilssen and Heide Görtz, piano.
153. Norwegian variations. Grieg, Valen, Tveitt. Pro Musica ; PPC 9053. Einar Røttingen, piano.
154. Female fates and fortunes. Simax: PSC 1145. Randi Stene, mezzo. Burkhard Kehring, piano.
155. Soledad. Tango for 3 & Per Arne Glorvigen. MSCD 1117

Chronology

ca. 1770:
Alexander Greig, Edvard Grieg's great-grandfather, emigrates from Scotland to Bergen, and becomes established as a merchant. He changes his name to Grieg.

1814:
Edvard Hagerup, Prefect and grandfather of Nina and Edvard Grieg, takes part in the constitutional assembly at Eidsvoll.

1840:
Johan Svendsen is born.

1842:
Rikard Nordraak is born.

1843:
15th June: Edvard Grieg is born in Bergen. The Leipzig Conservatory is founded by Felix Mendelssohn-Bartholdy and others.

1845:
Nina Hagerup is born on 24th November.

1853:
Edvard Grieg begins attending Tank's school in Bergen. Grieg's mother inherits the estate of Landås Hovedgård.
Magnus Brostrup Landstad publishes *Norske Folkeviser* (Norwegian Folk Songs). Ludvig Mathias Lindeman publishes the first book of *Older and Newer Norwegian Mountain Melodies*. The piano maker Steinway & Sons is founded in New York.

1858:
Edvard Grieg: *Larvik polka*, one of his first compositions. Travels to Larvik in the summer with his father. Edvard Grieg is admitted to study at the Leipzig Conservatory.

1860:
Edvard Grieg contracts a serious lung disease and is forced to disrupt his studies. Convalesces in Bergen; returns to Leipzig in the autumn.

1861:
Edvard Grieg: *String Quartet in D minor* (now lost) is performed at the Leipzig Conservatory. Grieg's first public concert takes place in Karlshamn in southern Sweden.

1862:
Grieg completes his studies in Leipzig. Grieg's first concert in Bergen.

1863:
Edvard Grieg goes to live in Copenhagen. Grieg composes the Symphony in C minor. Rikard Nordraak composes the melody to *Yes, we love this country*.

1864:
Grieg's first encounter with the Norwegian composer Rikard Nordraak. The music society "Euterpe" is established in Copenhagen. Grieg spends the summer in Bergen, and visits Ole Bull. Returns to Copenhagen in the autumn and becomes secretly engaged to his first cousin, Nina.

1865:
Grieg's breakthrough works: *Melodies of the Heart*, Op. 5 – *Humoresques*, Op. 6 – *Piano Sonata*, Op. 7 and *Violin Sonata No. 1*, Op. 8. Grieg's first trip to Rome.

1866:
Edvard Grieg meets Henrik Ibsen for the first time. Grieg moves to Kristiania (now Oslo) and becomes the music director of "Det philharmoniske Selskab" (The philharmonic Society). Rikard Nordraak dies.

1867:
Edvard Grieg marries Nina Hagerup on 11th June in Copenhagen. Grieg publishes his first book of *Lyric Pieces*. Edvard Grieg and Otto Winter-Hjelm found the Academy of Music in Kristiania.

1868:
Alexandra, Nina and Edvard Grieg's only child, is born on 10th April. Grieg composes his *Piano Concerto in A minor* in Søllerød outside Copenhagen. Grieg receives a letter of encouragement from Franz Liszt.

1869:
Grieg's daughter Alexandra dies on 20th May. Debut performance of the *Piano Concerto in A minor* in Copenhagen.

1870:
Edvard Grieg meets Franz Liszt in Rome. Edvard Grieg: *25 Norwegian Folk Songs and Dances*, Op. 17.

1871:
Grieg meets Frants Beyer for the first time Grieg founds the music society "Musikforeningen" in Kristiania, whose orchestra he conducts along with Johan Svendsen. Spends the summer at Landås (Bergen), and the rest of the year in Kristiania.

1872:
Edvard Grieg spends all year in Kristiania Collaborates with Bjørnstjerne Bjørnson, including composing incidental music for the play *Sigurd Jorsalfar*.

1873:
Edvard Grieg spends the summer in Bergen, and the rest of the year in Kristiania. Concert in Bergen with Ole Bull and Bjørnstjerne Bjørnson.

1874:
Edvard Grieg composes incidental music for the first two acts of *Olav Trygvason*.

Grieg receives a pension from the Norwegian government. Grieg leaves Kristiania, and now lives most of the time abroad. Grieg is contacted by Henrik Ibsen and asked to compose incidental music for a theatrical performance of the poem *Peer Gynt*.

1875:
Edvard Grieg travels to the Danish island of Funen, Weimar, Copenhagen, Bergen. Both Grieg's parents die in the autumn, with only a few weeks between them. Edvard Grieg: *Ballad i G minor*, Op. 24.

1876:
Peer Gynt receives its first performance at the Christiania Theater. Edvard Grieg: *Six Poems by Henrik Ibsen* and *Five Poems by John Paulsen*. Grieg visits the first Festival in Bayreuth (R. Wagner: *Der Ring des Nibelungen*). Writes six articles about the Festival for the newspaper Bergensposten.

1877:
Edvard Grieg spends the spring in Kristiania followed by a stay in Lofthus in Hardanger.

1878:
Edvard Grieg stays at Lofthus until the end of summer. Grieg receives a grant and travels to Germany, where he stays for the rest of the year.

1879:
Edvard Grieg spends the spring in Leipzig The summer is spent in Lofthus in Norway, where Ole Bull visits him. Grieg spends the autumn in Bergen and Leipzig, and Christmas in Copenhagen. Edvard Grieg: *String Quartet No.1 in G minor*, Op. 27.

1880:
Edvard Grieg spends the spring in Copenhagen, Leipzig, Kristiania and Bergen. Summer holiday in Lofthus. Edvard Grieg: *12 Melodies to Poems by A.O. Vinje*, Op. 33. Grieg becomes the Music Director of Musikselskabet Harmonien (Bergen Philharmonic Orchestra). Ole Bull dies.

1881:
Edvard Grieg spends most of the year in Bergen. Grieg seeks treatment at the spa in Karlsbad, summer holiday in Lofthus.

1882:
Edvard Grieg spends most of the year in Bergen. Treatment at Karlsbad spa, summer holiday in Lofthus.

1883:
Marital crisis and temporary separation from Nina. Edvard Grieg travels to Bayreuth, Thüringen, Rudolstadt, Weimar, Dresden, Leipzig, Meiningen, Breslau, Cologne, Karlsruhe, Frankfurt, Arnhem, The Hague, Rotterdam, Amsterdam. Spends Christmas with Julius Röntgen in Amsterdam.

1884:
Edvard Grieg is reunited with Nina in Leipzig. Together they travel to Rome, Sorrento and Lake Maggiore. Grieg meets Ibsen in Rome. Grieg purchases a plot of land and starts building the villa at Troldhaugen. Edvard Grieg: *Holberg Suite*,

Op. 40. Travels to Amsterdam, Leipzig, Rome, Lake Maggiore, Leipzig, Bergen and Hardanger (Lofthus).

1885:
22nd April: Nina and Edvard move into their new home at Troldhaugen. *Lyric Pieces III*, Op. 43. Summer holiday in Lofthus, walking tour in the Jotunheimen mountains with Grieg's friend Frants Beyer.

1886:
Edvard Grieg spends the spring in Copenhagen. Grieg meets the painter and composer Holger Drachmann. Drachmann visits Grieg at Troldhaugen and accompanies him on a tour of Jotunheimen.

1887:
Edvard Grieg spends the spring in Kristiania, and the summer at Troldhaugen. Grieg has treatment at Karlsbad spa in September – October, and spends the rest of the year in Leipzig. Edvard Grieg meets Peter Tchaikovsky. Edvard Grieg: *Violin Sonata No. 3 in C minor*, Op. 45.

1888:
Edvard Grieg spends the spring in Berlin and London, and the summer in Copenhagen. Concert in Birmingham, otherwise spends the rest of the year at Troldhaugen arranging *Peer Gynt Suite No. 1*, Op. 46 Travels to Berlin, Leipzig, London, Copenhagen, England.

1889:
Edvard Grieg leaves Troldhaugen in January, and travels to Berlin, Leipzig, Manchester, London, Paris, Brussels, Kristiania. Christmas in Copenhagen.

1890:
Edvard Grieg travels to Paris, Stuttgart, Leipzig, Berlin, Copenhagen, Kristiania. Edvard Grieg meets Emperor Wilhelm II in Bergen.

1891:
Edvard Grieg: *Lyric Pieces V*, Op. 54. Edvard Grieg: *Peer Gynt Suite II*, Op. 55 is finished. Grieg spends the spring in Copenhagen. Travels via Kristiania to Troldhaugen. Frants Beyer, Grieg and Julius Röntgen stay at Lofthus and in Jotunheimen. Grieg first encounters Gjendine Slaalien and meets her again each summer for the next 10 years. The composer's cabin at Troldhaugen is built. Grieg spends the autumn in Kristiania. Grieg's portrait is painted by Erik Werenskiold and Eilif Pettersen.

1892:
Nina and Edvard Grieg celebrate their silver wedding at Troldhaugen on 11th June Autumn spent in Kristiania, Copenhagen, Berlin and Leipzig. Peder Severin Krøyer: *Nina and Edvard Grieg.*

1893:
Edvard Grieg spends the winter in Leipzig, and the spring in Menton. June: Treatment at Grefsen sanatorium, summer in Troldhaugen and in Jotunheimen. Spends the autumn in Kristiania and Copenhagen. Edvard Grieg receives an honorary doctorate from Cambridge University.

1894:
Travels to Copenhagen, Leipzig, Munich, Geneva, Menton, Paris, London. Summer

at Troldhaugen and in Jotunheimen. Autumn in Copenhagen.

1895:
Edvard Grieg spends the spring in Copenhagen, summer at Troldhaugen, and the autumn in Kristiania, Copenhagen and Leipzig. Winter in Leipzig.

1896:
Edvard Grieg spends the spring in Leipzig, Vienna, Copenhagen. Summer at Troldhaugen, with a stay at Lofthus, where he celebrates his 53rd birthday in the company of his parents-in-law and good friends. The autumn is spent in Stockholm, Kristiania and Vienna.

1897:
Edvard Grieg spends the spring in Vienna, Amsterdam, The Hague, Amsterdam, Berlin, Copenhagen. The summer is spent at Troldhaugen, and the autumn in Liverpool, Manchester, Birmingham, Edinburgh, Cheltenham, Brighton, London. Christmas at Troldhaugen. Edvard Grieg: *Norwegian Folk Songs*, Op. 66. Grieg becomes a member of the Academy of Arts in Berlin. Performs before Queen Victoria at Windsor Castle.

1898:
The Bergen Music Festival is inaugurated – the first festival of music in Norway. Grieg spends the spring and summer at Troldhaugen. Part of the summer spent in Jotunheimen. Autumn and winter in Copenhagen. Edvard Grieg: *Haugtussa*, Op. 67 (text: Arne Garborg).

1899:
Edvard Grieg spends the spring in Copenhagen and Rome, the summer at Troldhaugen, and the autumn in Kristiania, Stockholm and Copenhagen. Grieg visits Bjørnstjerne Bjørnson at Aulestad. Declines invitation to give a concert in Paris (because of the Dreyfus Affair).

1900:
Edvard Grieg spends the spring in Copenhagen and Kristiania, summer at Troldhaugen, and autumn in Kristiania, with treatment at Voksenkollen sanatorium.

1901:
Edvard Grieg spends the spring in Copenhagen, and summer at Troldhaugen. Edvard Grieg: *Lyric Pieces, Book 10*, Op. 71. Grieg makes a speech at the unveiling of the statue of Ole Bull in Bergen on 17th May.

1902:
Edvard Grieg spends the winter in Copenhagen, and the spring and summer at Troldhaugen. In the autumn Grieg visits Warsaw, among other cities. Grieg's portrait is painted by Erik Werenskiold.

1903:
Edvard Grieg spends the winter and spring in Kristiania, Prague, Paris (his first concert after the Dreyfus affair). Summer at Troldhaugen. Autumn and winter in Kristiania. Edvard Grieg: *Slåtter*, Op. 72. On 15th June Edvard Grieg celebrates his 60th birthday at Troldhaugen. Bjørnstjerne Bjørnson visits Troldhaugen for the first time.

1904:
Edvard Grieg travels to Copenhagen and Stockholm. Summer at Troldhaugen, autumn in Kristiania. Grieg meets Emperor Wilhelm II in Bergen. Grieg visits Bjørnstjerne Bjørnson at Aulestad.

1905:
Edvard Grieg spends the spring in Copenhagen, the early summer in Kristiania, and then travels to Troldhaugen. Spends the autumn and winter in Kristiania. Edvard Grieg meets King Haakon VII and Queen Maud. The Norwegian parliament, Storting, declares the dissolution of the union between Sweden and Norway. King Oscar II of Sweden and Norway abdicates from the Norwegian throne and Håkon VII becomes King of Norway.

1906:
Edvard Grieg spends the spring in Kristiania, Prague, Amsterdam, The Hague, London, Copenhagen. Summer at Troldhaugen. Autumn and winter in Kristiania. Edvard Grieg is awarded an honorary doctorate by Oxford University. The violinist Adolf Brodsky visits Grieg at Troldhaugen.

1907:
Edvard Grieg spends the winter in Kristiania. In the spring he travels to Copenhagen, Munich, Berlin, Kiel, Leipzig and Copenhagen. Grieg's last concert in Kiel on 26th April. Summer at Troldhaugen. Edvard Grieg: *Four Psalms*, Op. 74. Julius Röntgen and Percy Grainger visit

Grieg at Troldhaugen. In August Grieg seeks recreation at Fleischers Hotel in Voss. 4th September: Edvard Grieg dies in Bergen Hospital. 9th September: Grieg's funeral procession goes from the Hall of the West Norway Museum of Decorative Art in Bergen.

1911:
Carl Nielsen stays at Troldhaugen and begins work on his violin concerto in the composer's cabin.

1918:
Nina Grieg sells Troldhaugen to Consul Joachim Grieg. (Title deed from Nina Grieg to Joachim Grieg, dated 27.12.1918).

1923:
Consul Joachim Grieg gives Troldhaugen to Fana Municipality (Deed of gift from Joachim Grieg to Fana Municipality, dated 18.12.1923).

1928:
Troldhaugen is opened to the public on 25th May.

1935:
Nina Grieg dies in Copenhagen, on 9th December.

1936:
On 15th June, on Edvard Grieg's birthday, the urn containing Nina Grieg's ashes is placed in the cliff-side grotto at Troldhaugen.

Edvard Grieg's travels and tours

1858: Bergen – Larvik – Bergen – Leipzig

1859: Leipzig

1860: Leipzig – Bergen – Leipzig

1861: Leipzig – Bergen – Karlshamn – Leipzig

1862: Leipzig – Bergen – London – Paris – Bergen

1863: Bergen – Copenhagen

1864: Copenhagen – Bergen – Copenhagen (Rungsted)

1865: Copenhagen – North Zealand – Berlin – Leipzig – Dresden – Vienna – Venice – Ferrara – Bologna – Pisa – Livorno – Rome

1866: Rome – Capri – Rome – Civitaveccia – Florence – Como – Colico – Rorschach – Lindau – Augsburg – Nuremberg – Leipzig – Berlin – Copenhagen – Oslo – Bergen – Oslo

1867: Oslo – Copenhagen – Oslo

1868: Oslo – Bergen – Copenhagen (Søllerød) – Oslo

1869: Oslo – Drammen – Bergen – Oslo – Copenhagen – Rome

1870: Rome – Copenhagen – Bergen – Larvik – Oslo

1871: Oslo – Drammen – Oslo – Bergen – Oslo

1872: Oslo – Stockholm – Leipzig – Oslo – Copenhagen – Oslo

1873: Oslo – Stockholm – Oslo – Drammen – Arendal – Kristiansand – Stavanger – Bergen – Oslo

1874: Oslo – Bergen – Kristiansand – Copenhagen

1875: Brobyværk (on the Danish island of Funen) – Leipzig – Weimar – Copenhagen – Bergen

1876: Bergen – Oslo – Bergen – Bayreuth – Gossensass – Oslo – Stockholm – Uppsala – Oslo

1877: Oslo – Hardanger (Børve) – Bergen – Hardanger (Lofthus)

1878: Hardanger (Lofthus) – Cologne – Bonn – Leipzig

1879: Leipzig – Copenhagen – Hardanger (Lofthus) – Leipzig – Bergen – Leipzig

1880: Leipzig – Copenhagen – Oslo – Bergen

1881: Bergen – Karlsbad – Hardanger (Lofthus) – Bergen

1882: Bergen – Stavanger – Haugesund – Karlsbad – Oslo – Bergen

1883: Bergen – Rudolstadt – Frankfurt am Main – Weimar – Leipzig – Meiningen – Leipzig – Breslau – Leipzig – Cologne – Karlsruhe – Frankfurt am Main – Arnhem – The Hague – Rotterdam – Amsterdam

1884: Amsterdam – Leipzig – Rome – Sorrento – Rome – Pallanza, L. Maggiore – Leipzig – Bergen – Hardanger (Lofthus) – Bergen

1885: Bergen – Jotunheimen – Oslo – Copenhagen

1886: Copenhagen – Århus – Ålborg – Randers – Horsens – Vejle – Århus – Ribe – Brobyværk (Fyn) – Copenhagen – Lofthus – Bergen – Oslo – Bergen

1887: Bergen – Karlsbad – Leipzig

1888: Leipzig – London – Ventnor, Isle of Wight – Copenhagen – Bergen – Birmingham – Scheveningen – Bergen

1889: Bergen – Berlin – Leipzig – London – Copenhagen – Manchester – London – Bergen – Jotunheimen (Gjendebu) – Bergen – Oslo – Copenhagen – Oslo – Copenhagen – Brussels – Paris

1890: Paris – Stuttgart – Leipzig – Bergen – Sogn – Oslo – Copenhagen

1891: Oslo – Copenhagen – Oslo – Bergen – Paris – Bergen – Jotunheimen – Oslo – Bergen

1892: Bergen – Oslo – Copenhagen – Leipzig – Berlin

1893: Leipzig – Menton – Bellagio – Meran, Schloss Labers – Oslo – Bergen – Jotunheimen (Eidsbugarden) – Bergen – Oslo – Copenhagen

1894: Copenhagen – Leipzig – Munich – Geneva – Menton – Paris – London – Cambridge – St Leonards on Sea – London – Oslo – Bergen – Oslo – Copenhagen

1895: Copenhagen – Oslo – Copenhagen – Bergen – Oslo – Leipzig

1896: Leipzig – Vienna – Semmering – Leipzig – Copenhagen – Bergen – Hardangervidda (Tronsbu) – Bergen – Stockholm – Oslo – Vienna – Semmering

1897: Vienna – Leipzig – Berlin – Leipzig – Amsterdam – The Hague – Amsterdam – Copenhagen – Oslo – Trondheim – Molde – Bergen – Hardanger (Fossli) – London – Hastings – London – Liverpool – London – Manchester – Birmingham – Edinburgh – London – Windsor – Cheltenham – London – Brighton – London – Amsterdam

1898: Amsterdam – Düsseldorf – Leipzig – Copenhagen – Bergen – Hardanger (Fossli) – Bergen – Odense – Copenhagen – Fuglsang (on the Danish island of Lolland)

1899: Copenhagen – Rome – Napoli – Milano – Leipzig – Bergen – Ålesund – Hjørundfjord – Norangfjord – Geiranger – Stryn – Loen – Vadheim – Bergen – Oslo – Copenhagen – Stockholm – Copenhagen

1900: Copenhagen – Oslo – Bergen – Oslo

1901: Oslo – Copenhagen – Bergen

1902: Bergen – Copenhagen – Warszaw – Copenhagen – Bergen – Oslo

1903: Oslo – Copenhagen – Prague – Berlin – Warszaw – Paris – Leipzig – Berlin – Oslo – Bergen – Framnes (Hardanger) – Bergen – Oslo – Aulestad (Lillehammer)

1904: Aulestad – Oslo – Stockholm – Oslo – Bergen – Oslo – (dep. Copenhagen 30.12)

1905: Copenhagen – Oslo – Bergen – Oslo

1906: Oslo – Gothenburg – Copenhagen – Berlin – Leipzig – Prague – Berlin – Leipzig – Amsterdam – London – Oxford – St Leonards on Sea – London – Cologne – Hamburg – Copenhagen – Oslo – Bergen – Oslo

1907: Oslo – Copenhagen – Berlin – Munich – Berlin – Leipzig – Kiel – Korsør – Copenhagen – Skodsborg – Hellerup – Skodsborg – Copenhagen – Oslo – Fagernes – Grindaheim – Lærdal – Bergen – Voss – Bergen *

* When Grieg died on 4 September 1907, he was about to take another trip abroad, this time to Leeds in England.

Edvard Grieg's life was like a continuous travel all over Europe. When you consider how poor his health was, it is amazing that he endured the strenuous touring life. It was actually the conductor Edvard Grieg who was the major attraction in the European metropolises. But in addition to directing, he also continued to give concerts with his wife Nina and other musicians.

Edvard Grieg's concerts

1861: Karlshamn

1862: Leipzig – Bergen

1864: Bergen

1865: Copenhagen – Leipzig

1866: Copenhagen – Bergen – Oslo

1867: Oslo

1868: Oslo

1869: Oslo – Drammen – Bergen – Copenhagen

1870: Bergen – Larvik – Oslo

1871: Drammen – Oslo – Bergen – Oslo

1872: Oslo

1873: Oslo – Stockholm – Oslo – Drammen – Arendal – Kristiansand – Stavanger – Bergen – Oslo

1874: Oslo – Copenhagen

1875: –

1876: Bergen – Stockholm – Uppsala

1877: Oslo – Bergen

1878: Cologne – Bonn – Leipzig

1879: Leipzig – Copenhagen – Bergen – Leipzig

1880: Copenhagen – Oslo – Bergen

1881: Bergen

1882: Bergen – Stavanger – Haugesund

1883: Bergen – Weimar – Dresden – Leipzig – Meiningen – Breslau – Cologne – Karlsruhe – Frankfurt am Main – Arnhem – The Hague – Rotterdam – Amsterdam

1884: Amsterdam – Rome – Bergen

1885: Bergen – Oslo – Copenhagen

1886: Copenhagen – Ålborg – Randers – Århus – Horsens – Vejle – Ribe

1887:   Leipzig

1888:   Leipzig – London – Copenhagen – Birmingham

1889:   Berlin – London – Manchester – London – Oslo – Copenhagen – Brussels – Paris

1890:   Paris – Stuttgart – Leipzig – Oslo

1891:   Oslo

1892:   Oslo – Copenhagen

1893:   Leipzig – Oslo – Copenhagen

1894:   Copenhagen – Leipzig – Munich – Geneve – Paris – London – Bergen – Copenhagen

1895:   Copenhagen – Oslo

1896:   Vienna – Copenhagen – Stockholm – Oslo – Vienna

1897:   Vienna – Amsterdam – The Hague – Arnhem – Liverpool – London – Manchester – Birmingham – Edinburgh – London – Windsor Castle – Cheltenham – Brighton – London

1898:   Bergen

1899:   Copenhagen – Rome – Oslo – Stockholm – Copenhagen

1900:   Copenhagen – Oslo

1901:   Copenhagen – Bergen

1902:   Warszaw – Bergen – Oslo

1903:   Prague – Warszaw – Paris – Bergen

1904:   Gothenburg – Stockholm – Uppsala – Stockholm – Oslo

1906:   Oslo – Prague – Amsterdam – London – Oslo

1907:   Oslo – Copenhagen – Munich – Berlin – Kiel

«Music friends in Bergen presented us with a beautiful Steinway grand piano»

EDVARD GRIEG

The centerpiece of Edvard Grieg Museum – Troldhaugen is the polished Steinway, Grieg's very own grand piano. It looks like he has just left it for a brief moment. The Steinway was built in Hamburg in 1892 and imported to Bergen by an instrument dealer called Carl Rabe. On the morning of Nina and Edvard's silver wedding anniversary, some of their friends had managed to install it in their sitting room before the couple had gotten out of bed! There was room for both of them on the low piano chair. Nina was not only a wonderful singer, but a good pianist, so she and Edvard often played four-handed piano. In fact, that was the prelude to their engagement in Copenhagen in 1864; «We played Schumann's Spring Symphony four-handed – and then we were engaged!» said Nina.

STEINWAY & SONS